W9-BNT-575

Praise for *Theft of a Nation*

"*Theft of a Nation* offers a rich history of regulation in the United States: the forces that promoted it; the forces that sought (and still seek) to undo it; the consequences of deregulation. Timely and insightful, *Theft of a Nation* will generate research for years to come."

—**GRAY CAVENDER**,
Arizona State University

"Finally! In *Theft of a Nation*, Gregg Barak reviews the actions that led to the so-called mortgage crisis on Wall Street in terms of their underlying criminality, not only of the individual economic players but also of the Wall Street system itself. This is a book that applies traditional (and Barak's new) criminological models so we can understand the underlying causes of systemic conduct that would, in any other context, be viewed as simple and blatant criminal conspiracies. I recommend it to all of us who are still trying to understand how our nation not only tolerated but also eventually rewarded the actors and the system—the thieves—that stole our nation's economic security."

—**HON. DONALD SHELTON**, chief judge,
Washtenaw Trial Court, Ann Arbor, Michigan

"This is an intelligent and disturbing analysis of how Wall Street interests and governmental policies have, time and again, colluded in the fleecing of America. It is nothing short of a tour de force in the areas of white-collar crime and victimology."

—**A. JAVIER TREVIÑO**, Wheaton College

Other Books by Gregg Barak

In Defense of Whom? A Critique of Criminal Justice Reform

Crimes by the Capitalist State: An Introduction to State Criminality (editor)

Gimme Shelter: A Social History of Homelessness in Contemporary America

Varieties of Criminology: Readings from a Dynamic Discipline (editor)

Media, Process, and the Social Construction of Crime: Studies in Newsmaking Criminology (editor)

Representing O.J.: Murder, Criminal Justice, and Mass Culture (editor)

Integrating Criminologies

Integrative Criminology (editor)

Crime and Crime Control: A Global View (editor)

Violence and Nonviolence: Pathways to Understanding

Violence, Conflict, and World Order: Critical Conversations on State-Sanctioned Justice (editor)

Battleground: Criminal Justice (editor; a two-volume encyclopedia)

Criminology: An Integrated Approach

Class, Race, Gender, and Crime: The Social Realities of Justice in America, 3rd Edition (coauthored with Paul Leighton and Jeanne Flavin)

ISSUES IN CRIME AND JUSTICE

Series Editor
Gregg Barak, Eastern Michigan University

As we embark upon the twentieth-first century, the meanings of crime continue to evolve and our approaches to justice are in flux. The contributions to this series focus their attention on crime and justice as well as on crime control and prevention in the context of a dynamically changing legal order. Across the series, there are books that consider the full range of crime and criminality and that engage a diverse set of topics related to the formal and informal workings of the administration of criminal justice. In an age of globalization, crime and criminality are no longer confined, if they ever were, to the boundaries of single nation-states. As a consequence, while many books in the series will address crime and justice in the United States, the scope of these books will accommodate a global perspective and they will consider such eminently global issues such as slavery, terrorism, or punishment. Books in the series are written to be used as supplements in standard undergraduate and graduate courses in criminology and criminal justice and related courses in sociology. Some of the standard courses in these areas include: introduction to criminal justice, introduction to law enforcement, introduction to corrections, juvenile justice, crime and delinquency, criminal law, white collar, corporate, and organized crime.

TITLES IN THE SERIES

Effigy: Images of Capital Defendants by Allison Cotton

The Prisoners' World: Portraits of Convicts Caught in the Incarceration Binge by William Tregea and Marjorie Larmour

Perverts and Predators: The Making of Sexual Offending Laws by Laura J. Zilney and Lisa Anne Zilney

Racial Profiling: Research, Racism, Resistance by Karen S. Glover

State Criminality: The Crime of All Crimes by Dawn L. Rothe

Punishment for Sale: Private Prisons and Big Business by Donna Selman and Paul Leighton

Forensic Science in Court: Challenges in the Twenty-first Century by Donald E. Shelton

Threat Perceptions: The Policing of Dangers from Eugenics to the War on Terrorism by Saran Ghatak

Gendered Justice: Intimate Partner Violence and the Criminal Justice System by Venessa Garcia and Patrick McManimon

Murder Stories: Ideological Narratives in Capital Punishment by Paul Kaplan

The Complexities of Police Corruption: Gender, Identity, and Misconduct by Marilyn Corsianos

Theft of a Nation

Wall Street Looting and Federal Regulatory Colluding

Gregg Barak

ROWMAN & LITTLEFIELD PUBLISHERS, INC.
Lanham • Boulder • New York • Toronto • Plymouth, UK

WAUKESHA PUBLIC LIBRARY

IWPL0010448346

Published by Rowman & Littlefield Publishers, Inc.
A wholly owned subsidiary of The Rowman & Littlefield Publishing Group, Inc.
4501 Forbes Boulevard, Suite 200, Lanham, Maryland 20706
www.rowman.com

10 Thornbury Road, Plymouth PL6 7PP, United Kingdom

Copyright © 2012 by Gregg Barak

All rights reserved. No part of this book may be reproduced in any form or by any electronic or mechanical means, including information storage and retrieval systems, without written permission from the publisher, except by a reviewer who may quote passages in a review.

British Library Cataloguing in Publication Information Available

Library of Congress Cataloging-in-Publication Data Available

ISBN 978-1-4422-0778-3 (cloth : alk. paper)
ISBN 978-1-4422-0779-0 (paper : alk. paper)
ISBN 978-1-4422-0780-6 (electronic)

∞™ The paper used in this publication meets the minimum requirements of American National Standard for Information Sciences—Permanence of Paper for Printed Library Materials, ANSI/NISO Z39.48-1992.

Printed in the United States of America

In memory of Glass-Steagall, 1933–1999

Contents

Acknowledgments

I would like to acknowledge the following people for their feedback and support during the course of researching, organizing, and writing this book: Maya Pagni Barak, Ron Barak, Michael Braswell, Werner Einstadter, David Friedrichs, Gil Geis, Jessica Kruger, Stuart Henry, Paul Leighton, Charlotte Pagni, Henry Pontell, Don Shelton, Adam Trahan, and Ben Wilcox. I would also like to thank three anonymous peer reviewers whose careful readings, comments, and suggestions were invaluable to the final product. Finally, I would like to thank Sarah Stanton of Rowman & Littlefield for her acumen and backing throughout this book project.

Additionally, I would like to acknowledge "realist criminology," a research tradition that is both empirically based and theoretically driven, and "social constructionism," a sociological body of relative truth formation. Taken together the material realities of crime and justice are derived from those labels created by empirically grounded social interactions. These labels in turn have both symbolic meanings and practical consequences. First, they enable people to identify and distinguish between types of harms or social injuries. Second, when criminal events occur these labels facilitate the likelihood that "justice" is done or not.

For example, as philosopher of law Hyman Gross has argued in his classic work, *A Theory of Criminal Justice*, "The rules of conduct laid down in the criminal law are a powerful social force upon which society is dependent for its very existence."[1] Yet, from a social constructionist perspective, Wayne Morrison has emphasized in the British anthological textbook, *Criminology*, "It is a social choice to recognize such and such as a crime, or such and such a person as a 'criminal.' Some other term and therefore some other course of action could be used."[2] Or as the Dutch abolishment lawyer Louk Hulsman has pointed out, "Crime has no ontological reality. Crime is not the object but the product of criminal policy. Criminalization is one of the many ways of constructing social reality."[3] At the same time, from the vantage point of realist criminology, crime is not only a social construction produced in tandem by control agents, mass media, and political ideologies. Crime is also a material phenomenon that has a reality of its own.[4]

Accordingly, the social problem of Wall Street securities fraud is as much a problem of how it is defined and represented as it is a matter of how finance criminal activities are organized and institutionalized across society. This inquiry that you are about to experience embodies an examination of both the realities and the representations of Wall Street looting and federal regulatory colluding.

Introduction

The U.S. Constitution mentions three federal crimes that citizens may be found guilty of: treason, piracy, and counterfeiting. At the turn of the twentieth century, this number had climbed to several dozen criminal statutes. By the 1980s the criminal code consisted of some three thousand offenses and twenty-three thousand pages of federal law. Today, nobody knows the exact number of offenses despite efforts at counting. According to a 2008 study there were an estimated forty-five hundred crimes in the federal code. In addition, there are thousands of federal regulations that carry criminal penalties. Many of the newly enacted federal laws have also lowered the bar for a conviction in that they no longer require the prosecutor to demonstrate the criminal intent of the defendant. For example, a 2010 joint study by the conservative Heritage Foundation and the liberal National Association of Criminal Defense Lawyers "analyzed scores of proposed and enacted new laws for non-violent crimes in the 109th Congress of 2005 and 2006. The study found of the 36 new crimes created, a quarter had no *mens rea* requirement and nearly 40% more had only a 'weak' one."[1]

As a result of these and other legal changes in punishment over the past thirty years, the U.S. Bureau of Justice Statistics reported that the total number of federal prisoners for 2009 had grown to two hundred thousand, representing more than an eightfold increase compared to a fourfold increase of state prisoners that grew to a little over two million.[2] The diminished requirements to prove criminal intent in order to convict, however, do not necessarily make the prosecutions of the crimes of the powerless or of the powerful any easier. For these legal developments are always subject to the vagaries of discretionary enforcement and selective application of the law.[3] At the same time, prosecutions are also subject to the number of street and suite crimes in relation to the total systemic capacities of the agencies of crime control and financial regulation.

Rising criminal demand without increasing prosecutorial or penal capacity intensifies the inversely related criminal justice/punishment patterns of severity and leniency experienced by relatively powerless offenders versus the relatively powerful offenders. In effect, scarce resources result in criminal prosecutors selecting out those less demanding and more winnable legal cases. Demand and winnability are defined by the complexity of the involved illegalities and by the availability of potential defendants' resources.[4] Thus, the collective impact of system incapacity (i.e., scarce or shrinking resources) tends to suppress, or decrease, the likelihood of criminally prosecuting those complex white-collar offenses committed by persons with the deepest of financial pockets, like any of the Wall Street miscreants.

For example, as both the number of federal criminal statutes mushroomed in recent decades and the number of federal prosecutions rose annually from a little over 30,000 or 192 per one million adult citizens in 1980 to some 83,000 or 395 per one million in 2009, offenses prosecuted and offenders subject to criminalization and the penal sanction as indicated by the bar graph of the top ten federally prosecuted offenses for 2010 (see figure I.1) varied considerably. Some 63 percent of all those prosecuted and incarcerated were for immigration and drug-related offenses. Out of the total, only about 11.7 percent of these involved white-collar offenses, and the number of those convicted for fraud was 8,028.

None of those criminal prosecutions involved any of the wealthiest banks for securities frauds,[5] precluding one pathway to insolvency or bankruptcy. Moreover, in the wake of an epidemic of high-stakes financial fraud, Wall Street was brought to its knees only temporarily, thanks to the Troubled Asset Relief Program signed into law by President Bush on October 3, 2008. However, be-

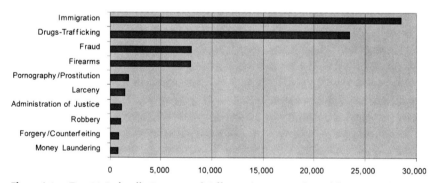

Figure I.1.   Top 10 Federally Prosecuted Offenses in 2010. Adapted from "Tracking the Growth in Federal Criminal Sentences," U.S. Sentencing Commission, 2011.

fore and after the TARP bailouts, a larger pattern of collusion still exists in the forms of waivers and exemptions from punishment. These "plea bargain" deals have been negotiated between the mega investment banks of Wall Street, the Securities and Exchange Commission, and the U.S. Department of Justice in numerous agreements and settlements pertaining to securities fraud.

The relative incapacities of the systems of criminal and civil/regulatory bureaucracies that normally address the separate and related worlds of street crime and suite crime are also affected by the recent appellate and U.S. Supreme Court decisions regarding corporate liability and victim compensation involving security violations.[6] Other legal and political developments have specifically protected "crimes of capital accumulation" from aggressive prosecution, effectively establishing a non-criminal reality where banking and related investment frauds are, in effect, *beyond incrimination*.[7] Notwithstanding politics, law enforcers are not pursuing Wall Street fraud for several reasons:

- Statutes of limitations on securities litigation are effectively three years.
- Deferred prosecution agreements were established under the new 2008 guidelines of the U.S. Department of Justice that allow financial companies to avoid indictments if they agree to investigate and report their own crimes.
- The Securities and Exchange Commission and other federal/state regulators are not up to the potential case demand because of inadequate agency resources and staffing.
- The revolving door between the government-private sectors has created a situation in financial litigation where the ties between the DOJ and the white-collar-corporate legal defense community have become particularly strong.
- To pursue these securities frauds criminally would not only potentially bring about the demise of these financial institutions but in the process would also certainly hurt investors.

Bottom line: The federal prosecution of financial fraud in the United States by the end of 2011 had fallen to a twenty-year low. In fact, 2011 recorded the lowest number of securities fraud prosecutions in at least two decades. Trend wise, every year since 1999, the number of federal criminal prosecutions has gotten smaller and smaller as the banking oligopoly in the United States has gotten bigger and bigger. According to a recent Transactional Records Access Clearinghouse (TRAC) report from Syracuse University, the Department of Justice was on track to file just 1,365 prosecutions for financial institutional fraud in fiscal year 2011. At the same time, during 2011 the Securities and Exchange Commission filed a record-high 735 enforcement actions, going to trial in 19 cases, settling as many cases as possible with fraudulent defendants who neither admit nor deny wrongdoing while they agree to pay fines worth a fraction of the losses to their investors.[8]

Theft of a Nation is about finance capital and institutionalized crime. This book explains how the federal government, despite its rhetoric to the contrary, came to dismiss the crimes of Wall Street and to rebuff the victims of Main Street.[9] It examines the means by which a combination of governmental actions and omissions absolved Wall Street bankers, mortgage lenders, and associated swindlers from any accountability for their criminally fraudulent behavior. More broadly, *Theft of a Nation* is the story of the cultural and ideological histories of investment banking and Washington, DC, and how the interdependent cooperation by the nation's economic and political elites enabled Wall Street not to be held liable for the millions of people it victimized, for the billions of dollars it looted from investors, and for the trillions in capital that it destroyed worldwide. Finally, within the circumstances of both a mature democracy and a free-market society, this book provides an explication of the contradictions between the forces of institutionalized financial crime and the forces of institutionalized regulatory control.

FRAMING THE CASE

Theft of a Nation is not only about financial fraud and its control. More fundamentally, it's about the interactions of law, power, and wealth. As Marx and Weber would have understood, this investigation is about the interplay of the developing political economy[10] and the bureaucratically rational legal state.[11] Both thinkers despite their different emphases would have agreed that it's a study in the structural contradictions of *bourgeois legality*. Specifically, it's about the ways that finance capitalists who have great wealth, prestige, and access to politicos at the highest levels of government were afforded ample opportunities to make, break, and neutralize, if not capture, the laws of regulation. It is also about how these financiers were able to push back against or circumvent those unacceptable regulations that manage to get passed into law.

This happens for essentially two reasons. First, within the worlds of monopoly and financial capital, Wall Street investment bankers have become the dominant economic players. Second, within the current rise of global capitalism, finance capital is both the product and generator of forces that are transforming the contradictory governmental processes of regulation and deregulation. Furthermore, because of the dominance of finance capital and the concentration of wealth into a small number of Wall Street firms and institutions, a banking oligopoly[12] or a banking cartel[13] now exists in the United States (see figure I.2).

For a quick historical perspective: Back in 1947 the federal "government sued 17 leading Wall Street investment banks, charging them with effectively

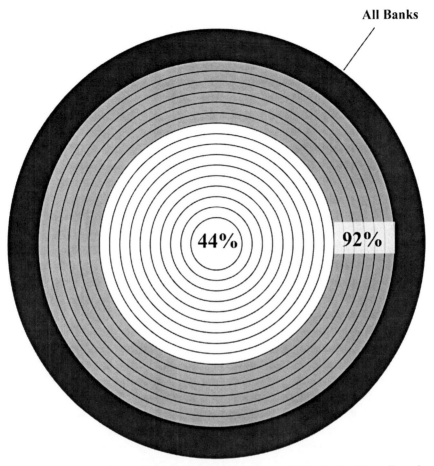

All Banks

44%

92%

Figure I.2.   The Banking Oligopoly in America. Represented in the banking oligopoly figure are the top three banks with 44 percent of market share, the top twenty banks with 92 percent of market share, and some eight thousand other banks dividing the remaining 8 percent of market share. From Barry Ritholtz, "The Big Picture," December 25, 2011, http://www.ritholtz.com/blog/2011/12/the-banking-oligopoly.

colluding in violation of antitrust laws."[14] The Department of Justice in its complaint alleged that these firms, among other things, had created "an integrated, overall conspiracy and combination" that began in 1915 and was in continuous operation thereafter, by which they developed a system "to eliminate competition and monopolize 'the cream of the business' of investment banking."[15] The United States argued further that these Wall Street investment banks, including Morgan Stanley as the lead defendant and Goldman Sachs, had created a cartel that set the prices charged for underwriting securities. The cartel also set the prices for providing mergers-and-acquisitions advice, while "boxing out weaker competitors from breaking into the top tier of the business and getting their fair share of the fees."[16] Finally, the government argued that the big firms had placed their partners on their clients' board of directors as a means of knowing what was coming down the pike internally and of keeping competitors at bay externally.

As journalist, former Wall Street banker, and best-selling author of *House of Cards*, *The Last Tycoons*, and *Money and Power*, William D. Cohan has recently contended, "The government was spot on" in their 1947 case: "The investment-banking business was then a cartel where the biggest and most powerful firms controlled the market and then set the prices for their services, leaving customers with few viable choices for much needed capital, advice or trading counterparties."[17] Today, the very same arguments can be made, only more so, as the capital worth of the leading firms (e.g., Goldman Sachs Group, Inc., Morgan Stanley, JP Morgan Chase & Co., Citigroup Inc., and Bank of America Corp.) is even more concentrated. In effect, this banking cartel or oligopoly with its political allies pretty much control what does or does not constitute securities violations in the world of fraudulently based market transactions.

More fundamentally, capitalism has always been a system of control and domination. Central to control and domination is the law and the state apparatus of enforcement that stands behind the law. Within the capitalist mode and relations of production, the state and law in tandem "operate to sanction the exploitation of direct producers—the workers—on behalf of the capitalists—the bourgeoisie—while giving the impression that state and law are in fact neutral, separate from the capital relation of exploitation."[18] This is not to imply that the interests of the state and of capitalists are one and the same. There are all types of competing interests within and between capitalists and state authorities. Thus, the state-legal criminalization of securities fraud hangs literally in the balance of the contradictory forces of free-market capitalism.

William Chambliss developed a *structural contradictions* theory of crime, law making, and enforcement.[19] This theory reflects the position that fundamental to all historical eras and societies are the contradictory forces of survival and destruction. While societies produce the means of survival, they also produce the means of decline, creating perpetual dilemmas and conflicts. Under free-market capitalism, the fundamental contradictions are between labor and capital. The laborers or employees pursue better working conditions and/or higher wages. Meanwhile, capitalists pursue greater profits and resist the demands of workers, as these will reduce their bottom lines.

Within the developing political economy of capitalism, the dilemma for capital, labor, and the state is how to reconcile their conflicts and differences, considering that the fundamental contradiction between them cannot be re-solved short of a revolutionary transformation of society. As a consequence, the resolution of lesser conflicts may result in still other conflicts or contra-dictions. From a structural rather than an instrumental position on the nation-state, regardless of which political parties occupy the White House or who fills the various offices of the other branches and agencies of government, the state remains deferential to the interests of the capitalist economy. At the same time, from an instrumentalist position and in terms of the ongoing class struggle between labor and capital, the capitalist classes are always putting pressure on the state to pass and repeal laws in their interests, winning most of the time, often in the face of much resistance and opposition from other classes.

Chambliss identified two fundamental contradictions in a capitalist po-litical economy that lead to crime: "wages, profits, and consumption" and "wage-labor supply." The first contradiction has to do with whether or not workers have sufficient money to purchase commodities based on what capitalists pay them in wages and benefits versus whether or not capitalists have more or less profits available for reinvestment. When workers lack the money to purchase goods and services, the economy becomes sluggish. On the other hand, higher salaries for workers cut into profits and reinvesting. The second contradiction has to do with the capitalist maintenance of a sur-plus labor force, inclusive of outsourcing, too, that helps both to keep wages down and to provide a supply of labor from which capital can draw upon when the demands of workers threaten their profits. These inherent contra-dictions of free-market capitalism can culminate in crimes of theft from both the under and over classes, as each group goes about its respective business of economic survival.

With respect to the crimes of capitalist survival, these "arise from the particular forms of social relations associated with the processes of capital accumulation, concentration, and centralization."[20] The control of these types of financial crime call for an examination of: (1) the particular dynamics of accumulation that develop when capital is privately owned and the process of accumulation is managed largely for private rather than public interests, and (2) the contradictory political and economic forces that permeate the social relations of criminalization and law enforcement. Accordingly, this inquiry's evaluation and treatment of the "crimes of capitalist control" include not only those acts prohibited under criminal or regulatory law, but also those reflected in civil laws and torts. To be precise, the socio-legal topography covered in this investigation addresses the criminal and civil/administrative processes as well as those processes of regulatory and other legal bodies that have had some kind of Wall Street oversight capacity.

Lastly, before turning to the rest of the book, let me tend to a housekeeping matter that revolves around how I collected the evidence for this analysis of Wall Street looting and federal regulatory colluding. Virtually all of the "data" presented herein are based on the public record. This research is of a secondary order. It has relied on major media networks, online news services, journalistic accounts, Internet blogging, and the digital retrieval of relevant documents—past and present—as these are related to the socio-historical documentation of the Wall Street crisis of 2007–8 and its aftermath. In turn, these empirically available records have been informed by and are subject to an array of theories not only from criminology but also from the disciplines of law, economics, and political science.

Chapter One

Law, Power, and Wealth

On the Rhetoric and Reality of Fighting Financial Abuse

Six weeks before Attorney General Alberto Gonzales was forced to resign for having approved one year before the forced resignations of nine U.S. attorneys, he stood before hundreds of federal prosecutors and investigators in the Great Hall of the Justice Department to celebrate the fifth anniversary of the creation of the Corporate Fraud Task Force and to declare victory over white-collar corruption. Established by an executive order in July 2002, the task force was President George W. Bush's signature response to what was viewed at the time as an epidemic of criminal wrongdoing in corporate America. As Bush's first attorney general, John Ashcroft, stated in his address to the CFTF's national conference on September 27, 2002:

> We cannot—we will not—surrender freedom for all to the tyranny of greed for the few. Just over a year ago, Americans were called to defend our freedom from assault from abroad. Today we are called to preserve our freedom from corruption from within. You are the answerers of this call; you are the defenders of this freedom. I am grateful to you all for your leadership, and I thank you for your sacrifice and your steadfast commitment to returning integrity to American markets through justice.[1]

Three months earlier, the Sarbanes-Oxley Act (SOX) had become law, endorsed by many as the most important corporate law reform measure since the passage of the securities and exchange laws of the 1930s.[2] While this law addresses regulatory issues such as accounting oversight, insider trading, the transparency of financial statements, auditor independency, conflicts of interests, and the resource needs of the Securities and Exchange Commission, SOX did not address the effects of the "re-opened" market conditions created by President Bill Clinton when he signed into law the Financial Services

9

Modernization Act of 1999, which repealed that portion of the 1933 Glass-Steagall Act making "it a felony for anyone—banker, broker, dealer in securities, or savings institution—to engage in the deposit-taking and securities businesses at the same time."[3]

Otherwise known as Gramm-Leach-Bliley, the FSMA had the effect of eliminating the separation between commercial and investment banks in place since the 1930s, turning the financial markets into a free-for-all and establishing a criminogenic environment. The passage of this legislation was the culmination of economic and political elites struggling successfully to fully dismantle the regulatory regime of old, which had prevented since the stock market crash of 1929 economic meltdowns like the Wall Street catastrophe of 2007–8. It was after the 1929 crash that regulations such as Glass-Steagall were created to prevent future speculative debacles. Lynn Turner, former chief accountant of the SEC, has argued that the existing regulatory system was not broken or outdated, but that it did stand in the way of making a lot of "risky money" by way of derivatives[4] and other types of financial instruments. In the name of opening up larger financial supermarkets and allowing "all these businesses under one roof, without a single word in the law requiring regulation of the inherent conflicts," and by "prohibiting the SEC from being able to require regulation of investment holding companies," Congress enabled the financial environment that would become one massive system of abuse and fraud.[5]

Both Sarbanes-Oxley and the Corporate Fraud Task Force (CFTF) responded to an avalanche of revelations occurring over an eight-month period from 2001 to 2002. Enron had collapsed in the fall of 2001. In March of 2002, Arthur Andersen, the accounting firm that handled the books for Enron, was charged with obstruction of justice. A few months later, Adelphia Communications announced it was adjusting its earnings statement by a billion dollars to cover hundreds of millions of dollars looted by senior executives. By the time allegations surfaced in June 2002 about the $3 billion fraud by WorldCom executives, "the leading stock indexes seemed locked in a death spiral, with investors panicked about which public company holding their retirement funds might topple next."[6] As G. W. Bush told a gathering of federal prosecutors who were discussing the implications of SOX in September 2002, the "high-profile acts of deception in corporate America have shaken people's trust in corporations, the markets and the economy. The American people need to know we're acting, we're moving, and we're moving fast."[7]

Like the CFTF, previous and subsequent white-collar task forces are essentially designed to: (1) coordinate the firepower of multiple federal law enforcement agencies, (2) deter wrongdoing in corporate suites, and (3) restore investor confidence. At the five-year commemoration, Gonzales boasted that the task force had won an unprecedented 1,236 corporate fraud convictions, including those of 214 chief executive officers and presidents, 53 chief financial officers, 23 corporate lawyers, and 129 vice presidents. The attorney general claimed, "Our victories have been about more than just compiling statistics or making an example out of one or two bad actors. They have been about preserving the integrity of our corporate boardrooms and our financial markets . . . about changing a culture . . . about redefining the way companies do business."[8]

Since task forces actually have no prosecutorial authority, Gonzales had really been referring to the work and convictions accomplished by local U.S. prosecuting attorneys. More important, given the number of high-profile acquittals, hung juries, and appellate reversals, not to mention "the precipitous decline in the number of major corporate fraud indictments" following Bush's re-election in 2004, *The American Lawyer* (TAL) wanted to know: "Has the problem of corporate fraud really been solved, as Gonzales suggested at his celebration in July? Or has the Justice Department stopped trying as hard to prosecute it?"[9] In the spring of 2006, TAL investigated the Justice Department's record on corporate fraud prosecutions. This massive undertaking was not made any easier by the fact that the U.S. DOJ does not keep statistics on corporate fraud (or most other serious white-collar crimes) and could not provide a complete list of the cases Gonzales had counted among his victories.

The American Lawyer was able, nevertheless, to create a detailed portrait of the major corporate fraud prosecutions between 2002 and 2007, by examining publicly available case records and win-loss performance statistics as well as interviewing dozens of current and former prosecutors, task force members, and white-collar criminal defense lawyers. TAL found "a highly publicized, top-down strategy that encouraged local prosecutors to charge both corporations and individual defendants with fraud."[10] The effort had resulted in hundreds of convictions—337 in the cases they tracked from their data on 124 investigations and 440 indictments—with the vast majority, 76 percent, coming through plea deals. Many of these corporate criminals were given significant punishments with more than fifty sentenced to upward of five years in prison. Among those high-profile CEOs sentenced to prison were Bernard Ebbers of WorldCom and John Rigas of Adelphia.

Prosecutions of high-profile defendants were also lost or failed, some resulting from questionable tactics employed by the DOJ, such as compelling corporate defendants to waive their legal rights. From TAL's tracking data:

- Twenty-seven defendants were acquitted at trial, including executives at Adelphia, Online Inc., PurchasePro.com Inc., and Qwest Communications Inc.
- Twenty-two mistrials occurred.

• Nine convictions were overturned on appeal, including high-profile defendants from Credit Suisse First Boston and from Merrill Lynch.

TAL's investigation also found that after issuing detailed reports in 2003 and 2004, the task force stopped reporting its efforts in 2005, just as corporate fraud indictments slowed to a trickle. While their analyses revealed 357 indictments in major corporate cases between 2002 and 2005, there had been only 14 indictments in 2006 and 12 during the first ten months of 2007. As for such defeats in the "war on corporate crime," many were blamed on insufficient manpower and money to properly investigate and prosecute complex fraud cases. For example, a co-leading prosecutor in the investigation and prosecution of former Enron chairman Kenneth Lay and CEO Jeffrey Skilling stated that the DOJ was "challenged by a lack of resources, both technical and in terms of personnel . . . we often felt that the defense was outgunning us on both levels."[11] David Meyer, the principal deputy assistant attorney general at the time, acknowledged that the U.S. attorneys were not given extra staff to help prosecute corporate fraud, so they had to prioritize the cases to prosecute. Meyer also stated that the low number of prosecutions in 2006 and 2007 had resulted from the remarkable successes of the CFTF: "You're getting a lot more focus on compliance, and on ethics internally in corporate structures. . . . We do believe that the success of the Corporate Fraud Task Force, in conjunction with the Sarbanes-Oxley Act, is making it more likely that fraud is being detected by corporations themselves."[12]

A reduction in fraud was hardly the social reality because eighteen months later, on May 20, 2009, President Barack Obama signed into law the Fraud Enforcement and Recovery Act of 2009. The new law was designed to "improve enforcement of mortgage fraud, securities and commodities fraud, financial institutional fraud, and other frauds related to Federal assistance and relief programs, for the recovery of funds lost to these frauds, and for other purposes."[13] Then, on November 13, 2009, the DOJ, as part of an annual exercise, announced its top ten management and performance challenges for the upcoming year. One year earlier financial crimes were nowhere to be found on the top ten list. In 2009, these crimes had risen to number five on the list. As part of the financial crimes challenge, it is noted that there are shortages of resources due to the costs of the counterterrorism efforts. The number five challenge also underscored that while "many types of financial fraud have increased in recent years, mortgage fraud has seen a dramatic spike, with the FBI reporting more than double the number of criminal mortgage fraud investigations over the past three years."[14] It was also noted that the bureau "has seen significant growth in corporate fraud and misconduct in the securities and commodities markets at the institutional, corporate, and private investor levels" and is "currently investigating over 189 major corporate frauds, 18 of which have losses over $1 billion."[15]

A few days later, on November 17th, when the Obama administration unveiled its own task force to target the financial crimes that played a role in the Wall Street meltdown of 2007–8, the attorney general, Eric Holder, was joined at his side by Secretary of the Treasury Tim Geithner, Secretary of Housing and Urban Development Shaun Donovan, and Director of Enforcement at the Securities and Exchange Commission Robert Khuzami. During his announcement of the formation of the Financial Fraud Enforcement Task Force, Holder had this to say:

> We face unprecedented challenges in responding to the financial crisis that has gripped our economy for the past year. Mortgage, securities, and corporate fraud schemes have eroded the public's confidence in the nation's financial markets and have led to a growing sentiment that Wall Street does not play by the same rules as Main Street. Unscrupulous executives, Ponzi Scheme operators, and common criminals alike have targeted the pocketbooks and retirement accounts of middle class Americans, and in many cases, have devastated entire families' futures.[16]

Reading from prepared remarks, the AG explained that the new task force to replace Bush's CFTF was larger in scope than its predecessor. Holder also emphasized that:

> In the tough economic environment we face today, one of this Administration's most important missions is to draw upon all of the resources of the federal government to *fight financial fraud in all its forms*. The Task Force will wage an aggressive, coordinated, and proactive effort to investigate and prosecute financial crimes. We will marshal the criminal and civil enforcement resources of the executive branch to investigate and prosecute financial fraud cases; recover stolen funds for victims, address discrimination in lending and financial markets, and enhance coordination and cooperation among federal, state, local, tribal, and territorial authorities responsible for investigating and prosecuting significant financial crimes and violations (emphasis added).[17]

FERA, the DOJ, and the "new and improved" task force on financial fraud all appeared to be on the same page back in 2009 as each stressed the same four areas of deception:

- **Mortgage fraud**, from the simplest of "flip" schemes to systematic lending fraud in the nationwide housing market
- **Securities fraud**, including traditional insider trading, Ponzi schemes, and misrepresentations to investors

- **Recovery Act (rescue) fraud**, to make sure the taxpayers' investment ("bailout") is not siphoned away by the dishonest few
- **Discrimination**, to ensure that the financial markets work for all Americans, and that nobody is unfairly targeted based on impermissible characteristics

Nevertheless, for example, as note 9 from the introduction underscores, by the beginning of 2012 Obama and Holder's Financial Fraud Enforcement Network had not criminally prosecuted a single case involving any of the six largest banks in the United States. In fact, so invisible or non-existent had the work of Obama's first financial fraud team been that when the president made a big deal about establishing a Financial Crimes Unit in the DOJ in his 2012 State of the Union address, few people recalled that the Obama administration had already played the "special task force card" in its alleged fight against financial crime back in 2009. Amazingly, the "old" and the "new" financial fraud teams were composed of the same key legal, economic, and political players, including Holder, Geithner, Donovan, Khuzami, and Lanny Breuer, the head of the DOJ's Criminal Division. All of these individuals have very close ties to the banking industry.

Further on down the fraudulent financial food chain, however, the Department of Justice has been busy busting and prosecuting "low-level" mortgage fraudsters, for example, from an updated news report on June 20, 2011, covering two mortgage fraud cases from Operation Stolen Dreams.[18] The first case involved a nine-count indictment returned from a grand jury in Sacramento against Alonzo Jackson Brown III, 44, charging him with an investment fraud scheme and a mortgage fraud scheme. In a separate and unrelated case, Leonard Bernot, 46, of Laguna Hills, California, had "pleaded guilty today before U.S. District Judge Kimberly J. Mueller to conspiracy to commit mail fraud for his part in a wide-ranging 'foreclosure rescue' scheme involving Head Financial Services Inc."[19] Only a little over a year before, between March 1 and June 18, 2010, Operation Stolen Dreams had become the largest collective enforcement effort to confront mortgage fraud in U.S. history. The nationwide sweep involved 1,517 criminal arrests, resulting in 525 indictments representing estimated losses of more than $3 billion. The operation also yielded "191 civil enforcement actions and the recovery of more than $196 million."[20]

In reference to the Eastern District of California that charged forty-six defendants with felony mortgage offenses and secured eleven guilty pleas, Herb Brown, Special Agent in Charge of the Sacramento FBI, stated that these "cases provide a glimpse of just how pervasive Mortgage Fraud is. We must and will continue to pursue fraudsters in the real estate and mortgage industries."[21] Echoing those sentiments were U.S. Attorney Wagner for the Eastern District: "Mortgage fraud continues to be a major problem in this region, which has cost banks, borrowers, and homeowners tens of millions of dollars." Wagner also commented that future indictments were in the works as "we will continue to pursue those industry insiders who abuse and exploit the mortgage and real estate process for their own personal gain."[22]

For perspective on the magnitude of these types of mortgage frauds, white-collar criminologist and former senior deputy chief counsel for the Office of Thrift Supervision, William Black, underscored in a 2008 paper delivered at the annual Minsky Conference that the number of fraud incidents found in file reviews for fiscal year 2007 indicated around one million fraudulent loans.[23] Needless to say, the Mortgage Fraud Working Group certainly has a "caseload" too large to make much of a dent in, or to have much of a deterrent effect on, this kind of fraudulent behavior. Inquiring minds might want to know where are the working groups to target the other financial crimes identified not only by FERA, the DOJ, and the Obama administration, but also from the findings of the 652-page report, "Wall Street and the Financial Crisis: Anatomy of a Financial Collapse," released in April 2011?

Specifically, where is the Securities and Commodities Fraud Working Group or the Financial Institutional Fraud Working Group? In terms of financial recovery, targeting these major types of frauds would considerably up the ante from hundreds of millions or tens of billions to hundreds of billions or even trillions in dollars lost and/or stolen from real estate holdings, pension funds, and other institutional investments, assuming that enough resources were allocated for this charge. For example, take the estimated $5 to $7 trillion in lost home equity. In the case of the working group of leaders and the number of people assigned to the investigative unit of Obama's 2012 Financial Fraud Enforcement Network, there were initially fifteen attorneys, investigators, and analysts as well as ten FBI agents. An additional thirty attorneys, investigators, and support staff from the U.S. attorneys' offices were scheduled to join the unit some time in early 2012.

That's a total of fifty-five persons and amounts to "about $100 billion of lost home equity per person assigned to this task force."[24] By comparison, one hundred FBI agents were assigned to the Enron case, and there were about one thousand agents assigned to the Savings and Loans (S&L) scandal. In the latter financial fraud, there were one hundred times as many agents assigned to a much simpler task than investigating Wall Street, which equaled about one-fortieth of the losses in dollars. In short, this underallocation of investigators does not represent "a serious deployment of government resources to unmask a complex economy-shaking financial scheme."[25]

A SHORT HISTORY OF FRAUD AND
LOOTING IN THE UNITED STATES

Major financial frauds and lootings have rich histories and active lives throughout their risk-taking adventures up to the present crises in housing, real estate, and finance capital. Historically, what is believed to be the largest single management fraud in post-Revolutionary America revolved around the federal government's efforts to establish a national or central bank and the abuses (e.g., "insider trading," "cooking the books") perpetrated by bank executives, directors, and branch managers of the Second Bank of the United States from 1816 to 1836.[26] Despite the congressional investigation into the fraud that found the perpetrators to have blatantly violated the bank-operating rules and laws, there were no punishments administered for these illicit actions.[27] In 1836, however, President Andrew Jackson put an end to these "crimes" by vetoing a bill to renew the Second Bank's charter. More specifically, he put an end to the rampant looting by these fraudulent executives who had purchased controlling shares in the Second Bank while establishing their own financial firm as a means of manipulating Second Bank stock.

The discontinued charter of the Second Bank would forestall the implementation of central banking for more than seventy-five years in the United States. During the so-called Free Banking Era (1836–1913), bankers could issue their own currency or banknotes and investors could shop around from state to state looking for the "best" deals. In 1867, there was the infamous collapsing of Crédit Mobilier, "a construction company-turned-financial institution indirectly owned by the financial promoters of the Union Pacific Railroad, which was itself controlled by the federal government."[28] Shortly before Congressman Oakes Ames took over this "bank" he had "generously spread Crédit Mobilier shares among numerous Congressional colleagues to secure votes on additional federal funding that was purportedly needed to complete the railroad's construction."[29] This first major incident of pre-twentieth-century financial looting made all the history books because $23 million of loan proceeds ended up in the pockets of the owners of Crédit Mobilier.

Enter the era of the "Gilded Age" with its unprecedented industrialization, rapid population growth, and concentration of wealth. During this period, there were associated changes in finance capital and in investment banking that led to both market and shareholder expansion. Helping to build the modern securities markets, JP Morgan established the first major investment-banking firm. Not too long after that, Morgan and a community of Wall Street bankers and financiers became the subjects of the Pujo Committee investigations carried out by the U.S. Congress from 1912 to 1913. Although this "money trust" of connected bankers and industrialists exerted powerful control over the nation's finances, manipulated control of the New York Stock Exchange, and attempted to evade interstate trade laws, there was no actual contractual agreement among them that was in violation of the law.[30] In reaction to the recommendations of the Pujo Committee, the Federal Reserve Act was enacted on December 23, 1913, setting up the Federal Reserve Bank and establishing the centralization of banking in the United States.

In the late nineteenth and early twentieth centuries, the growth of finance capital and the increasing number of banks and investment houses were also accompanied by "individual would-be investors who suffered most at the hands of swindlers peddling bogus securities to a public delirious with visions of overnight riches."[31] By the mid-1920s the speculative spirit had gripped the U.S. stock market and roughly two million investors. At the same time, there was also the frenzy over government debt that had spread to equities as well as to residential real estate. Within very short periods, both had experienced huge price growth. When the inevitable bursting of the Roaring Twenties' bubbles finally came crashing down in the 1929 stock market implosion, financial fraud had played a major role in the large amounts of bogus stock sold to investors, rich and not-so affluent or middle class, alike.

The investigation of the stock market crash by the U.S. Senate Banking and Currency Committee's Pecora Commission (1932–34) concluded that the major banks, investment houses, and even law firms had marketed hundreds of millions of dollars of worthless stock. These Wall Street firms included Chase National Bank; JP Morgan & Co.; Kuhn, Loeb and Co.; and National City Bank and its "securities affiliate," National City Co. The Pecora Commission also discovered that Chase's boss, Albert Wiggin, made a $4 million profit as his bank's stock price rapidly tanked, not unlike chieftains of Lehman Brothers, Merrill Lynch, and other sinking super-investment institutions like AIG and Countrywide during the 2007–8 meltdown. One of the more audacious frauds of the 1920s involved large New York banks that sold "massive amounts of worthless securities to their securities 'affiliates,' thereby applying copious layers of financial cosmetics to their own balance sheets."[32] The simultaneous investigation and exposure of these Wall Street financial institutions and their criminal investment activities leading up to the crash undoubtedly played an important role in the drafting and passage of the major regulatory reforms such as the Glass-Steagall Act, the Securities Act of 1933, and the Securities Exchange Act of 1934.

When I present the historical story of deregulation, bailouts, and too big to fail in chapter 3, I will return to this overview of fraud and looting beginning with the S&L scandals of the 1980s. Aside from these types of market-driven and market-driving frauds as well as the looting that tends to accompany the rises and falls in the cycling of "free" economies, there is an array of more common frauds involving petty white-collar offenders. Together, the costs of these internal and external frauds are staggering. Current estimates are that U.S. organizations collectively sustain $1 trillion in internal fraud losses alone each year. According to the Association of Certified Fraud Examiners (ACFE), these organizations lose approximately 7 percent of gross revenue annually to fraud as contrasted with those losses from external frauds, such as those that emanate from identify thefts, organized crime syndicates, disgruntled employees, and dishonest employees or consumers. Interestingly, the data on twenty-one industries studied by the ACFE from 2006 revealed that banking/financial services topped the list of internal fraud incidents. Government and public administration was a distant second followed by health care services.[33] In 2008, the Federal Trade Commission reported that 643,195 Americans filed complaints regarding their victimization from fraudsters, a 50 percent increase from 428,394 in 2006.[34]

These social realities of the history of financial frauds or of fraudsters more generally can be connected to a body of criminological knowledge that has accumulated no shortage of hypotheses and theories involving the etiology and control of various forms of white-collar crime. Outside of white-collar crime circles, however, these ideas have been downplayed, dismissed, or ignored altogether by mainstream media, journalistic accounts, and by traditional "fraud minimalists." The latter economists and politicos not only deny "that there is any significant degree of fraud in financial markets," but they also limit their analyses of the "major meltdowns, when they do occur," to the "larger structural disorders, mismanagement and incompetence, government and regulatory interference, overzealous enforcement efforts, and 'risky' business."[35] These fraud minimalists ascribe further to the uncritical analyses of free-market relations whose hegemonic view holds that Wall Street firms may have been guilty of a lot of "moral hazard" and of too much "gambling for resurrection," but that none of these corporations or their CEOs should be held legally responsible for business fraud.[36]

Similarly, the revelations of the U.S. Senate's report of the Anatomy of the Financial Collapse (AFC) provides useful data and valuable insights into the Wall Street meltdown from both the material shared and the discourse used to describe and explain the Wall Street behavior. For example, the AFC has identified the "root causes," and the report seeks to show how these in combination were responsible for the Wall Street financial crisis and the subsequent government bailout. The AFC's four causal factors include: (1) high-risk mortgage lending, (2) regulatory failures, (3) inflated credit ratings, and (4) investment banking abuses.[37] Consistent with the spirit of fraud minimalists and echoing the same conclusions reached by other official investigations into financial crises, such as the 1993 report "Origins and Causes of the

S&L Debacle: A Blueprint for Reform" issued by the Financial Institutional Reform, Recovery and Enforcement Commission,[38] the majorities from each of these commissions, some eighteen years apart, identified numerous ways in which the environments of thrifts in the 1980s and of investment banks and mortgage companies at the beginning of the twenty-first century were operating in ways that encouraged lawbreaking and material fraud. In their final reports, however, both commissions to varying degrees "whitewash" the nature of these securities fraud.[39]

PRESENTING THE EVIDENCE

Chapter 2 presents a comparison of the similarities and dissimilarities between Bernie Madoff's Ponzi scheme that victimized tens of thousands of mostly innocent investors and the fraudulent schemes of Wall Street that drove the housing bubble and 2006 crash in real estate that resulted in history's largest financial meltdown, victimizing hundreds of millions of innocent people. In the case of the financially structured crimes of Wall Street, references are made to thousands of collateralized mortgage obligations (CMOs)[40] that were

Figure 1.1. "What crime?" By permission of Steve Kelley and Creators Syndicate, Inc.

recklessly invested en masse throughout the United States and elsewhere as alternative debt-financing instruments, including millions of fraudulent subprime and adjustable-rate mortgages. These mortgage loans were, in turn, bundled, sliced into different risk pools, and fraudulently pushed and resold all around the globe not as the "junk" or even worse, "toxic," derivatives that they were, but as triple-A-rated securities, the best that money can buy.

Chapter 3 presents an overview of the contradictory histories of financial regulation and deregulation in the United States from the early 1900s to the present. This "schizophrenic" history provides the necessary background, contextual information, and explanation of how over time the usual crimes of capital have been viewed alternately as the costs of doing either "illegal" or "risky" business. At the same time, from the S&L debacles of the 1980s to the Wall Street implosion of 2007–8, this chapter locates the government bailout policies within the dualistic rise to power of finance capitalists and free-market ideologies.

Chapter 4 is the theory chapter that drives this inquiry and holds my narratives together. To achieve these ends, the chapter does several things: First, it makes definitional distinctions between the types of white-collar crime, primarily contrasting the differences of occupational and corporate offenses. Second, it presents a general overview of the theories of organizational crimes and the etiology of the crimes of the powerful. Third, it describes five integrated theories of and/or approaches to the worlds of corporate and financial crimes. Fourth, it introduces both an interactive model of *organizational control fraud* and an interactive model of *institutional financial control fraud*. In turn, these mutually reinforcing interactive models of fraud are brought together in a Reciprocal Model of Wall Street Fraud that explains the political economy of Wall Street looting and federal regulatory colluding. Finally, I use the public record on the material relations of Washington Mutual Bank, the Office of Thrift Supervision, Moody's and Standard & Poor's, and the Goldman Sachs Group to substantiate the veracity of these models.

Chapter 5 frames its discussion by utilizing Donald Black's theory of the law and several of his scientific principles of "the behavior of law" to help make sense of the tracking of those financial fraud cases initiated against executives at relatively large companies through the different governmental agencies, paying close attention to the identities of these defendants, the charges against them, and the outcomes of their cases. All but three of these thirty fraud cases were civil, and eighteen were brought by the SEC. In most of these cases, the government negotiated a settlement before ever filing a complaint, announcing both the case and the settlement on the same occasion. Chapter 5 also provides an overview of the monetary settlements, where no criminal charges were ever filed and no criminal behaviors were ever admitted to. These cases involved the largest financial institutions in America, including the very same corporations that were bailed out by TARP. The overall distribution of punishment in relation to stratification is consistent with both Black's theory of the law and Chambliss' theory of structural contradictions.

Chapter 6 presents an overview of consuming victims, victimless identities, and the re-emergence of state-sanctioned victimization. Focus revolves around a historical discussion of victimology and victimization in the context of the comparative political responses to victims of both ordinary criminal offenses and white-collar offenses. In the course of this examination of recognized and unrecognized victims, similarities and dissimilarities between the two types of injured parties are identified. Finally, this chapter reviews the legal prospects and remedying efforts of investors, mostly comprised of institutional groups, who as their only means of pursuing compensation have civilly sued various financial firms to recover their monies lost to Wall Street's fraudulent securities transactions.

Chapter 7 is the political chapter describing those individuals and parties who prepared the legislation as well as those who lobbied for and against the new regulatory rules and procedures that became the Dodd-Frank Wall Street Financial Reform and Consumer Protection Act of 2010. The chapter then follows the unfinished business of finalizing the actual rules of the new regulatory regime and the continued struggle over these and their implementation throughout 2011. In the course of this review of the Dodd-Frank political tug-of-war between re-regulators and de-regulators, I also examine the strengths and weaknesses of the accepted or rejected rule changes from the perspectives of consumers, politicos, Wall Streeters, and policy wonks.

The conclusion summarizes the general argument of *Theft of a Nation*. This chapter also underscores the contradictory relations of the crimes of capitalist control and the torts of financial litigation. The final portion of this book explores the types of changes in our financial arrangements that move beyond Dodd-Frank, toward the socialization of finance capital, and away from riskier victimization. The book ends with a People's Tribunal in the spirit of Occupy Wall Street, in which I imagine what a redistribution of the bailouts or of compensation for the pain and suffering of the American people would look like.

Chapter Two

Bernie Madoff's Ponzi Scheme and Wall Street's Financial Meltdown

A Primer on Investment Fraud and Victimization

On December 10, 2008, Bernard Madoff, or "the Jewish T-bill" as affluent Jewry of New York and Florida respectfully referred to him, purportedly told his wife and two sons that his investment business was a Ponzi scheme. The next day two FBI agents showed up at Madoff's front door and placed him under arrest for numerous federal crimes. In addition to the felony charges, the government sought at least $170 billion in forfeited assets. This figure "counts all the money that moved through Madoff bank accounts during the years of the fraud as the proceeds of illegal activities."[1] Legally speaking, as a market maker—the middleman between buyers and sellers of stocks—Madoff intentionally engaged in the deprivation of people's rights and property. He stole some $18 billion from tens of thousands of investors, and most unknowingly became victims. A few others "knowingly" became benefactors of Madoff's slight of the invisible hand—the largest Ponzi scheme in the history of modern capitalism. His financial con of cons had taken a lucrative wealth management business and had grown it, over the course of some two decades, into a $50 billion securities fraud that finally collapsed when too many investors wanted to pull out their funds during the worst economic crisis since the Great Depression.

At the time of Madoff's public exposure and his criminal demise, one question was often asked: Why did one of the most successful broker-dealers in the financial industry; a legendary Wall Street figure who had been a co-founder and former chairman of the NASDAQ; and a loving husband, father, and brother as well as an admired and beloved philanthropist operate what became the biggest, unregistered, and imaginary "hedge fund" (e.g., a mutual fund for millionaires and other institutional investors) the world has ever known? Unless Madoff, now confined for 150 years in the Butner Federal Correctional Institution, decides to write his memoirs or a "tell all" book, inquiring minds will probably never know what exactly prompted Bernie to commit his "crime of choice."[2]

A more interesting question has to do with why a sizable number of wealthy and savvy investors could be taken for large sums of money? Relatedly, how did a fraudster like Madoff and a team of five persons over the course of some 16 years establish a global network of investors from more than 40 countries, 339 funds of funds (e.g., mutual funds that invest in other mutual funds), and 59 asset management companies get away with this pecuniary swindle for as long as they did? As Madoff stated from his prison cell in early 2011, "They had to know. But the attitude was sort of, 'If you're doing something wrong, we don't want to know.'"[3]

In fact, criminological research suggests there were a host of psychological factors as well as organizational interests at work "not to know." In addition to his status as a "trusted criminal" by his clients and regulators alike, his fraudulent enterprise was run as a "secret society" consisting of a handful of well-paid individuals that escaped the purview of his closest family members.[4] In the face of both knowing, for some of Madoff's investing victims, and the negative consequences of disclosing the truth after so long, for some of his regulators, the result became concerted ignorance.[5] Neither his investors nor his regulators wanted to believe that Madoff was actually running under their noses a multibillion-dollar financial scam.

A similar but expanded answer comes from the book *No One Would Listen* (2010) by Harry Markopolos.[6] Markopolos, an independent financial fraud investigator for institutional investors and others seeking forensics accounting expertise, has emphasized the cultural and social acceptance of free-market ideologies and the political denial over the past three decades of the harmful consequences of widespread deregulation. He and other insiders have also elaborated on the declining enforcement activity of the financial regulatory agencies of the United States during this period. For example, despite the detailed evidence of Madoff's fraud provided by outside informers and independent investigators to the Securities and Exchange Commission beginning in the late nineties, the SEC never took any official steps against his Ponzi scheme.

The same kinds of explanation may be applied to those too-large-to-fail financial institutions like AIG, Countrywide Financial, or Goldman Sachs. Despite all the red flags, warnings, and concerns raised by people inside and outside of the SEC, the Federal Reserve Board, and the DOJ over the "questionable," "risky," and "unsound" practices of these financial transactions, these firms were given a free pass to persist in their behavior without interference until the meltdown began in the fall of 2007. It has also been argued by academics and commentators that in the case of the frauds committed by both Madoff and Wall Street, professionals were acting "without understanding the underlying logic of the transactions they made, and those who knew better ignored the signs of impending disaster. And in both cases, agencies failed to exercise oversight delegated to them as 'guardians of trust.'"[7]

This argument, although correct, is too generous and does not get close to the most germane legal issues surrounding the sanctioning and punishment of Wall Street financial fraud.[8] For example, by the end of 2011, with no shortage of existing evidence on the widespread and institutionalized fraud committed by Wall Street firms and with the statute of limitations on securities litigation about to expire, not one of these "defrauding banksters" or their fraudulent corporations had been criminally prosecuted by the United States. Moreover, with the billions of dollars looted and the trillions of dollars lost and the millions of victims harmed, the U.S. Congress and G. W. Bush bailed out the highest-rolling bankers, mortgagers, and insurers in October 2008 when the president signed into law the Troubled Asset Relief Program (TARP). Had the government not purchased the assets and equity from these Wall Street financial institutions to cover the losses wrapped up in their toxic derivative investments,[9] these corporations would have collapsed, as Washington Mutual Bank and Lehman Brothers did a few weeks earlier in September 2008.

Comparatively, Madoff's Ponzi scheme was unique in the annals of Ponzi schemes. Its longevity, size, and global reach make similar Ponzi schemes highly unlikely in the future. By contrast, the episodic orgies of speculation, manipulation, and rigging of financial markets by Wall Street bankers are as old as "leveraged based investments," according to the late John Kenneth Galbraith, a former president of the American Economic Association.[10] Historically, when these institutional fraudsters have been "caught" with smoking guns in their hands, they are rarely, if ever, criminally prosecuted for securities fraud. When occasional sanctions do occur, they usually involve civil, administrative, or regulative enforcement. If financial penalties are incurred, they are a small fraction of the monies "illegally" gotten, and none of the fined parties or corporations has to admit publicly or otherwise to any intentional misdeeds or wrongdoing. Such lawful dishonesty exemplifies the contradictions of bourgeois legality and the crimes of capitalist control alike.

BERNARD MADOFF AND HIS VICTIMS

Madoff's secretary for twenty years, Eleanor Squillari, speaks:

> Bernie stole our trust. Most of us were honest, hardworking people with families. We thought we were living the American Dream and felt privileged to work for such a brilliant, wonderful generous man who was doing such good and charitable things. Now we feel like fools.[11]

Madoff speaks:

> When I began the Ponzi scheme, I believed it would end shortly and I would be able to extricate myself and my clients from the scheme. [But] as the years went by I realized that my arrest and this day would inevitably come.[12]

Though Madoff did not look directly at any of the victims when they spoke of their pain and suffering in U.S. District Court during the sentencing phase, he did turn to them during his remarks before the sentence was pronounced by Judge Denny Chin and simply uttered, "I'm sorry. I know that doesn't help you." He also acknowledged that there were no excuses for his behavior:

> I cannot offer you an excuse for my behavior. How do you excuse betraying thousands of investors who entrusted me with their life savings? How do you excuse deceiving 200 employees who spent most of their working life with me? How do you excuse lying to a brother and two sons who spent their entire lives helping to build a successful business? How do you excuse lying to a wife who stood by you for 50 years?
>
>   I will live with this pain, with this torment, for the rest of my life . . . I have left a legacy of shame . . . to my children and grandchildren.[13]

A Few Victims, a Couple of Judges, and an Expert Speak

Tom Fitzmaurice, 63, who was working three jobs to make ends meet, stated, "There will be no retirement, no trips to California to visit our 1-year-old grandson." He also read from a statement by his wife, Marcia, who stood by his side. It read, "I cry every day when I see the pain in my husband's eyes. . . . I cry for the life we had." In a letter shared by Judge Chin from one widow who had gone to see Madoff two weeks after the death of her husband to invest their life savings, Madoff was quoted as saying, "Your money is safe with me," as he put his arm around her. Another victim, Miriam Siegman, born blocks away from the District Court in New York City and now living a new life of poverty in Stamford, Connecticut, stated, "I now live on food stamps . . . I scavenge in dumpsters at the end of the month." On the other hand, Burt Ross, a former mayor of Fort Lee, New Jersey, having lost $5 million in retirement funds and trusts for his children, stated that he was not in bad shape personally, but was speaking on behalf of victims, including the renowned Holocaust survivor and author, Elie Wiesel, who had invested millions of dollars on behalf of nonprofit charities. Ross had commented, "As if Mr. Wiesel hasn't suffered enough in his lifetime."[14]

Recognizing that sentencing a seventy-one-year-old man to 150 years is largely symbolic, Judge Chin explained that "symbolism is important for victims" because a "substantial sentence may in some small measure help the victims in their healing process."[15] On the other hand, another criminal trial judge with more than twenty years of experience on the bench and that the author knows views symbolic sentences or "dispensing a sentence length" for the benefit of victims as "irrelevant at best and pandering at worst."[16] Jayne Barnard, a law professor at William & Mary who wrote a 2001 law review article that was influential in expanding victims' rights in the law in 2004 was also in attendance at the sentencing of Madoff. Like Judge Chin, she joined other victim advocates in arguing that fraud victims suffer emotionally and socially. Barnard had this to say: "The proof of the value of the process is exactly what we saw in the courtroom today. The victims were eloquent, they were dignified, and they told very powerful stories."[17]

These victims also referred to Madoff as a "monster" and a "low-life." When the tough sentence was imposed, the victims present also burst into applause and cheers.[18] Whether or not criminal sentences and victim impact statements help with the healing process is debatable. Research findings on victim redress from both domestic and international crimes are mixed at best, and unsatisfying and alienating at worst.[19] Nevertheless, testimonies from victims, or victim impact statements, are of value as they give voice to the injured or harmed person, compel the perpetrator to acknowledge, face, and/ or recognize his victim, and legitimate to the bystanders and larger society that real criminality and real victimization has occurred.

Not All Investors/Victims Are Similar or Treated the Same

In the case of Madoff's victims, not all investors were the same: "Not all victims were weak, defenseless, unsuspecting 'lambs' who, through tragic or ironic circumstances or just plain bad luck, were pounced upon by cunning, vicious 'wolves.'"[20] While there were many investors of modest means who had lost most, if not all, of their life savings, there were some forty-eight hundred clients including those who invested directly, assuming that they had $1 to $2 million dollars to invest. Madoff's victims also contained some of the world's largest banks and wealthiest people, including Access International CEO René-Thierry de la Villehuchet. A French aristocrat and money manager with access to rich investors throughout Europe, he committed suicide in his Manhattan office two weeks after Madoff surrendered to the police. De la Villehuchet lost more than $1 billion of his own, his family's, and his clients' money.[21] By contrast, the vast majority of people invested indirectly and had their much smaller sums of money bundled together through "feeder" accounts. Naturally, the material and psychological suffering that these groups of fraud investors/victims experience is not the same.

For example, although there were tens of thousands of investment victims, there were just 113 letters filed with the federal court, and only 9 victim statements were recorded live the day of sentencing. Not surprisingly, the victims who spoke that day, with one exception, were not wealthy. They were ordinary people with median incomes, including a physical therapist, a retired correctional officer, and an accountant. Collectively, their stories of financial devastation where life savings were lost lasted about one hour. By contrast, those investors/victims who did not testify publicly and who were able to invest their money directly were obviously more capable of "writing off their losses" as a bad investment (assuming that they were not compensated for their losses). In any case, these were not life-altering losses, as they represented only a portion of these investors' net worth. On the other hand, those who invested their life savings of far smaller denominations could not avoid financial devastation and they are less likely to receive any restitution. There are also those anonymous non-beneficiary victims of the not-for-profit charities. These "victims" are quite probably unaware of their victimization altogether.

Moreover, only those elite victims who invested directly with Madoff, and who should have known better about the size of the returns but whose enthusiasm and/or greed got the best of them, were eligible for insurance claims of up to $500,000 and to whatever billions might be legally recovered. The other indirect investors are virtually out of luck, subject to litigation relief that may or may not occur after years of protracted legal proceedings. In fact, around the time of Madoff's admission of guilt and sentencing, many of his victims were lawyering up in contending groups in order to fight one another for the limited dollars in restitution.

In addition to victims' differential eligibility for recovery and economic restitution, there is the more complicated issue of separating out the victims and perpetrators. In some instances, even neutral "observers may have reasonable doubts and honest disagreements over which party in a conflict should be labeled the victim and which should be stigmatized as the villain," obscuring further the "determination that one person should be arrested, prosecuted, and punished, and the other defended, supported, and assisted."[22] For example, even before the sentencing of Madoff, some of his clients had already been sued to recover more than $10 billion that they had withdrawn in recent years. In the case of the trust funds and partnerships run by investors Jeffry Picower and Stanley Chais, it was alleged that they had withdrawn $6.1 billion over and above their principal investment. Although Picower and Chais had not formally responded by the time of sentencing, their lawyers claimed that they too were victims of the Madoff fraud.

Another lawsuit was also filed a few weeks before the sentencing against Cohmad Securities Corporation, one of the firms that helped feed investors to Madoff. The suit sought "more than $100 million in commissions earned by the Cohmad principals, who also were sued for civil fraud by the SEC."[23] The suit was also seeking "more than $105 million in profits Cohmad employees and their families withdrew from the investment accounts they had with Mr. Madoff."[24] Lawyers for Cohmad's principals denied any connection to the fraud. Similarly, Irving Picard, a court-appointed trustee who is recovering assets for Madoff's fraud victims, unveiled new allegations in October 2009 against investors who allegedly benefited from the multibillion-dollar Ponzi scheme.[25] Picard announced that he would also go after the assets of certain relatives of Madoff who worked at the New York firm.

In May 2010, about 720,000 overseas Madoff investors who had organized in 2009 into a global alliance of 60 firms settled with their banks, receiving about $15.5 billion. In theory, according to law firms representing those victims of the fraud, this represented 100 percent of their clients' invested monies. Unlike those overseas investors, U.S. investors are not likely "to see similar compensation any time soon, partly because their investments were with Mr. Madoff or through conduits that lack the deep pockets of the big European banks."[26]

Finally, while most investors/victims from whatever group of victims/ investors remain relatively invisible, there were other wealthy individuals and institutional investors who may have actually made a lot of money off of this Ponzi scheme by withdrawing their money before Madoff "folded up shop." After all, there is a vast amount of "missing money" or the difference between the magnitude of Madoff's alleged fortune of some $50 billion and the reported losses of some $15 to $18 billion claimed by his victims. Accordingly, Picard, making good on his earlier claims to seek money from those who benefitted from the scheme, announced on July 27, 2010, through the *New York Times* that he would begin filing lawsuits "against approximately 1,000 investors who have been dubbed 'net winners' from the scam."[27]

Making good on his claim to file numerous lawsuits, including one against JP Morgan for $19 billion, Picard had already collected about $10 billion for Madoff victims by May 2011. However, much of the money could not be given out pending the resolution of other legal actions by some investors that could change the eventual size of the payouts and who would receive them.[28] At the same time, Picard had also filed papers with the court seeking permission "to distribute $272 million to compensate victims who held 1,224 accounts at Mr. Madoff's firm, an average of about $222,000" per victim.[29] In the meanwhile, some of the world's biggest banks were "jumping into a multi-billion-dollar market that buys up victims' claims in the Bernard Madoff Ponzi scheme, including two banks that have been sued in connection with the fraud."[30] Back in June 2010, investors were receiving offers of just twenty to thirty cents on the dollar. One year later, offers on claims had risen to roughly seventy to seventy-five cents on the dollar.

WALL STREET BANKERS AND THEIR VICTIMS

The central role played by Wall Street banks in the housing crash of 2006 that led to the financial meltdown of 2007–8 is not difficult to document. In the old days, before the passage of Gramm-Leach-Bliley in 1999, which integrated commercial and investment banks, the big four at the time—Goldman Sachs, Lehman Brothers, Morgan Stanley, and Salomon Brothers—would not have been allowed to unleash their various financial products that bundled hundreds of thousands of bad, risky, or subprime housing loans. Without these exotic instruments there would not have been the kind of growth in the mortgage markets that drove the housing bubble and crash, the real estate crisis that still persists, and the worst epidemic of mortgage foreclosures in U.S. history. Moreover, without this deregulatory reform there would not have been the wide-scale and institutionalized network of defrauding, involving the cooperative interactions of thousands of brokers, lenders, appraisers, and escrow and title people, operating throughout the derivative-driven and crime-facilitative mortgage environment.

Using "techniques of neutralization," these networks of criminality rationalized away their illegal behaviors to the tune of creating more than one million fraudulent mortgages in 2007 alone. The outcome from this institutionally organized mortgage fraud also cost the financial industry between $946 million and $4.3 billion in 2006.[31] Back in 2010, former investigative reporter and creator of *USAWatchdog*, Greg Hunter, in combining mortgage fraud and foreclosure fraud estimates, was blogging about "The Perfect No-Prosecution Crime"[32] and the $6.4 trillion problem in real estate, referring to "fat cat bankers" who could not legally prove what they owned. Meaning quite simply that

> trillions of mortgage-backed securities HAVE NO BACKING. I think this is the biggest fraud in history. This was not an accident made by someone pressing the wrong button or a few documents that weren't handled properly, but fraud on a massive scale that took years and tens of thousands of people to pull it off.[33]

"Back in the day," before mortgage-based securities were applied to home loans, mortgage dealers required that home buyers were able to produce a down payment of 10 percent or more, had a steady income, and a good credit rating. At the turn of the twenty-first century, the borrowing standards were radically lowered, the traditional protections against the risks of home fore-closures were swept aside, and mortgage dealers started writing mortgages for as little as zero down and zero interest for a period of time. In the past, few if any banks would have wanted these mortgages on their books, know-ing how likely they were to fail. Yet in a few years a mass market for these toxic mortgage debts was thriving.

How were those high-risk mortgages sold around the world to investors, pension funds, insurance companies, municipalities, county governments, boards of education, and so on? To package and sell these subprime mort-gages not as the junk-rated mortgages that they were but rather as triple-A-rated investments, which they weren't, the big banks employed essentially three methods. First, they bundled thousands of mortgage loans into collat-eralized mortgage obligations.[34] Second, the banks "co-opted" inflated credit ratings from Moody's and Standard & Poor's.[35] Third, they sold investors on the idea that CMOs as a whole were sound because most of those mortgages in the bundled packages were solid. Well, the percentages or ratios of solid to not solid mortgages involved here are critical. For example, once upon a time, the old thrifts or savings and loans liked to keep their subprime or riskier loans to no more than 7 percent of their portfolio of loans.[36] By the peak year of the housing boom in 2006, Goldman Sachs had underwritten "$76.5 billion worth of mortgage-backed securities—a third of which were sub-prime."[37]

Then in order to protect themselves from these toxic financial instruments, the megabanks hedged their investments of other people's money by getting companies like American International Group (AIG) to provide insurance—known as credit default swaps[38]—on the CMOs. These swaps represented essentially wages between the banks and AIG. The banks were betting that borrowers of home loans would default; AIG was betting that they would not.[39] Although the investment banks won these bets, the losers of these bets would come back to bite them (or not). In other words, the bursting of the fraudulently induced housing bubble led effectively to the collapse of Bear Stearns, Washington Mutual Bank, and Lehman Brothers.

However, in the convoluted world of the TARP bailouts for those institutions that were deemed too big to fail like AIG, "whose toxic portfolio of credit swaps was in significant part composed of the insurance that banks like Goldman bought against their own housing portfolios,"[40] at least $1.3 billion of taxpayer money given to AIG ultimately found its way back to Goldman Sachs. Hence, like bandits, Goldman Sachs made out twice on the housing bubble. That is to say, the firm looted both their investors and the taxpayers: first, when they bet against their own toxic CMOs and second, when they colluded with Bush II and company to make the taxpayers indirectly pay off on those lost CMOs, as well.[41]

Not All Taxpayers/Victims Are Similar, Nor Are the Payouts to the Winners and the Losers

The economic fallout or victimization of the American people from the Wall Street meltdown and its aftermath is difficult to measure. Even an approximate figure of the number of victims who suffered financial losses is difficult to grasp because of distinctions that can be made between direct and indirect victims. By the summer of 2011, there were 13.9 million people looking for work and the official unemployment rate was near double digits (9.1). Perhaps more significantly, one out of four mortgagees in the United States were "underwater," owing more money on their homes than they are worth. Putting aside the fact that virtually all of the "portfolios" in the United States have lost net worth due to this financial debacle, it is safe to assume that we are talking on the order of upward of fifty million victims.

A non-exhaustive list of individual and institutional victims would include: the tens of thousands of employees and investors of the bond house Bear Stearns, of the investment bank Lehman Brothers, and of the brokerage house Merrill Lynch, as each of these firms met their demise, destroying billions of dollars in shareholder values. By the end of 2008, as housing prices fell precipitously across America, homeowners had already collectively lost some $13 trillion in the value of their homes from their "peak" before the housing bubble burst in 2006. Similarly, looking at the Dow Jones Industrial Averages and the NASDAQ, the former dropped more than 50 percent from its October 2007 high of around fourteen thousand to about sixty-five hundred in March 2009, and the latter witnessed the disappearance of some $5 trillion in wealth. Globally, estimates have placed the decline in wealth at close to $50 trillion.[42]

While most mainstream economists and fraud minimalists are still in denial about the workings of the "free-market" and the "causes" of the banking crisis, this is no longer the case for Alan Greenspan, the former and longest-lasting chair of the Federal Reserve System. During his congressional testimony on the financial crisis in October 2008, Greenspan made a striking apology when he admitted that the assumptions about self-correcting financial markets were wrong. After nearly three decades at the economic helm, Greenspan has finally exited from the public stage and with him his long-overdue admission that the free market without regulation is a flawed system. Unfortunately, most of the nation's economic and political elite prefers to ignore Greenspan's call for serious re-regulation. They have also dismissed Greenspan's endorsement for breaking up those behemoth banks regarded as "too big to fail."[43]

Unlike Madoff or Greenspan, Wall Street institutions have still not recognized or accepted culpability for their erroneous and misguided behavior.

Although the investment firms have acknowledged their role in the financial crisis as well as that their institutional survival depended on taxpayer bailouts, they have never come clean or branded specifically what things went wrong. For example, one of the unrivaled overseers of financial risk, Lloyd C. Blankfein, CEO of Goldman Sachs, admitted late in 2009 during a public mea culpa that the megabanks made "mistakes" and "we participated in things that were clearly wrong . . . we apologize."[44] Again, there is no identification or discussion of those "things" that were clearly wrong. Nor is there any commitment or promise or rhetoric to disengage from any of these practices. Instead, these patterned mistakes of "business as usual" are framed ideologically by Blankfein as doing "God's work" in order to sustain the free-market system.

Of course, what neither Blankfein nor most on Wall Street or Capitol Hill want to address are the crimes of capitalist control, whether it's the everyday practices of securities fraud or the institutionalized looting facilitated by a corrupt U.S. taxing system. For example, in the case of Goldman Sachs, the bank paid out $10 billion in compensation and benefits in 2008 before netting a profitable income of $2 billion, which yielded an effective corporate tax rate of 1 percent or $14 million paid to Uncle Sam. For the same year, God's helper, Blankfein, was the recipient of $42.9 million in pay.[45] In 2010, compensation and benefits for twenty-six of the top thirty-five publicly held securities and investment-services firms set a record of $144 billion, "a 4% increase from the $139 billion paid out in 2009." Moreover, the "data showed that revenue was expected to rise at 29 of the 35 firms surveyed, but at a slower pace than pay."[46]

Not surprisingly, in response to the fallout from their self-inflicted wounds, the TARP bailouts, huge quarterly profits, and million-dollar bonuses, these Wall Street institutions found themselves on the defensive and under popular attack. In October 2009, for example, a couple thousand protesters marched at the American Bankers Association's annual conference in Chicago. Foreshadowing Occupy Wall Street two years later, these demonstrators brandished cutouts of bank chief executive officers. One month later, Goldman Sachs announced that it would spend $500 million to help thousands of small businesses recover from the recession. This public relations exercise represented a paltry sum of money when compared to the $16.7 billion the bank had already set aside for its bonus pool during the first nine months of 2009. In the same period, as a tax-deductible expense, the financial industry had also spent $344 million lobbying Capitol Hill against substantive financial reform.

What did Wall Street get in return for spending more of the taxpayers' money? In one of many examples from the *Time* cover story for July 24, 2010—"Government for Sale: How Lobbyists Shaped the Financial Reform Bill"—$15 million paid by money managers "to protect the favorable carried-interest tax treatment" yielded "about $10 billion in lower taxes" over ten years.[47] In the larger scheme of things, $10 billion is "chump change" compared to what has been at stake over Wall Street's continued "free hand to keep peddling the indecipherable derivatives beyond the reach of regula- tors."[48] At the outbreak of the Great Recession, the Gang of Six—Bank of America, Citigroup, Goldman Sachs, JP Morgan Chase, Morgan Stanley, and Wells Fargo—held more than 95 percent of the exposed derivatives whose total contract value exceeded $290 trillion. To put it simply, these bankers were not about to relinquish their control over the right to exploit these fi- nancial markets without a fight. Nor were these banksters about to turn their backs on their deregulatory and non-regulatory gains accomplished during the administrations of Presidents Bill Clinton and G. W. Bush.

During the financial reform hearings in 2009, Paul Barrett, editor of *BusinessWeek*, summed up the state of affairs on substantive regulatory reform this way:

> Neither the Federal Reserve nor the Securities and Exchange Commission ap- pears to have the mettle to impose strict limits on the kind of gambling with borrowed money that drove storied investment banks out of business or into the hands of taxpayer-backed rescuers. And no one has had the temerity even to suggest that we ought to revisit the deregulatory moves of the 1990s.[49]

Moreover, as business reporter and journalist Andrew Ross Sorkin argued in his best-selling *Too Big to Fail* (2009), these goliaths of the banking industry were protected by an implied taxpayers' safety net. Hence, they have a built- in incentive to start taking risks again.[50]

Banker Not Bankster: Perpetrator and Victim Non-recognitions

The relatively small number of victims and dollars lost as a result of the Ponzi scheme pulled off by Bernie Madoff weighted against the humongous economic losses caused by the banksters of Wall Street in alliance with such other financial institutions as Countrywide Financial, AIG, and so on, reveal important dissimilarities in the legal reactions to individualized versus institutionalized organizational fraud and victimization. Unlike Madoff and his conspirators to defraud, Wall Street bankers and their financial networks have not only "gotten off easy," but they have also been rewarded with bail- outs and bonuses for their fraudulent behaviors. At the height of the financial crisis, the "shakedown" or maximum at-risk government commitment was for $13.89 trillion. By May 2010, $4.73 trillion had been disbursed and $2.71 trillion had been repaid.[51]

For perspective, restoring the Bush II tax cuts for millionaires and billion- aires would have generated roughly a trillion dollars, more than enough to have bailed out Wall Street. Better yet, with a bit more "equitable" taxation and/or billing of Wall Street directly for the meltdown it caused in 2007–8 and/or toward the prevention of future meltdowns, both the costs for one meltdown as well as for reducing the risks of future meltdowns would be borne by those responsible. Though all of these ideas were suggested at the time of the TARP bailouts, there was no support in Congress for anything that might resemble the jurisprudence of "just deserts."

These differences in accountability, blame, culpability, and sustained political and economic vilification of the institutionalized victimization of the American people by Wall Street, when compared to the repetitive negative reconstruction of the individualized victimization caused by fraudsters like Madoff or by rogue corporations like Enron or WorldCom, has resulted in a "restorative justice" of sorts for those perpetrators of toxic financial implosion and in an "equal neglect" of sorts for the tens of millions of "invisible" Main Street victims. Without the necessary financial reform, enforcement, and legal control, securities fraud remains essentially an invisible crime of capitalist control. We remain all the more vulnerable as market financial relations often make it "difficult to distinguish white-collar crime from ordinary business transactions,"[52] making accountability all the more unlikely.

So long as there are no criminal prosecutions, let alone convictions, for securities fraudulent behavior, Wall Street will remain unconcerned about criminal or social responsibility for the wrongdoing and damage that it has caused. Unless held criminally liable for their widespread victimization, Wall Street and the American public will not regard these bankers as the banksters they are. Unlike the thieving Madoff, who had to face his victims in a court of law and acknowledge his wrongdoing, the looters of Wall Street share no sense of culpability for their victimization of others. There is no recognition of the harm and injuries to millions, no legacy of shame, real or unreal. Concurrently, the pain of their victims remains largely abstract and unacknowledged. Finally, without the debatable symbolic value of these victims experiencing some form of meaningful sanction against their violators, such as compensation for their losses, if not for their pain and suffering, then there are high risks that the same types of securities-related frauds will be repeated in the future.

CRIME, THE AMERICAN DREAM, AND VICTIMIZATION: A FINAL INTRODUCTORY CONTRADICTION

The historian James T. Adams coined the term "the American Dream" in his 1931 book, *The Epic of America*. He was referring to a country where life should be better and richer and fuller for everyone. He was not necessarily emphasizing material success, but rather the idea or belief that regardless of birth or circumstances, American society existed as a place where all people could pursue happiness and attain the fullest stature of which they were capable. In a few words, security and self-actualization through equal opportunity. Subsequent commentaries on the American Dream have tended to emphasize an abundance of social competition, winners and losers, and the ascendance of pecuniary values at the core. In *Social Theory and Social Structure* (1968), sociologist Robert K. Merton argued, as he had for some three decades, "In some large measure, money has been consecrated as a value in itself, over and above its expenditure for articles of consumption or its use for the enhancement of power."[53] As far back as his 1938 adaptation of Émile Durkheim's nineteenth-century theory of normlessness or "anomie" into "strain" theory, he located the cause of crime in the failure of the political economy "to provide an adequate means for all those whose aspirations had been raised by advertising and media to achieve the monetary success of the American Dream."[54]

Echoing Merton's sentiments on the cultural pursuit of material wealth are Steven Messner and Richard Rosenfeld in *Crime and the American Dream* (2001). These criminologists argue that the American Dream "offers 'no final stopping point.' It requires 'never ending achievement.'"[55] This pecuniary dream, they argue, can't be satiated, and it has no financial limits. Specifically, in expanding the criminogenic stimuli involved in individual behavior offered by Merton's theory of criminal motivation, Messner and Rosenfeld base their theory of crime and "institutional anomie" on three selfish or ego-centric premises about the American Dream: (1) it requires a never-ending pursuit of money for its own sake; (2) the means of monetary acquisition are of little importance; and (3) the consequences of individual attainment are viewed as independent from their affects on others. No longer are economically motivated crimes limited to the adaptive illegitimate opportunities available to the disadvantaged pursuing the American Dream of success. Instead, illegitimate opportunities to acquire material wealth are open to all those who are not disadvantaged, especially to those who are most advantaged because their decisions to act socially irresponsible, to loot the American people, and to defraud the American Dream have been "decriminalized" by the contradictions of the political economy of bourgeois legality, which effectively prohibits the criminal prosecution of institutionalized securities fraud.

As for the victims of at least some financial crimes, there may be some kind of identification with the more powerful perpetrators. For example, in one intriguing study of a classic Ponzi scheme that unfolded in Houston, Texas, in the late 1990s, the authors of the research argue that the victims and perpetrators of this financial fraud shared similar criminogenic stimuli. They contend further that fraud offenders and fraud victims accept means that are more alike than different:

> Despite the fact that both held the same potential "benefit" (i.e., wealth), they had very different potential "costs." The victims believed they were risking the loss of money they had invested and the offender was risking imprisonment. However, both the offender and the victims reached the same conclusion—that these costs were acceptable viabilities for the chance to attain wealth. This suggests that both forms of means/costs were similar enough in that they are both less threatening than wealth is valuable.[56]

Among the conclusions reached by Trahan et al., the majority of these fraud victims were behaving in accordance with the values of the American Dream. Furthermore, rather than viewing the solicitation by the offenders as the causative agent, the "cause" was primarily the American culture that instilled behavioral tendencies conducive to fraud victimization. Moreover, it was found that those Americans who ascribed to the inherent value of money may be at greater risk for this type of victimization. Their argument is less about the individual and more about the sociopolitical context in which the fraud occurs. In other words, those victims of this particular Ponzi scheme were not exceptionally greedy Americans because the "greed" upon which this fraud thrived was "not a function of the individual attributes of its victims," rather it was a function or "characteristic of American economic culture."[57]

Making matters of securities fraud and financial crime more complicated are the facts that these transgressions take many forms, some obvious and others opaque. As already implied, in the financial world of fraud it is sometimes difficult to prove, if not to actually distinguish, between legal and illegal enterprises. Moreover, as journalist Carol Lloyd wrote about mortgage fraud back in 2006, it is not only "difficult to disentangle victim from criminal" but also "crime from business as usual."[58] More generally, as Trahan et al. have argued about financial crime, risk taking, and innovation, "The economic system's reliance on free market structures allows entrepreneurial ventures to closely resemble fraud crimes."[59]

In sum, looting is more about the illegitimate opportunity thing than the greed thing. Testifying before the U.S. Banking Committee in 2002, Greenspan stated, "It is not that humans have become any more greedy than in generations past. It is that the avenues to express greed have grown enormously."[60] In terms of striking the correct "balance" between too much and too little allure in licit and illicit markets, white-collar criminologists Peter Grabosky and Neal Shover argue that the "challenge is to enable the use of lure for legitimate purposes, while reducing its potential as an instrument or target of crime."[61] The struggle to reduce the cultural lure is formidable because of a rising stream of opportunities that accompany the developing policies of complex societies:

> Absent credible oversight, every new tax becomes an opportunity for evasion. Every new program of public expenditure is a potential lure for those who would appropriate from it unlawfully. This is no less true of policies implemented with the best of intentions: programs designed to extend opportunities for home ownership to those previously excluded from the residential housing market helped create the subprime mortgage debacle.[62]

Chapter Three

Unenlightened Self-Interest, Unregulated Financial Markets, and Unfettered Victimization

From the Savings and Loan Bailouts to Too Big to Fail

For the first time in U.S. history the 1980s witnessed "me generation" graduates from elite colleges and universities flocking to Wall Street to become investment brokers, arbitrage dealers, and over-the-counter derivative traders.[1] These new vocational choices were not unrelated to the changing market relations of a post-industrial service economy and to an upgraded version of the older pecuniary American Dream. The new American Dream (2.0) "was to make tens of millions of dollars on Wall Street or as a hedge fund manager in Greenwich, Connecticut." The new dream "was also connected to the old American Dream—to own a house of one's own."[2] In the unregulated environment of derivatives, these two dreams became a dangerous mixture. One consequence was that Wall Street bankers and related financial service providers dealing in mortgages, real estate, and insurance took illegal advantage of both investors and homebuyers. Together, Wall Street firms not only defrauded the dream of homeownership, but they also effectively appropriated and transformed the government-guaranteed subprime lending program, significantly contributing to the financial collapse of 2007–8.

In the not too distant past, these types of loans constituted about 7 percent of a firm's portfolio of investments rather than the 50 percent or more that they would become for the biggest lending institutions prior to the meltdown. Previously, subprime loans had been used primarily as a tool for refinancing homes for low and moderate-income people. Only secondarily was it used for buying homes. This began to change in the late 1990s and was very different by the early 2000s. In the new world of derivatives, investment bankers abandoned most, if not all, of the "old" lending standards as they bundled together mortgage-backed securities into collateralized debt obligations.[3] In the process, subprime abusive lending took off and "homeownership" became available essentially to anyone able (or not) to afford a particular mortgage regardless of socioeconomic class—"no questions asked."

The combination of low interest rates, expanding subprime loans, and a refinancing bonanza inflated the housing market. In turn, the housing bubble would peak and burst in the first decade of the twenty-first century. When the real estate market crashed in 2006, millions of Americans ended up losing their homes as foreclosure rates and numbers began to climb to record highs.[4] The imploded housing market, the toxic loans and derivative investment withdrawals, and the creation of a debtor class of homeowners contributed to the financial crisis in 2007–8 as well as to the government bailouts in 2009 that addressed the needs of Wall Street but not the needs of Main Street. As Damon Silvers, a lawyer at the AFL-CIO and member of the TARP Congressional Oversight Panel explained just before the August Panic of 2011:

> If your personal wealth is predominantly in capital markets [then] you had a hell of a scare, but you're 70 percent of the way back to where you were in 2007. If your personal wealth is predominantly in your home, you're fucked. And for approximately 80 percent of the people in the US, their only asset is in their home.[5]

These changing and developing free-market relations cannot be separated from the rising monopolization of the financial sector and the bourgeoning of a Wall Street oligarchy in particular. From the savings and loan bailouts in the 1980s to the contemporary policies of too big to fail, these controversial courses of action are at the heart of the economic and political conflicts over state intervention into the financial relations of abuse and fraud. The TARP bailouts have set into motion years of fierce lobbying and intense congressional debate concerning the appropriate responses to the Wall Street debacle. Early on, the product of this infighting and lobbying resulted in President Obama signing the Wall Street Reform and Consumer Protection Act of 2010, otherwise known as Dodd-Frank.

The twenty-three hundred pages of legislation was not the end of policy formation, but a ratcheting up of an ongoing conflict. The law established a catalog of rules and unresolved issues to be worked out by regulators, lobbyists, and congressional committee members. A year after the law's passage most of these rules/issues had not been resolved, let alone implemented. Although the dotting of the i's and the crossing of the t's were supposed to be completed by July 2012, they were not. These conflicts between the forces of regulation and consumer investment rights versus the forces of deregulation and securities trader rights vary over time. While the ideologies of laissez-faire and deregulation have recently lost much of their allure on Main Street, the cultural capital of "free enterprise" on Wall Street and in Washington, DC, is still very much alive.

These ideological differences over the proper roles or relationship between the private sector and governments are not new to the history of the

United States. At least as far back as the skirmishes between founding fathers Thomas Jefferson and Alexander Hamilton over the establishment of a publicly chartered bank in 1791, there have been social and cultural tensions between those Americans who favor centralized and those who favor decentralized forms of political and economic power. For example, those politicos who advocated for decentralized power and opposed a strong central bank, the Jeffersonians, had concerns over the abuse and control of banking's crucial economic functions—to mediate financial transactions and to manage the supply of credit. Their argument was that the creation of the (First) Bank of the United States would give too much power to those bankers, enabling them to "gain leverage over the federal government as its major creditor and payment agent," as well as facilitating the picking of "economic winners and losers through its decisions to grant or withhold credit."[6]

For Jefferson, "banking institutions [were] more dangerous than standing armies" and he argued that with the increasing importance of finance to society came the increasing power of banks.[7] Jefferson and the minority of presidents that have historically lined up with him, such as Andrew Jackson, Theodore Roosevelt, and Franklin Delano Roosevelt, have all believed that armed with too much power, banks could use it to primarily benefit themselves rather than their investors. Even worse, banks could use their power to undermine both democracy and the general welfare.

On the other side of the political aisle, Hamilton, neither an agrarian nor a slave owner like Jefferson, favored a strong federal government that actively supports economic development. Hamiltonians believed, for example, that a strong central bank manages the federal government's money more efficiently than a decentralized system of banking. They also believed that by providing an important source of credit to both the government and the economy, a central (federal) bank allows for entrepreneurial development and long-term prosperity. Historically, the United Stated government has tended to side with the Hamiltonians rather than the Jeffersonians. Yet, on more than a few occasions, the central financial policies and/or abuses of capitalist control have been checked or constrained by Jeffersonian inclinations to curtail the vast economic power of investment bankers. This has typically occurred following severe economic crises like the 1929 stock market crash and during the 1930s Great Depression when a host of financial reforms and other New Deal policies, such as the Social Security Act of 1935, were introduced.

REGULATING BANKING (1908–2002)

After the Panic of 1907, also known as the Bankers Panic, when the New York Stock Exchange had fallen close to 50 percent from one year earlier,

Congress passed the Aldrich-Vreeland Act in 1908, which activated the
National Monetary Commission. This law prompted national banks to start
currency associations. In groups of ten or more banks, these associations
with a minimum of $5 million in capital were backed by a combination of
governmental bonds and the securities held by the banks in common. The act
also permitted the distribution of emergency currency by the Comptroller of
the Currency. It also did some of the early planning for and recommended the
passage of the Federal Reserve Act of 1913.

President Wilson signed the Federal Reserve Act into law, which created
the Federal Reserve System (FRS) or the central banking system of the United
States. The nation had been without a central bank since President Jackson
declined to renew the charter for the Second Bank of the United States when
he vetoed the bill in 1836. The new banking and currency reform required
that all nationally chartered banks become members of the FRS, headed
initially by the Federal Reserve Board and subsequently since 1935 by the
Board of Governors, appointed by the president and approved by the U.S.
Senate. State-chartered banks have had the option of becoming dues-paying
members of the FRS. The act also established a single U.S. currency and a
twelve-member Federal Advisory Committee. It required that all member
banks purchase specified non-transferable stock in their regional Federal Reserve Bank and set aside a stipulated amount of non-interest-bearing reserves
with their respective reserve banks. Member banks are entitled to lower
interest loans at the discount window, usually on a short-term basis to meet
temporary shortages of liquidity caused by internal or external disruptions.

Over the years the Federal Reserve Act has been amended some two hundred times and continues to be one of the principal banking laws of the United
States. Three of the more significant amendments have been: (1) amended
Section 13 in 1932, which gave the Fed the authority in "unusual and exigent
circumstances" to make loans to anybody so long as the collateral provided in
exchange arose "out of actual commercial transactions"; (2) the Banking Act
of 1935 that created the Federal Open Market Committee consisting of the
seven-member Board of Governors of the FRS and five representatives from
the Federal Reserve banks whom are empowered to direct all open-market
operations of these banks; and (3) the 1977 charge to the FOMC to "promote
effectively the goals of maximum employment, stable prices, and moderate
long-term interest rates" (Section 2A, FRA).

In 1932 President Hoover signed the Federal Home Loan Bank Act into
law. The act was designed to lower the cost of homeownership. It established
both the Federal Home Loan Bank Board to charter and supervise federal
savings and loan institutions and the Federal Home Loan Banks that lend to
savings and loans in order to finance home mortgages. After the S&L debacle

peaked in the late eighties, the Financial Institutions Reform, Recovery, and Enforcement Act of 1989 transferred the regulation of thrifts (S&Ls) to the Office of Thrift Supervision with the Department of Treasury. Like other federal bank regulators, the banks that OTS regulates pay their salaries. Initially viewed as an aggressive regulator, the office became increasingly lax as both revenues and the OTS staff declined in the 1990s. At the same time, the OTS expanded its oversight to non-banks and was supervising such companies as AIG and Washington Mutual when each failed leading up to the financial crisis of 2007–8.

The Banking Act of 1933, or the Glass-Steagall Act as it is more popularly known, was passed into law in response to the collapse of a substantial portion of the commercial banking system earlier that year. The goals of the law were to prohibit "commercial banks from collaborating with full-service brokerage firms or participating in investment banking activities," on the one hand, and to protect "bank depositors from the additional risks associated with security transactions," on the other hand.[8] This act also established the Federal Deposit Insurance Corporation (FDIC) and Regulation Q that provided the Federal Reserve with the authority to regulate or set interest rates for savings deposit accounts.

The 1933 Securities Act (also known as the Federal Securities Act or the Truth in Securities Act) and the 1934 Securities Exchange Act (also known, as the Exchange Act) were two sweeping pieces of legislation that formed the modern basis of the regulation of financial markets and its participants. The 1933 law was the first major federal legislation to regulate the original issuing or the offer and sale of securities by companies and their direct investors. The 1934 law was the first major federal legislation to regulate the secondary trading of securities in the case of stocks, bonds, and debts between persons who may or may not be related to the issue, typically through the activities of brokers or dealers. Both of these acts required companies that sell securities to the public to disclose material information in periodic reports. They also prohibited deceit, misrepresentation, and other fraud in the sale of securities. Finally, the 1934 law created the Security and Exchange Commission, the agency with the primary responsibilities for enforcing the regulations of these two acts.

The National Housing Act of 1934 created both the Federal Housing Administration (FHA) and the Federal Savings and Loan Insurance Corporation (FSLIC). Designed in an effort to stop the tide of bank foreclosures during the Great Depression and to make housing and home mortgages more affordable for the middle class, the FHA and the FSLIC became the anchor of the mortgage and homebuilding industries. For the next four decades, the regulation of thrifts (savings and loans) allowed for the relative stability of these financial institutions and for the affordability of housing. Some thirty-six years later in 1970, Congress would pass the National Credit Union Share Insurance Fund for credit unions to perform the same functions as the FDIC did for banks and the FSLIC did for thrifts—guarantee or secure deposits.

Three related regulatory laws that were aimed at protecting the consuming public in financial transactions with lending institutions were the 1968 Truth in Lending Act, the 1992 Broker-Dealer Risk Assessment Program, and the 1994 Home Ownership and Equity Protection Act. The Truth in Lending Act was designed to protect consumers in credit and requires lenders to disclose in clear terms and in standardized form the arrangements, costs, and rates of all loans. The Broker-Dealer Risk Assessment Program was the result of the SEC implementing Section 17(h) to the Securities Exchange Act of 1934 as amended by the Market Reform Act of 1990. The amended law required broker-dealers to file quarterly risk assessment reports, providing disclosures about materially associated persons, organizational charts, policies and procedures, and legal representation as necessary. The Home Ownership and Equity Protection Act banned predatory lending, referring to those practices where lenders do not care whether or not the home borrowers can make their payments because the lenders can then foreclose and snatch up these homes below market value. The Truth in Lending Act was further amended in 1994 and reads in part: "A creditor shall not engage in a pattern or practice of extending credit to consumers under [high-cost refinance mortgages] based on the consumers' collateral without regard to the consumers' repayment ability, including the consumers' current and expected income, current obligations and employment."[9]

The last major regulatory act passed by Congress before the Wall Street Reform and Consumer Protection Act of 2010 was the 2002 Sarbanes-Oxley Act also known as the Public Company Accounting Reform and Investor Protection Act (in the Senate) and as the Auditing Accountability and Responsibility Act (in the House), or simply as SOX. The bill was enacted in response to the public's lack of confidence in the nation's security markets due to the numerous accounting and corporate scandals early in the twenty-first century. While not applicable to privately held companies, SOX contains eleven sections, ranging from corporate board responsibility to criminal penalties. The act created the quasi-public agency, the Public Company Accounting Oversight Board, charged with specifically overseeing those accounting firms engaged in auditing public companies. The act also mandated the SEC to implement new rulings or requirements to comply with the law. When President George W. Bush signed the bill into law, he stated that SOX included "the most far-reaching reforms of American business practices since the time of Franklin Delano Roosevelt."[10] As true as that statement may have been, the law quickly fell into disfavor with businesses and many regulators alike.

FREE-MARKET IDEOLOGIES AND DEREGULATION

During the last quarter of the twentieth century the basic philosophy and practice of free-market theories, often referred to as nineteenth-century laissez-faire theory or as neo-classical rational economics today, became the governing justifications for policies of deregulation and non-intervention. By the 1980s, these empirically undemonstrated theories had come to capture academia by way of Milton Friedman, a pioneering, Nobel-winning economist at the University of Chicago.[11] Subsequently, these unproven theories of "free markets" along with their accompanying anti-government and anti-regulation ideologies came to dominate the imaginations of nearly all of the Republican and Democratic politicians alike. Although free-market theory and practice has never worked as explained, "free market" rhetoric has served as a powerful ideological weapon and rationalizing tool for redistributing wealth upward. This is not to argue that the neo-classical ideologies of free markets, governmental hands off, and privatization in general, as well as the deregulation of financial securities and the lack of an economic-systemic delegitimation crisis in particular, have not been without their vocal critics and non-believers.

On the contrary, within academic and policy circles both inside and outside the official corridors of Wall Street and Washington, there have been alternative analyses and interpretations of economics, regulation, and state intervention. For the most part, those non-conforming perspectives have been dismissed, ignored, or marginalized by elite policy wonks of the prevailing political economy of neo-liberal capitalism. Those excluded outsiders with a difference in approach to the Wall Street implosion of 2007–8 and the future of financial markets have included such esteemed economists as Nobel Prize winners Maurice Allais and Joseph E. Stiglitz. Excluded insiders have included, for example, the recent demise of Brooksley Born, a former chair of the Commodity Futures Trading Commission (CFTC), or the earlier departure of Reagan appointee Ed Gray. By the mid-eighties, Gray, the seventeenth chairman of the Federal Home Loan Bank Board, understood the ill consequences and inherent risks in new thrift deregulation, particularly as these related to brokered deposits and the quest for high-yield investments. Armed with the experiences of the collapses of Penn Square Bank in Oklahoma City in 1982 and Empire Savings and Loan in Mesquite, Texas, in 1984, Gray became very concerned about thrift speculation. He also became too persistent in his criticisms of and opposition to the new deregulations stemming from the Garn-St. Germain Act (1982). As a direct result, President Reagan accepted Gray's early resignation from his appointed three-year term to spend more time with the family.[12]

Ironically, before Friedman's ascension to free-market guru status, he was a soft-spoken Keynesian. During the time he worked in government post–World War II and before introducing his monetary theory of economics in the 1960s, Friedman—a self-described political and economic libertarian—had supported Keynes' economics of high taxation and social spending as a means of combating the contradictions of capitalism. After all, these ideas were working and they were politically popular as in the Great Society and War on Poverty programs promoted by President Lyndon Johnson (1963–68). In contrast to Keynesianism, Friedman's theory of monetarism emphasizes the key role played by the money supply. Monetarism argues that the government should keep its supply of money steady, expanding it each year only slightly to allow for the natural growth of the economy. Taking issue with Keynes' theory about a lack of investment causing the Great Depression, Friedman argued instead that the crisis of the thirties was due to the contraction in the supply of money.

In his best-selling book *Capitalism and Freedom* (1982), which became the bible of neo-conservatism, he argued for the eradication of the economic and social policies of the New Deal and Great Society. These, he claimed, were based on an unnatural system of progressive taxation and the welfare of the public good, all of which inhibited individual growth and free enterprise. Moreover, according to the theory of monetarism and free markets, when left to their own devices, inflation, unemployment, and production will naturally adjust themselves to the fixed money supply.[13] Finally, because Friedman assumed that private sector enterprises are naturally more efficient than public sector enterprises, he became an advocate for institutionalizing three types of policies: (1) non-interference and deregulation that would foster the faster accumulation of profits; (2) privatization or the selling off of state assets so corporations could profiteer in the transference of capital from the public to the private sector as in the cases of government retirement funds and pensions, school vouchers and education, or expenditures on prisons and detention facilities; and (3) lower taxes and equal rates for rich and poor alike.

Compared to virtually all of the other developed nations in the world, U.S. "exceptionalism" has rendered an underdeveloped welfare state with both lower and less progressive taxation rates. At the same time, our country has never actually subjected itself to the full wrath of free-market theory or practice. By contrast, what have been the experiences of those underdeveloped or developing countries that from time to time have been forced to apply these theories? These real-world exercises in unrestrained free markets and neo-liberal economic policies have turned out to be nothing short of dismal failures.[14]

As far back as the 1970s, with the military coup d'état and murder of democratically elected socialist president Salvador Allende, when Friedman became the American economic advisor to the ruling dictator, General Augusto Pinochet, his debut experiment in free-market theory never delivered the goods. Not even to the repressive military regime, let alone to the majority of the Chilean people. Two decades later, following the conclusion of the Cold War and the fall of the Eastern Bloc nations and the USSR, similar free-market efforts were tried first in Poland and later in Russia by so-called Friedman disciples like Jeffrey Sachs. At a time when strategies of tax cuts, free trade, social austerity, privatization, and deregulation were riding high in ideological value, these policies in combination proved themselves once again to be unworkable.[15] By the turn of this century, Sachs had abandoned the theories and policies of free markets. Currently, he is employing a mixed or balanced approach to economic development. Unfortunately, the same has not been the case for those economic and political elites who occupy the seats of power on Wall Street and in Washington, DC.

After more than two centuries, the contradictory policies of laissez-faire and centrally controlled (regulated) financial institutions in the United States have created unrivaled periods of development and prosperity, interrupted by times of downturn, economic crisis, and panic. In 2012, the nation finds itself still trying to recover from its most recent economic-financial crisis brought about when three decades of easing credit and an expanding money supply accompanied by high leveragability[16] and the deregulation of financial securities turned combustible. Also, because the Wall Street Financial Reform and Consumer Protection Act of 2010 does not adequately address these crisis-generating conditions, the long-term structural problems of risk and volatility remain. Similarly, because the same financial relations are still in place and because the concentration of wealth has shrunk the number of megabank players, the risks and stakes of derivative investments have actually become greater now than before the financial collapse.

Nevertheless, adherents to the ideologies of free markets with their often-distorted view of Adam Smith's "invisible hand" typically believe that economic self-interest invariably leads to the best possible outcomes. According to this ideological orthodoxy, "Any restrictions on the profit-seeking activities of individuals and corporations interfere with the invisible hand, and therefore are 'inefficient' and nonsensical."[17] Ignored by most of these ideologues in their deferential references to *The Wealth of Nations* (1776) were Smith's concerns about self-interests leading to exploitation, injustice, and financial ruin. For example, Smith was critical of "how employers colluded with each other to keep wages low, as well as the 'savage injustice' that European mercantilist interests had 'commit[ted] with impunity' in colonies in Asia and the Americas."[18]

Two hundred and thirty-six years later, not much has changed with respect to the unrestricted pursuit of profit and the savage injustices committed by many global corporations on the world stage today. As for Wall Street mega-banks, not only do they prey on their competitors with the money of their customers, but they also prey on themselves. In fact, it was "their efforts to loot their own firms [that] nearly destroyed the industry and the entire global economy."[19] In addition, over the past twenty years, the change in the size of incentives and investments has "led to large-scale looting, with firms running with too little equity and taking on undue risk to maximize short-term prof-its."[20] Likewise, a publication by the Brookings Institute in 1993, "Looting: The Economic Underworld of Bankruptcy for Profit," argued that business-people were profiting from bankrupting their own firms because of "poor ac-counting, lax regulation, or low penalties for abuse," which "give owners an incentive to pay themselves more than their firms are worth and then default on their debt obligations."[21]

Contrary to free-market ideology and fraud minimalism, criminologists and others seeking understanding of Wall Street looting and mass victimiza-tion need to approach these material relations with the realization that the political economy of capitalism is not some kind of unified system dominated by "free markets." Rather, capitalism is an economic system of fragmented, contradictory, and uneven markets of risks and rewards. Consequently, the winners and losers of the current financial crisis are framed not only by the markets they have access to, but also to the bodies of rule enforcement that may be applied (or not) in legal practice.

DEREGULATING FINANCIAL MARKETS (1980–2008)

Deregulation and lax/non-enforcement of the federal securities laws and rules can be traced back to Democratic president Jimmy Carter (1976–80). However, it is during the two-term Republican presidency of Ronald Reagan (1980–88) that the crusade to deregulate financial markets took off, launched by Reagan's first inaugural address on January 20th where he is remembered for having declared, "Government is not the solution to our problem, govern-ment is the problem." Two months later, on March 31st, the age of deregula-tion was formally born and ushered in when Reagan signed into law the De-pository Institutions Deregulation and Monetary Control Act of 1980. Since then, under Republican and Democratic administrations alike, the general direction of the federal government has been away from business-financial regulation, which does not mean away from intervening into the national af-fairs or international relations of both economic and financial markets.

To appreciate the broader impact that legal deregulation has had on dete-riorating the standards and weakening the external checks and balances on financial markets, one has to first understand the ways that "cheap capital and deregulation . . . fuelled the growth of over-the-counter markets, in particular negotiated, customized, or unique [financial] products, where customers would have difficulty evaluating the quality of prices they were being offered or the true risks they took on."[22] Second, one has to grasp how the innovating instruments in the realm of Wall Street's over-the-counter derivatives were subject only to self-management (or regulation). For example, the 1974 Commodity Futures Trading Act gave the Commodity Futures Trading Commission the broad authority over futures and options, and its Treasury amendment removed or "carved out foreign exchange, government securities, and other types of financial instruments."[23] These regulatory exemptions allowed for the explosive growth in OTC markets, and they posed a new challenge to the existing regulatory framework. Over the years, because these derivatives did not directly involve either deposits or traditional securities and because they defied the conventional treatment of accounting balance sheets, Wall Street and Congress would periodically revisit the struggle over whether or not to regulate these financial transactions.

Traditionally, by way of the National Housing Act of 1934, Congress' solution to rising home prices had been an interest rate cap that thrifts were allowed to pay on deposits. The reasoning was that so long as S&Ls did not have to pay too much for their deposits, they would not have to charge too much to those who borrowed from them to purchase their homes. For an expanding middle class, with the exception of a mildly inflationary period in the 1960s, the comfortable world of thrifts and the American Dream of affordable homeownership had been working quite nicely. In the early seventies, besieged by economic stagflation, these market conditions began to worsen. By the mid-seventies, the interest rate cap had become a serious impediment to attracting new business. As the decade came to an end, inflation was running at 13.3 percent and thrifts could typically still not pay more than 5.5 percent on deposits. On top of this investment disadvantage, money market funds[24] had become quite popular earlier in the decade and were also cutting into their deposits. Although not insured, money market funds were paying much higher interest rates, sometimes higher than the rate of inflation. By 1980, the outflow of money from thrifts had reached crisis proportions: "85 percent of savings and loans were losing money" and regulators were warning "that if nothing were done, all thrifts would collapse by the end of 1986."[25]

The prevailing logic of Reaganomics had been that increased federal regulations and governmental intervention was inhibiting competition and free markets. Moreover, regulation had not regulated away runaway inflation. And the tightening of the money supply by the FRB in 1979 to reduce inflation resulted in interest rates soaring to their highest level in the twentieth century, which had also set off an economic recession. Brashly and without hesitation the policy direction became one of deregulation. Designed to phase out the interest rate controls on deposits placed with banks and thrifts, the Monetary Control Act of 1980 also increased the FSLIC insurance coverage on deposits from $40,000 per account to $100,000. Overnight, without a cap on interest rates and an increase in deposit insurance by $60,000, "thrifts could attract $100,000 blocks of (insured) money with which they could wheel and deal at no risk."[26] In addition, a new FSLIC deregulation took effect in 1980 allowing thrifts for the first time to make real estate loans anywhere in the country. Previously, loans were restricted to local market areas.

The new law increased thrift deposits. At the same time, the law created a profit squeeze for the savings and loan industry:

> As the cost of deposits increased, the spread between the prices thrifts paid for the short-term deposits and the rate thrifts had charged for the long-term loans they held (some of which they might have made 30 years earlier) decreased. Thrifts were paying significantly more interest on deposits than they were receiving on old loans. Thrifts from around the country found their balance sheets bleeding a sea of red ink, and lobbyists from the U.S. League of Savings Institutions and other trade organizations begged Congress to throw them another life preserver.[27]

In response, Congress passed the Garn-St. Germain Depository Institutions Act of 1982 and in the same year a Joint Current Resolution "placed the full faith and credit of the U.S. government" behind the FSLIC.[28] Together, these two pieces of legislation changed the very nature of the entire Savings and Loans industry.

Specifically, the Garn-St. Germain Act allowed savings and loans to offer other types of accounts, particularly money market funds, free from withdrawal penalties or interest rate regulation. The act not only expedited the phase out of interest rate caps and liberalized accounting practices, making it easier for balance sheets to be in compliance, but Garn-St. Germain was also buttressed by other deregulatory actions of the FHLBB between 1980 and 1983. These included doing away with regulations requiring (1) that a thrift have four hundred stockholders with no one owning more than 25 percent of the stock and permitting as few as a single shareholder owning 100 percent of a thrift; (2) that owners purchase thrifts with money, allowing them instead to substitute land and other non-cash assets; and (3) traditional down payments and fixed borrowing rates while allowing adjustable rate mortgages.

In the context of federal deregulation and competitiveness, state thrifts all across the country shortly thereafter deregulated as well, making the investment powers of these institutions limited only by the virtues and vices of their entrepreneurial imaginations. In fact, some regulators were saying quietly that these legal changes were really about the un-regulation rather than the deregulation of financial securities. As the investigative journalists of *Inside Job*, put it, "The ink wasn't dry" on the legislation "deregulating the thrift industry, before high-stakes investors, swindlers, and mobsters lined up to loot the S&Ls. They immediately seized the opportunity created by the careless deregulation of thrifts and lax supervision and gambled, stole, and embezzled away billions in a five-year orgy of greed and excess."[29] The fallout from these changes in regulatory law produced the biggest financial disaster since the Great Depression—the S&L crisis. At the time, this was also the biggest heist in U.S. history resulting in the biggest government bailout to date. Eventually, this bailout cost the American taxpayer $124 billion.

Presciently, at the suggestion of executives from Goldman Sachs, the next significant deregulation came with the passage of the Federal Deposit Insurance Corporation Improvement Act of 1991. Ensuring that the Fed could lend against *any* collateral in a time of crisis, this law amended Section 13 of the 1932 Federal Reserve Act. As I have already underscored, this section required that collateral could only be provided in exchange from "actual commercial transactions." Importantly, as economists Johnson and Kwak maintain in *13 Bankers*, "This change gave the Fed the power to widen its protective umbrella to encompass investment banks, at the same time that those banks were increasing the riskiness of their operations by expanding their derivatives and proprietary trading businesses and taking on additional leverage."[30] Seventeen years later, the dropping of this "miscellaneous provision" would come to the rescue of several megabanks and one very large insurance company, AIG, in the form of the controversial bailouts of 2008.[31]

In a review of deregulation and fraud, one non-legislative change that paved the way for subsequent securities fraud was the 1994 Supreme Court ruling in *Central Bank of Denver v. First Interstate Bank of Denver*, 511 U.S. 164. "In a stunning show of illogic," the 5–4 majority held that plaintiffs may not argue an aiding and abetting suit under Section 10(b) of the Securities Exchange Act, "reversing sixty years of court and administrative rulings."[32] In other words, the court all but wiped out investor protection by deciding that plaintiffs could no longer "sue advisors like investment bankers, accountants, and lawyers for aiding and abetting securities fraud. A suit against them could only proceed if the defendant was charged with primary liability, meaning the damaged party was his client."[33] Hence, investors were prohibited from recovering any losses from those accountants, for example, who had signed off on fraudulent financial statements and upon whom they had relied as investors.

1994 also witnessed major derivatives losses, most notably suffered by Orange County (California), Procter & Gamble, and Gibson Greetings. In response to these financial fiascos Congress took up the subject of derivatives regulation. There was a major investigation by the House Banking and Financial Services committee, and several proposed bills were introduced. These proposals represented a major test for Wall Street, and the industry, led by the International Swaps and Derivatives Association, countered with a major lobbying effort. Joined by the Group of Thirty, an international advocacy group comprised of mostly private sector bank executives, central bankers, and sympathetic academics, they produced a study overseen by Dennis Weatherstone, then CEO of JP Morgan and Company. The study concluded that the industry could be trusted to regulate itself and that no new regulations were necessary.[34] Alan Greenspan agreed, as did the Wall Street–friendly Clinton administration and Lloyd Bentsen, the secretary of the Treasury. This was the only one of several high-profile battles over regulation that Wall Street came close to losing. At the end of the day, as during other times of conflict over derivative regulation, any type of regulation went down to defeat.

Two years later in 1996 the Fed overhauled its regulations, making it easier for banks to expand and enter into new business activities. The Fed also allowed bank subsidiaries to earn up to 25 percent of their revenues from securities operations, up from 10 percent. Likewise, Congress changed the rules for banks entering new financial markets, eliminating the requirement of seeking approval first from the Fed, placing the burden on the regulators to challenge such actions. Then in 1998, the Federal Reserve Board of Governors decided not to "'conduct consumer compliance examinations of, nor to investigate consumer complaints regarding, nonbank subsidiaries of bank holding companies,' claiming it could not regulate nonbank entities (even though the Truth in Lending Act makes no distinction between banks and nonbanks)."[35] 1998 also saw another major political struggle over the regulation of derivatives.

This struggle pitted Brooksley Born, chair of the CFTC, against Greenspan, Robert Rubin (Clinton's first Treasury secretary and former co-director of Goldman Sachs), Larry Summers (Clinton's second Treasury secretary and Obama's director of the White House's National Economic Council), SEC Commission chair Arthur Levitt, and House Banking Committee chair Jim Leach. Born was on a campaign to regulate derivatives because of her concern that the buildup of large derivatives invisible to regulatory oversight created risks to the financial system as a whole. Once again, regulation went down to defeat as Rubin, Greenspan, and Levitt proposed draft legislation imposing a moratorium on regulation by Born's agency. The House Banking Committee, the Treasury, the SEC, and the major bank regulators lined up with Greenspan. Meanwhile, executives from several major banks also opposed Born because, as they argued, derivatives were functioning effectively without additional regulation. In October 1998, the moratorium was approved, and the next year, Born decided not to seek reappointment.[36]

1999 was a busy year for both deregulation and for resisting any ideas about regulating derivatives. In November, President Clinton signed into law the Gramm-Leach-Bliley Act, also known as the Financial Services Modernization Act of 1999. The law repealed part of the Glass-Steagall Act of 1933 and part of the Bank Holding Company Act of 1956, opening up markets among financial institutions and allowing consolidation between commercial banks, investment banks, securities firms, and insurance companies. In the same month, the President's Working Group on Financial Markets produced a report, "Over-the-Counter Derivatives Markets and the Commodity Exchange Act," signed by Treasury Secretary Summers, Greenspan, and the new CFTC chair, William Rainer. The report concluded that these derivatives should be exempted from federal oversight because regulation would not promote innovation, competition, efficiency, and transparency, nor would it reduce systemic risk or allow the United States to maintain its leadership in these developing markets.[37]

In May 2000, the House complied with the report and passed the Commodity Futures Modernization Act, but it was held up in the Senate because Senator Phil Gramm did not believe that the deregulation language was strict enough. Eventually, Gramm succeeded in foreclosing any chance of regulation by either the CFTC or the SEC. In December he was able to insert tougher language into the Consolidated Appropriations Act for fiscal year 2001, passed by a lame-duck Congress and signed into law by a lame-duck president. Once again, Wall Street and the financial sector had prevailed in protecting its high-risk gambling and profit-making OTC derivatives from the possibility of government interference.

Refinements in deregulation occurred during the first term of President George W. Bush. In 2003, the Office of the Comptroller of the Currency (OCC) ruled that state-lending rules did not apply to national banks preempting the attempts by the states, led by the Georgia Fair Lending Act and the New Jersey Home Ownership Security Act, to regulate the lending activities of these federally chartered institutions. The next year, the OCC exempted national banks from state mortgage regulations as well, disarming the states in their efforts to curtail the subprime mortgage boom. In 2004, the SEC agreed at the request of Goldman Sachs, Morgan Stanley, Merrill Lynch, Lehman Brothers, and Bear Stearns to allow investment banks to use their own models to calculate their net capital. Also in 2004 and 2005, because "shopping for ratings" had become part of the securitization business, the two major ratings agencies, Moody's and Standard and Poor's, modified their rating models in ways that made it easier to give higher scores to asset-backed CDOs, helping to extend both leverage and the structural financial boom. Finally, in the spring of 2008 the SEC ended its program to oversee investment banks while the FRB created the Primary Dealer Credit Facility, allowing investment banks to borrow directly from the Fed.[38]

BETS AND BONUSES

During the hearings of the Senate Subcommittee on the Investigation of the Financial Crisis in the spring of 2010, Senator Claire McCaskill in an exchange with Goldman Sachs had this to say: "You all are the house, you're the bookie" and your clients "are booking their bets with you. I don't know why we need to dress it up. It's a bet."[39] Economic Nobel Laureate Allais also talks in terms of a "casino economy" where "economic financialization" has "caused the market to increasingly resemble an enormous gambling table."[40] According to Allais, this casino economy provides limitless opportunities to make a lot of money, as profitable investments depend on speculative ventures, calculated risk-taking with minimal regulation, and all kinds of exotic derivatives. Similarly, Ellen Brown, an expert on the Federal Reserve Bank and author of *The Web of Debt*, now in its fourth edition, argues as an addendum to her research on the topic that derivatives markets have been transformed into gambling casinos and their brokers have become bookies:

> Derivatives are basically bets. Like at a racetrack, you don't need to own the thing you're betting on in order to play. Derivative casinos have opened up on virtually anything that can go up or down or have a variable future outcome. You can bet on the price of tea in China, the success or failure of a movie, whether a country will default on its debt, or whether a particular piece of legislation will pass. The global market in derivative trades is now well over a quadrillion dollars—that's a thousand trillion—and it is eating up resources that were at one time invested in productive enterprises. Why risk lending money to a corporation or buying its stock, when you can reap a better return from betting on whether the stock will rise or fall?[41]

Besides the loss of trillions of dollars available to invest in or to loan to companies for the production of real goods and services, the shift from investment markets to electronic casino markets also means that parties on one side of every speculative trade have a vested interest in seeing it fail. Worse yet, high-speed program traders—a field led by Goldman Sachs—can intentionally manipulate the market so that the thing bet on, whether a company, a movie, a politician, or a nation, is more likely to fail. As Brown explains, high speeders "use computer algorithms to automatically bet huge sums of money on minor shifts in price. These bets send signals to the market which can themselves cause the price of assets to shoot up or tumble down."[42] In other words, by placing high-volume bets (trades), the largest speculative bettors (traders) can actually "fix" prices in any direction they want. With this in mind, following the Wall Street implosion, some of the biggest losers of the financial bets on collateralized debt obligations and securitized subprime mortgages were bailed out to the chagrin of most Americans as were most of the megabank winners to prevent panics and runs against these "gambling houses." In short, protecting these financial casinos from the possibility of bankruptcy should all their bettors call in all their chits, as it were.

As part of the controversial bailouts, Obama's pay czar, Kenneth Feinberg, was appointed Special Master for TARP Executive Compensation. He was charged with recovering any excessive compensation that may have been distributed contrary to the public interest. Fienberg reviewed the pay of the top 25 executives at each of the 419 firms bailed out by TARP. He decided to focus on seventeen firms, including American Express, AIG, Boston Private Financial Holdings, Capital One, Bank of America, CIT Group, Citigroup, JP Morgan Chase, M&T Bank, Morgan Stanley, Regions Financial, SunTrust Banks, Bank of New York Mellon, Goldman Sachs, PNC Financial Services, U.S. Bancorp, and Wells Fargo, because these firms doled out $1.6 billion of the $1.7 billion in questionable pay to their employees in the five-month period immediately after the taxpayer bailouts began. Top bonuses for 2007 and 2009:

- Jamie Dimon (JPM): **$27.8M** in 2007; **$17M** in 2009
- Ken Lewis (BAC): **$20.4M** in 2007; **$9M** in 2008; retires with **$53.2M** pension in 2009
- Dick Fuld (Lehman): **$34M** in 2007
- Lloyd Blankfein (GS): **$70M** in 2007; **$9M** in 2009
- Gary Cohn (GS): **$72.5M** in 2007; **$15.1M** in 2009
- John Winkereid (GS): **$71M** in 2007
- Martin Sullivan (AIG): **$14M** in 2007
- John Mack (MS): **$1.6M** in 2007; **$0.9M** in 2009
- Colin Kelleher (MS): **$21M** in 2007
- Stan O'Neal (Merrill): **$160M** in 2007
- John Thain (Merrill): **$17M** in 2007
- Daniel Mudd (Fannie Mae): **$11.6M** in 2007
- Richard Syron (Freddie Mac): **$18M** in 2007
- G. Kennedy Thompson (Wachovia): **$21M** in 2007
- Chuck Prince (Citi): **$38M** in 2007
- Jeffrey Edwards (Merrill): **$14.7M** in 2006
- Tom Montag (BAC): **$29.9M** in 2009[43]

Although Feinberg did acknowledge at a press conference announcing his findings that the "payouts were 'ill-advised' and exhibited 'bad judgment'— some bankers were paid more than $10 million," he "refused to rule that any of the massive payouts [looting] went against the public interest."[44] Moreover, the pay czar let it be known that "banks told him that they had to pay out such huge sums because they were contractually obligated to."[45] Feinberg also let it be known that he thought the "firms should be free to restructure or even cancel those contracts." In fact, that's exactly what he told the banks in private discussions. He also stated that the banks told him (no doubt with a straight face) that "they'd take his recommendations 'under advisement.'"

At the end of his press briefing, Feinberg claimed that he thought "we did our best here at Treasury in balancing second-guessing, armchair-quarterbacking with a statutory mandate to seek reimbursement in appropriate cases," and "I am very comfortable with our findings." Additionally, he explained, as "a matter of fairness, to label these payments years later [eighteen months actually] as contrary to the public interest" would not be right and "I'm trying to minimize the likelihood that today's [July 23, 2010] decision will trigger another round of investigations and litigation. I've tried to strike that balance." As pointed out by *Huffington Post* bloggist Shahien Nasiripour, the "balance Feinberg struck means bailed out bankers get to keep their loot while taxpayers are left holding the bag." Finally, Feinberg thought it best that "we all move forward with lessons learned and that we put this sad chapter behind us."

Putting this sad chapter behind and moving forward may be easier done than said for a few thousand winning Wall Street bankers and vice versa for the millions of losers on Main Street. For the former, the below-the-fold article in Section B of the *Wall Street Journal* on July 24–25, 2010, captured the state of affairs quite accurately with the title: "Wall Street Exhales after Sidestepping Pay Czar's Wrath." In fairness to Feinberg, neither Congress nor TARP gave the Special Master for Executive Compensation any statutory authority to make Wall Street do anything with their ill-gotten loot. For the latter, the $1.7 billion represents "just the tip of the iceberg that needs to be recouped from Wall Street," said Stephen Learner, who directs the bank and financial reform campaign for the 2.2 million members of the Service Employees International Union (SEIU).[46]

"'This is a lead-in to a bigger problem,' Learner continued. 'We've got pension funds that lost hundreds of billions of dollars. We've got cities and states that are having to lay off firefighters because they got stuck in bad deals with Wall Street.'"[47] Not surprisingly, TARP did not charge the pay czar with recouping any of the lost pension funds, public and private jobs, mortgages, and more that disappeared almost overnight when Wall Street collapsed in

2008. "Told that Feinberg said he wanted to minimize the amount of new litigation and investigations, Learner said that the Pay Czar's findings should have opened 'a Pandora's box of why there aren't more efforts to recoup' Wall Street's 'ill-gotten gains.'"[48] However, for the same reasons—the fear of causing runs on those financial institutions, opening up all kinds of litigation, and further exposing the public to the workings of Wall Street—the government was not willing to allow these firms to declare insolvency or bankruptcy. For example, had the government permitted these too-big-to-fail banks to default on their debts, then the investors and other affected parties could have used bankruptcy fraud or fraudulent conveyance to claw back overpayments and lost revenues that could have been tied up for years in litigation. Instead, the bailout gains or loot went principally to a few winners, and the losses were covered by a nation of losers. President Obama thought this was a fair outcome, and he did not "'begrudge' the $17 million bonus awarded to JP Morgan Chase & Co. Chief Executive Officer Jamie Dimon or the $9 million issued to Goldman Sachs Group Inc. CEO Lloyd Blankfein" in 2009.[49]

As Obama explained in an early 2010 White House interview, "I, like most of the American people, don't begrudge people's success or wealth. That is part of the free-market system."[50] Moreover, in defending the $27.8 million and $70 million that Dimon and Blankfein received in bonuses in 2007 as not excessive, he had this to say: "I know both those guys" and "they are very savvy businessmen."[51] Indeed, they are very savvy derivatives salesmen who with collusion from the political leaders in the U.S. government are still running speculative investment empires at taxpayer and consumer expense. Part and parcel of American Dream 3.0, this casino capitalism gambles on little of social value other than mostly obscene gobs of currencies for building excessive personal fortunes by ways of fiddling with other people's money and life savings.

President Obama is well aware of these other interpretations or constructions of economic inequality. He is also aware of those economic constructions of financial realities that are out-of-bounds in the land of free markets. A place where producers extracted far more than they were worth, given the risks being taken. At the same time,

their outsize compensation moved the pay goalposts for all in the fold (recall that Merrill Lynch CEO John Train's driver earned $230,000 in a year). And pay is far and away the biggest expense at the firms, so systematic overpayment can and did leave them undercapitalized relative to the risks assumed. At Goldman, for instance, average compensation across the firm in 2007 was $630,000, totaling 44% of net revenues, and nearly twice net earnings.[52]

These types of extravagant compensation packages are reinforced by what retiring Senator Christopher Dodd had to say during a July 29, 2010, appearance on MSNBC's *Morning Joe* about banking executives. He noted that in his meetings with the Wall Street bankers over the course of the eighteen months running up to the passage of the Dodd-Frank Act, there were allegedly two things that mattered to them: (1) not losing any of their compensation structure in the form of salaries and bonuses and (2) not having to pay higher rates of taxes on their various investment instruments. As it turned out, the financial looting was left in place as Congress ultimately took a hands-off approach regarding compensation. The government also ended up receiving far less in future tax revenues on exotic instruments than what it had originally sought. Once again, Washington, succumbing to Wall Street lobbyists, failed to control another source of the gross accumulation of unequal wealth in America.

WINNERS AND LOSERS OF THE FINANCIAL CRISIS OF 2007–8

At the height of the Great Recession, the U.S. stock market had fallen 40 percent in value, the U.S. economy had lost more than four million jobs, and global output was declining for the first time since World War II. By the time the Obama administration was up and running in late winter, early spring of 2009, the financial markets were still in chaos, and the American people were becoming increasingly angered and hostile toward Wall Street. For example,

> Despite three government bailouts, Citigroup stock was trading below $3 per share, about 95 percent down from its peak; stock in Bank of America, which had received two bailouts, had lost 85 percent of its value. The public was furious at the recent news that American International Group, which had been rescued by commitments of up to $180 billion in taxpayer money, was paying $165 million in bonuses to executives and traders at the division that had nearly caused the company to collapse.[53]

It was during this time, March 27, 2009, that the new president hosted a meeting attended by CEOs from thirteen of the country's largest financial institutions, including two representatives of industry organizations.[54] These bankers/banks for some thirty years had been using their "huge balance sheets to place bets in brand-new financial markets, stirring together complex derivatives with exotic mortgages in a toxic brew that ultimately poisoned the global economy. In the process, they grew so large that their potential failure threatened the stability of the entire system, giving them a unique degree of economic leverage over the government."[55] In addition to becoming one of the wealthiest industries in the history of the American economy and one of the most powerful political forces in Washington, Wall Street was able to use the ideology of free markets to convince both sides of the political aisle "that unfettered innovation and unregulated financial markets were good for America and the world."[56]

During the course of the meeting, President Obama has been quoted as saying to the bankers, "My administration is the only thing between you [the megabanks] and the pitchforks" and "help me help you."[57] This is not to suggest that Obama was not at the same time trying to take advantage of the Wall Street crisis and to win concessions from the banks. As we will see in chapter 6, modest regulatory reforms did eventually pass into law, such as those measures to protect unwary consumers from predatory Wall Street. However, the undisclosed "bottom line" from the meeting was that even though these bankers played a central role in causing the financial crisis and recession, the country's future economic prosperity depended on these same megabanks, their leadership, and the continuation of the existing financial arrangements. The outcome would be pretty much business as usual. Only a bit bigger, more concentrated, and without serious regulation of those instruments connected to greater market risk and volatility.

The Obama administration did what it could to defend Wall Street from the angry masses, and the White House's talking points became that Wall Street, Main Street, and Washington were all on the same side of the financial implosion. As White House Press Secretary Robert Gibbs summed up the president's message from the meeting: "Everybody has to pitch in. We're all in this together." At the same press conference, CEOs Pandit of Citigroup and Stumpf of Wells Fargo were respectively chiming in: "I'm of the feeling that we're all in this together" and "the basic message is, we're all in this together."[58]

In an effort to prevent JP Morgan Chase, Goldman Sachs, and other megabanks from following in the footsteps of Bear Stearns, Lehman Brothers, Merrill Lynch, Washington Mutual, and Wachovia by "coming up short" and ending up in either acquisition or bankruptcy, the administration and the "high-rolling" bankers worked out a deal involving massive government bailouts. These bailout interventions for the bankers took the form of investing the taxpayers' money to pay the banks in full for their deals gone badly, for example, with AIG. These bailout mechanisms also included: (1) governmental guarantees for multiple markets, (2) lending controlled by the Federal Reserve Bank, and (3) historically low interest rates. Contradictorily, while the economic elites from Wall Street and the political elites from Washington were in this financial crisis together, average Americans found themselves on the "other side of the street." This was most obviously the case, for example, with respect to all those homeowners "underwater" (e.g., owing more than their homes are worth) and to the failure of the government to extend credit to millions of homeowners so they could avoid foreclosures.

In the immediate post-crisis era, 2009 to the present, the big losers have been all those Americans who have lost both their jobs and their mortgages. There are also the billions of lost dollars accounted for by all of the sour deals involving municipalities, school districts, and pension funds responsible for local government downsizing and laying off of teachers, firefighters, police, and so on. Smaller losers include all of those Americans who have retained their jobs, but whose retirement savings were suddenly worth significantly less dollars and whose median income during this century's first decade was declining for the first time since World War II. Other losers include the "smaller players" involved in banking, savings and loan institutions, and the mortgage service industry as market power continues to concentrate in the hands of the nation's largest banks. The big winners from the financial crisis have been those major banks that survived intact, such as JP Morgan Chase, Bank of America, and Wells Fargo. Helped in part in 2008 and 2009 when they were the recipients of $95 billion in capital from the U.S. government, these banks bought up their former rivals, including Lehman Brothers, Merrill Lynch, and Wachovia. Look how these firms grew in size:

> J.P. Morgan's takeover of Washington Mutual's failed banking operations in September 2008 increased the asset size of the New York company by more than $300 billion, or 20%. Bank of America bought Merrill Lynch & Co. and Countrywide as those two companies, with nearly $1 trillion in combined assets, were sinking. Wells Fargo acquired Wachovia, the biggest bank on the East Coast, when Wachovia was on the verge of collapse in late 2008. The three bulked-up giants now hold more than a third of all deposits in 25 metropolitan areas that are home to 70 million people, or nearly one-fourth of the U.S. population.[59]

Hence, those banks left standing were also allowed to grow even bigger in size, increasing both their market shares in everything from issuing credit cards to issuing new stock for companies. They also increased their likelihood of being labeled "too big to fail" in the future. By July 2010, these three banks held "33% of all U.S. deposits, up from 21% in mid-2007—the fastest shift of such a chunk of deposits in U.S. history."[60] Even more significantly, they were making "57% of all home mortgages in the first quarter" of 2010, up from 28 percent in 2008.[61] When measured in terms of loans and other assets, these three giants plus Citigroup, Inc. had "7.7 trillion as of March 31, up 56% since the end of 2007. Their combined assets [were] nearly twice as big as the assets of the next 46 biggest banks," according to SNL Financial, a research firm in Virginia.[62]

In the short term, Wall Street interests and the prevailing free-market ideologies had helped to "create the laissez-faire environment in which the big banks became bigger and riskier, until by 2008 the threat of their failure could hold the rest of the economy hostage."[63] Thus, when the U.S. government finally intervened to rescue the financial system, it did so on terms that were favorable to the megabanks as hundreds of smaller banks sank into insolvency and oblivion. Similar responses to earlier and lesser economic crises/downturns/recessions had prepared, if not conditioned, Wall Street and Washington to once again prop up the same risk-taking activities of too-big-to-fail financial institutions.

By avoiding these structural contradictions and by failing to address the root causes of these financial crises the political establishment remains "captive to the idea that America needs big, sophisticated, risk-seeking, highly profitable banks." As long as this is the case, Wall Street bankers will continue to have "the upper hand in any negotiation."[64] After all, politicians may come and go, but to date the banking oligopoly in the United States continues to grow exponentially. Meanwhile, the U.S. political economy, its infrastructure and institutions as a whole, continue to deteriorate from both a scarcity of financial credit and social capital as well as from an abundance of unenlightened self-interest and unfettered victimization.

Chapter Four

Theories of White-Collar Illegalities and the Crimes of the Powerful

A Reciprocal Approach to the Political Economy of Wall Street Looting and Federal Regulatory Colluding

Typologies on white-collar crimes are inclusive of a wide range of behaviors, both interpersonal and organizational in nature. Many of these behaviors have not been the focus of this examination. "Crimes of the middle classes," such as employee theft, embezzlement, recycling violations, and identity theft operate apart from financial securities fraud. Similarly, individual practices of illegality involving insurance or tax frauds and small-time "con games" or "confidence tricks" have little in common with Wall Street looting. The latter forms of financial deception (or mistrust) are commonly referred to by a variety of names. These include securities fraud, investment fraud, real estate fraud, mortgage fraud, insurance fraud, consumer fraud, professional fraud, financial fraud, corporate fraud, public corruption, institutional corruption, and manipulating the marketplace.[1] When all of these forms of securities fraud gelled in epidemic proportions during the run-up to the Wall Street collapse of 2007–8, they were in effect reinforcing illegal businesses as usual not only at the interpersonal and organizational level, but also at the institutional level of behavior.

Unlike the typical white-collar offenders, upper-world offenders refer to those illegal abuses committed "by upper-echelon businessmen in the service of their corporations, by high-ranking politicians against their codes of conduct and their constituencies, and by professional persons that are not in compliance with the interests of their governing bodies, multiple clients, and conflicts of interest."[2] Whether theories of white-collar illegalities are trying to explain the crimes of relatively powerless middle-class offenders or the crimes of very powerful Wall Street offenders, they are usually divided into one of two kinds of theories. Those that attempt to explain how people become violators or why they engage in criminal behavior, and those that attempt to explain why societies have the types of criminal events and crime controls they have. Among the "components" used in these theories are (1) the motivation or desire to deviate, (2) the freedom from social constraints or impunity from harms, and (3) the skill and opportunity to engage.[3]

While powerful offenders are social and reasoning animals, there are natural variations across individual humans, according to empirical studies on: rational choice theory and white-collar motivation, corporate crime, and the utility of cost-benefit analyses of deterrence[4] or the threat of sanctions and appeals to morality.[5] In the actual individual/organizational (e.g., corporate) commission of financial crime, the differential motivations and opportunities to violate the law converge around the legal doctrine of "collective knowledge" rather than around the requisite intent or knowledge to commit a crime.[6] Similarly, the organizational and institutional emphases in this study of Wall Street looting and federal regulatory colluding are less about how and why individual investment bankers or mortgage lenders committed fraud than about the changing political, economic, ideological, and legal relations of the contradictions of a developing capitalism that has historically facilitated and/ or impeded the theft of a nation.

A criminological challenge has also been to bring together those explanations of white-collar *criminality* that have traditionally focused on a range of theories from motive forces grounded in "biogenetic" risk-taking to "psychogenic" character traits to "sociogenic" organized behavioral norms. Or, theories that identify those interacting micro-, meso-, and macro-level factors and forces, which account for the various types of white-collar crime and victimization.[7] In taking these challenges on, corporate "organizational crime" theories have expanded the meaning of motivation to include such internal market variables as "the size of the corporation, the financial performance of the corporation and the degree of its emphasis on profit, the diffusion of responsibility through different divisions and departments, and a corporate subculture that promotes loyalty and deference to the interests of the corporation."[8]

Since the pioneering work of Edwin Sutherland in the 1930s and 1940s the study of white-collar crime has been dominated by sociological explanations that may be divided up into: (1) *social learning* theories, such as Sutherland's "differential association" (1940),[9] Sykes and Matza's "techniques of neutralization" (1957),[10] and Gottfredson and Hirschi's "a general theory of crime" (1990)[11]; (2) *structural* theories, such as Merton's "anomie" (1938),[12] Cohen's "status deprivation" (1955),[13] Cloward and Ohlin's "differential opportunity" (1960),[14] Chambliss' "structural contradictions" (1979), Miethe and Meier's "structural-choice" (1990),[15] and Braithwaite's "theory of greed" (1991)[16]; and (3) *rational choice* theories, such as Clarke and Cornish's "situational choice" theory" (1986),[17] Felson's "routine activities" (1987),[18] and Felson and Clarke's "crime pattern" (1998).[19]

By the 1980s criminologists had begun experimenting with integrated models of criminality/crime and crime control. Gradually, micro-, meso-, and/or macro-level integrated theories operating across individual, organizational, and institutional social relations began to develop explanations of white-collar offenses and social control.[20] Traditionally, integrations of white-collar offending have brought together differential association, anomie/strain, and rational choice/opportunity theories to explain criminal behavior. Each of these vantage points brings something to the theoretical table. When combined these integrated theories usually take on a whole greater than their parts. For example, through differential association the content of motivation and neutralization was explored to better explain how precisely criminal motives and attitudes were perceived, learned, and diffused between groups of people. Similarly, anomie/strain revealed the ways in which the social, structural, and cultural aspects of life shape the origins of criminal motivation. And rational choice/opportunity has provided details on how motivated offenders recognize criminal opportunities and make the decision to act accordingly.

INTEGRATED APPROACHES TO WHITE-COLLAR CRIME

One of the earliest integrated approaches that provided a general theory of crime and crime control, inclusive of street crime and suite crime, was elaborated by Richard Quinney in his 1977 *Class, State, and Crime*.[21] This Marxist formulation argues that crime/criminality and criminalization/crime control are the products of the developing contradictions of capitalism. This political-economic theory argues further that the social relations of production result in two related worlds of crime and crime control. The world of street crime consists of workers and ordinary people who commit "crimes of accommodation and resistance" that are subject to criminal law and penal control. The upper world of capitalists and agents of social control commit "crimes of domination and repression" respectively. These are primarily subject to civil law and regulative control.

Quinney's vertically integrated model posits that criminal activities are both occupationally and class specific. In other words, where people are positioned socioeconomically shapes the type of criminal options or illegal opportunities that they will engage in as well as the types of crime control that they will experience. Akin to Chambliss' theory discussed in the introductory chapter, Quinney's theory argues further that these crimes are driven primarily by the structural contradictions of survival in a capitalist society.

For those who are going about the business of trying to make ends meet and resisting social alienation, their personal and property crimes are often predatory and at times political acts of protest. For those who are going about the business of accumulating profits and surviving in a competitive marketplace, avoiding bankruptcy, resisting hostile takeovers, and subduing counterforces of capitalist regulation, their impersonal and financial crimes are often about economic domination, social harm, and governmental control.

The next contribution to the literature came from Stephen Box in his 1983 Integrated Theory of the Crimes of the Powerful—a conceptually comprehensive analysis of corporate crime.[22] Box's integrated model made use of the following criminological theories: anomie/strain, bonding/control, social learning, neutralization, subcultural, opportunity structure, and social control. For Box, corporate crime is the result of corporations striving to achieve their particular goals in an otherwise uncertain environment due to economic competition, the government, workers, the consuming public, and so on. Accordingly, corporations attempt to overcome uncertainties by illegally eliminating or otherwise reducing these through fraud, bribery, manipulation, price-fixing, inside trading, and other devious means.

Box employs anomie and strain as the motivational source of corporate crime. Motivational strains are translated into illegal acts through corporate cultures and differential associations. Elites learn to rationalize and neutralize their infractions with any social and moral contracts to which they may have previously ascribed. Box's integrated model reveals how the lack of rule enforcement of corporate misbehavior and the low risk of corporate punishment serve to reinforce rather than deter corporate crime. In his discursive scheme of things, elites come to view their behavior as not serious or threatening. They also come to believe that they are above or beyond the law. Finally, Box argues that ideologically and practically speaking, corporations are relatively free to commit violations without worry of being criminalized. This is because the general public and agents of control morally view corporate violations as regulatory rather than criminal offenses.

In his 1987 *AJS* article, "Toward an Integrated Theory of White-collar Crime," and his 1994 edition of *The Criminal Elite*, James Coleman provided one of the most referenced integrated theories of white-collar crime. This theory explains both occupational and corporate crimes. On the one hand, his micro-level analysis examines the motivations of "reckless" and "egocentric" offenders. On the other hand, his macro-level analysis probes the "structure of opportunities." In addition, Coleman's approach to "symbolic motivational" patterns moves beyond individual character. He views the origins of white-collar crime as rooted in "cultures of competition" and in the social structure of industrial capitalism that may or may not be subject to and checked by ethical standards, the media, or the social forces of the law depending on a firm's rate of increasing or declining profitability.

In terms of the offenders' point of view or symbolic construction of their social world, Coleman incorporates social learning, strain, rational choice, and interactionist theory as a means of comprehending white-collar crime. In particular, Coleman underscores the presence of the "techniques of neutralization" in the corporate world that erode ethical standards of conduct through various rationalizations. These excuses and justifications are the products of a corporate culture steeped in organizational conformity where efficient bureaucracies breed a kind of amoral pragmatism. He argues further that legitimate and illegitimate opportunities are differentially distributed according to the market and in reaction to the responses of the legal systems involved. This means that within large-scale organizational structures, white-collar crimes are the products of values and practices established by the vagaries of both the marketplace and law enforcement.

John Braithwaite's (1989) "reintegrative shaming," a general and integrated theory of crime, when applied to organizational crime and criminological etiology in particular, represents a social process by which several theoretical concepts of criminal behavior are linked together.[23] His micro-macro model of crime and crime control adds the idea of positive and negative reactions of lawbreakers to labeling, subcultural, control, opportunity, and learning theories. Braithwaite built his integrated theory on two traditions:

> Structural Marxist theory (first articulated by Dutch criminologist Willem A. Bonger), which links both white collar and conventional crime with the promotion of egoism in capitalist societies; and differential association theory (first developed by Sutherland), which holds that both white collar and conventional crime are learned relative to differential opportunity.[24]

Importantly, Braithwaite distinguished between two types of social disapproval or shaming—stigmatizing and reintegrative. Stigmatizing shaming frequently drives lawbreakers into further acts of misbehavior as they experience more deeply the negative feelings of deviance. By contrast, reintegrative shaming maintains community bonds by emphasizing mild rebuking and degrading ceremonies, followed by gestures of reacceptance. Accordingly, his model revolves around these two forms of shaming in relationship to each other so that the ongoing production of crime and deviance or of law-abiding and conforming behavior becomes a matter of differential shaming.

> Conduct tips in the direction that avoids the more potent shaming (disapproval), whether it comes from within the organization or the state. Involvement in white collar criminal conduct can then be understood as a function of

relative vulnerability to shaming; crime flourishes in organizations that shield members from shaming and pressure them to produce and is controlled in organizations that take proactive measures to expose law violators to shame.[25]

Braithwaite's theory also emphasizes social conditions, especially those penal characteristics that encourage or discourage reintegrative shaming. It also stresses the fact that some people are better bonded to society and more susceptible to shaming than others who may be more alienated. Similarly, at the cultural and organizational levels, societies like Japan that are more communal have more of an affinity for using reintegrative shaming, while those societies like the United States that are more individualistic have more of an affinity for utilizing stigmatizing shaming. Finally, based on his earlier worldwide empirical studies,[26] Braithwaite concluded that those societies with higher levels of inequality in wealth and power would have higher rates of both conventional and white-collar crimes than those with lower levels of inequality. This is not only the case because "unequal societies" produce a broader range of illegitimate opportunities, but also because these opportunities are often more financially rewarding than the legal opportunities.

Of particular relevance to this study of Wall Street looting were the empirical studies conducted by Calavita and Pontell on the deregulation of the U.S. savings and loan industry in the early 1980s, followed by the subsequent thrift frauds and "collective embezzlement" that resulted in staggering financial losses, a government bailout of approximately $88 billion, and the felony convictions of more than one thousand S&L insiders.[27] In their integrated analyses, Pontell and Calavita not only incorporate strain/anomie, social learning/differential association, and rational choice/ opportunity theories, but they also address the social, economic-structural, cultural, and ideological causes of fraud. In doing so, their comprehensive approach to the interaction between motivation and opportunity reveals how these fraudulent activities were directly caused by the changed laws regulating the thrift industry, which were themselves driven by or in response to developing market relations.

More specifically, their integrated research into the contradictions of financial development in general and the nature of the epidemic and system-wide thrift industry frauds in particular demonstrates how the deregulation and protectionist policies, the role conflicts within the regulatory systems, and the political ideologies and structural flaws in the financial system induced incentives and yielded opportunities for a wave of control frauds that resulted in the failure of some 747 savings and loan associations out of 3,234 nationwide. In further distinguishing between the fundamental differences inherent in finance capitalism and industrial capitalism, the authors have noted that in contrast to the latter where profits are made from the production and sales of goods and services, profits from the former are increasingly the result of "fiddling with money." In short, finance capitalism increasingly does not really produce anything of use value other than the exchange value of capital gains.

Quite recently, Ke Wang, a compliance officer in a leading Chinese securities firm with a PhD in criminal justice, introduced his Integrated Conceptual Model of Securities Fraud (see figure 4.1).[28] This model develops a multi-level integration of different theoretical perspectives to explain individual and organizational behavior in securities fraud cases from 1996 to 2001. Wang incorporates what he refers to as constant and time-varying covariates; the latter are included within the dashed rectangle in the figure. Wang's study examined "the role of individual executive incentive compensation as potential motivation for CEO and other top executives as a group to manipulate corporate stock prices by issuing false or misleading statements" (arrow 1).[29]

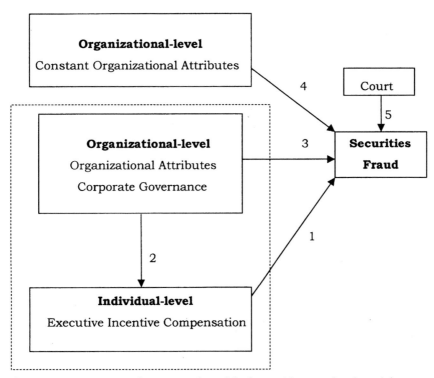

Figure 4.1. An Integrated Conceptual Model of Securities Fraud. Adapted from Ke Wang, *Securities Fraud, 1996–2001: Incentive Pay, Governance, and Class Action Lawsuits* (El Paso, TX: LFB Scholarly, 2010), 32.

At the individual level, rational choice theory is used as "an efficient way to analyze offenders' perceived benefits and risks when they are deciding whether to commit securities fraud."[30] Under the influence of self-interest, for example, "top executives may foster an aggressive business culture with an exclusive emphasis on economic goals. Under the pressure from the top or the influence from a deviant subculture, executives' subordinates may only report 'good' news to their supervisors and then to the investing public."[31]

At the organizational-level, Wang argues that there are the "constant organizational attributes" and the changing "organizational attributes" as well as the kind of "corporate governance" practiced. The former group of attributes, such as the type of financial institution, generally does not change across time and may influence the probability of securities fraud (arrow 4). The latter covariate groupings either directly or indirectly influence the probability that corporations will engage in securities fraud. The first group includes time-varying "organizational characteristics of corporations, which may shape the structure of executive compensation packages and then indirectly exert certain influence conducive to securities fraud" (arrow 2). At the same time, these organizational attributes may relate to other factors such as the "competitive pressure faced by corporations, or corporate resources and capabilities in fighting against civil and criminal prosecutions, which may have direct effects on the possibilities of securities fraud" (arrow 3).[32]

The second group includes time-varying corporate governance attributes and is reflected in such things as institutional ownership, shareholder rights, and the frequency of board meetings. These factors may or may not serve as direct or indirect deterrents against security fraud. Directly, as when governance maintains or loses control of individual deviant behavior (arrow 3). Indirectly, as when corporations check or let executive incentive compensation become excessive (arrow 2). Lastly, this model incorporates the effects of different federal court decisions of securities fraud cases (arrow 5), recognizing that what "may be viewed as fraud by one court may not be viewed as such by another court."[33]

Related to the above theoretical developments are the various transnational crimes of capital, from wealth accumulation to labor exploitation that are favored and shielded by the contradictions of "bourgeois law."[34] There are also the associated models of state-corporate crime[35] and of international law violations committed on behalf of ruling parties and/or the state.[36] Each of these integrated models seeks to breach the conceptual walls between economic crimes and political crimes stressing the social reality that there are neither pure economics nor politics. As Michalowski and Kramer have argued about state-corporate crime, there are only political economies.[37] Not unlike the other integrated theories discussed above, these models of "state complicit crime" also focus on multiple levels of analysis and dissect the motivations and constraints operating individually and organizationally. These theories also underscore the importance of the historical-social structure and the contradictory developments in the political economies that shape and/or constrain individual criminality, giving real meaning to these organizational crimes through the actualization of negative and/or positive legal reinforcements.

Ultimately, the reciprocal model of Wall Street fraud (see figure 4.4) introduced later in the chapter assimilates the rich theoretical traditions of white-collar crime discussed so far. My reciprocal model also extends Wang's linear model of securities fraud by bringing together explanations of control fraud, of market corruption, and of system capacity into an interactive model of *organizational control fraud* (see figure 4.2) and by presenting an interactive

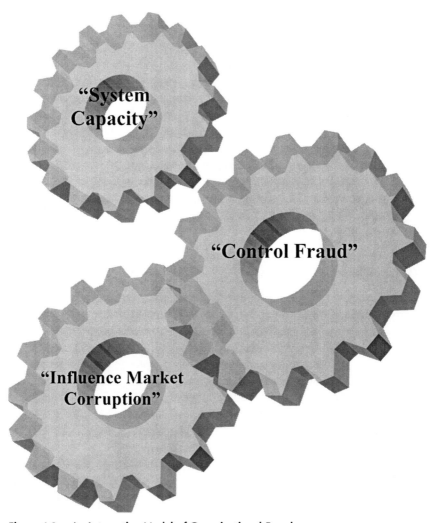

Figure 4.2. An Interactive Model of Organizational Fraud

model of *institutional financial control fraud* (see figure 4.3) with its parallel
and encompassing worlds of financial control fraud, governing corruption,
and regulatory colluding. In turn, these three models are incorporated into a
reciprocal model of securities fraud that explains the contradictory crimes
of capitalist control. This reciprocal model is inclusive of both the organizational and institutional relations across the financial landscape between Wall
Street and Washington, DC. Finally, these interactive approaches stress the
roles played in the "financial crisis by the breakdown of law and the failure
of governance and regulation," which allowed Wall Street and company to
escape criminal prosecution for their nefarious deeds.[38]

AN INTERACTIVE MODEL OF
ORGANIZATIONAL CONTROL FRAUD

This model, at the "organizational" or meso-level of interaction, links "control fraud," "market corruption," and "system capacity." These illegalities
typically involve defrauding behaviors that are confined to or originate within
an individual company, such as Enron, Galleon Hedge Fund, HealthSouth,
WorldCom, or other rogue companies within a given industry. These frauds
may also involve numerous businesses within the scope of a particular industry, such as the classic price-fixing conspiracy between General Electric and
Westinghouse in the 1950s or the more recent price-fixing cases involving,
for example, Nintendo Co., Ltd. in 2002 or the Archer Daniels Midland Corporation in 2004.

William Black's Control Fraud

Control frauds have typically referred to companies that use businesses as a
means of defrauding others and making it difficult to detect and punish the
frauds.[39] At the same time, William Black also connects control fraud to the
actual person who directs the theft by deception; a process that creates and
exploits trust in order to cheat those who were not party to the fraudulent
transactions. Black, who worked as a prosecutor for the SEC during the S&L
debacle and before that as the general counsel for the Federal Home Loan
Bank of San Francisco, has contended on several appearances on MSNBC's
The Dylan Ratigan Show that the Wall Street collapse represented a wave of
frauds led by men who control large corporations.

Black argues more generally that control frauds have caused massive
losses from property crimes such as those involving the Enron collapse in
late 2001.[40] He also contends that the epidemic in upper-world white-collar

crime in the early part of the past decade belied officially released data from the Department of Justice for this period. These data consistently reported that "property crimes had continued their downward trend and fallen to an all-time low."[41] This contradiction reflects the reality that the DOJ does not keep any official data on control frauds or any other serious white-collar crimes. This is unfortunate because control frauds can involve hugely insolvent firms. Experts, nevertheless, have touted these firms as among the very best firms in the world that money can buy, firms that probably would have brought down Wall Street in 2009 were it not for the government bailouts.

What makes control frauds uniquely dangerous is that like a person who controls a country, a person who controls a company "can defeat all internal and external controls because he is ultimately in charge of those controls. Fraudulent CEOs do not simply defeat controls; they suborn them and turn them into allies."[42] Those allies come from top-tier law and audit firms. Under the pretence of rendering zealous advocacy for their clients, lawyers can help fraudulent CEOs loot and destroy companies. Retained accountants are even more valuable to these fraudulent firms. As Black emphasizes:

> Every S&L control fraud, and all of the major control frauds that have surfaced recently, were able to get clean opinions from them. Control frauds, using accounting fraud as their primary weapon and shield, typically report sensational profits, followed by catastrophic failure. These fictitious profits provide means for sophisticated, fraudulent CEOs to use common corporate mechanisms such as stock bonuses to convert firm assets to their personal benefits.[43]

Similarly, fraudulent CEOs can place their firms in the line of businesses that offer the best opportunities for accounting frauds. This generally means investing in assets that have no readily ascertainable market value and arranging for reciprocal "sales" of goods that can transform actual losses into unreal profits. It can also mean targeting poorly regulated industries that can make a firm grow rapidly, turning it into a Ponzi scheme. To aid in these control frauds, fraudulent CEOs can also employ the vast resources of their firms to transform the regulatory environment through direct and indirect political contributions, lobbying against regulation and for tort reform, or seeking to remove a chief regulator or block the nomination of the next one. With this type of economic clout and political influence, "criminogenic environments" are formed where firms that appear healthy and legitimate are neither.

As the lessons of the financial collapse of 2007–8 have taught, control frauds are capable of fooling the most sophisticated market participants as well as many regulators. In the case of the S&L control frauds, they consistently deceived uninsured private creditors and shareholders alike. Waves of control fraud have occurred in other nations as well, often with devastating consequences to their economies. In the case of Russia's privatization campaign in the early 1990s, for example, hundreds of billions of dollars were looted and laundered, involving international banking schemes that used Swiss and offshore accounts, as well as U.S. banks, including The Bank of New York, the nation's oldest banking institution, founded in 1784 by Alexander Hamilton.[44]

These frauds have also occurred in cyberspace as when the dot-com Internet bubble burst on March 10, 2000. Similarly, the housing bubble that burst late in 2006, which had not bottomed out by the spring of 2012, was due primarily to the creation of artificial securities and the rise in derivative financial instruments. The most notorious of these investments include Wall Street's collateralized debt obligations (CDO) and credit default swaps (CDS). In an outbreak of control fraud "gone wilding" throughout the mortgage industry, these toxic Wall Street products were directly responsible for the financial meltdown of 2007–8.

Michael Johnston's Influence Market Corruption

Compared to Elite Cartel, Oligarch and Clan, or Official Mogul styles or forms of corruption, Influence Market corruption is the least visible expression of Michael Johnston's four "syndromes of corruption." Unlike the other forms of corruption, Influence Market is more domestic than it is international. The role of competitive politics in this style of corruption is also more complex than in the other forms. As a political scientist and innovative theorist of democracy, development, and corruption, Johnston explains, "Influence Market corruption revolves around access to, and advantages within, established institutions, rather than deals and connections circumventing them."[45] In other words, "Strong institutions reduce the opportunities, and some of the incentives, to pursue extra-system strategies, while increasing the risks. Moreover, the very power of those institutions to deliver major benefits and costs raises the value of influence within them."[46]

Basically, corruption entails "the abuse of a trust, generally one involving public power, for private benefit which often, but by no means always, comes in the form of money."[47] However, corruption may also include the abuse of trust involving private power to the detriment of the public that may, but by no means always, come in the forms of tax subsidies, lower interest rates, or bailouts for the rich. Of course, distinctions between the "public" and "private" control of banking can also be difficult to make, especially in the midst of neo-liberal policies of privatization and private-public partnerships working within the complexity of federal loans and insurance arrangements. Similarly, "Policy changes may redefine public roles as private, or delegate power and resources to organizations that straddle state/society boundaries, in the process changing rules and accountability." As a result, "benefits and costs may be intangible, long-term, broadly dispersed, or difficult to distinguish from the routine operation of the political system."[48] During the aftermath of the S&L crisis in 1989, a classic example surfaced with the alleged corruption involving one Republican and four Democratic U.S. senators—known as the Keating Five—and the very powerful Lincoln Savings and Loan Association.[49] In the case of market democracies, Johnston argues that "systemic corruption problems might involve uses of wealth and power that are legal but still impair institutions and preempt the participation of others."[50]

In sum, developed market societies with influence corruption are not very concerned with the social problem of transgressive corruption more common to developing economies, such as domestic institutions acting as banking repositories for laundered corrupt gains, or the activities of illicit international deals involving multi-national businesses. Such corrupt practices, of course, still exist in developed countries but the primary threat to advanced market democracies comes from those exchanges that occur mostly inside of the political-economic system. These include dealing in access to and influence within strong state institutions where politicians often serve as middlemen renting out their connections and power in return for contributions both legal and otherwise.

Henry Pontell's System Capacity

Henry Pontell has written extensively on system capacity/incapacity in the context of controlling and deterring both street and white-collar crime.[51] Both individually and in collaboration with his colleagues, Pontell has conducted primary research and published widely on the thrift industry and the savings and loan crisis in relation to control fraud, system capacity, and related legal issues.[52] Together, they have applied Pontell's model to the question of limited enforcement capacity in responding to white-collar crime in general and financial thrift crime in particular.

This model of system capacity assumes that "legal sanctioning—the celerity, certainty, and severity of punishment—depends, to a considerable degree, on the organizational structure of the court and also on factors external to the criminal justice system."[53] In short, "where resources are generous and demands light, sanctioning capacity is likely to be high. Sanctioning capacity is low where resources are scarce and demands heavy."[54] Pontell's model of the sanctioning process is also subject to the degrees of inequality and the amount of crime in society. In other words, the capacity of the judicial system to generate and administer penal sanctions depend not only on the organizational structures and workload demands of adjudicative bodies, but also on the relative power of the resources between prosecutors and defendants. Finally, legal sanctioning of street and suite crimes are both subject to the complexity of the offenses.

In particular, corporate and financial frauds are viewed as difficult to pursue because "they are well disguised within ordinary transactions" that "complicate enforcement efforts" and strain resources further.[55] In other words, because these crimes are usually difficult to detect and sanction, there are "built-in" disincentives to prosecute. Even in the case of enforcing thrift fraud where special resources were allocated and prosecutorial task forces were created, enhancing cooperation among the various sanctioning agencies and resulting in more than one thousand successful felony convictions, the sheer magnitude of fraud cases overwhelmed the capacity of the state to effectively respond, falling well short of the level of response necessary for the control or deterrence of crime. Accordingly, the number of these crimes that "officially" existed at the end of the day depended not on the actual occurrences but rather "on the state's capacity and willingness to ferret" these crimes out and so label them.[56]

AN INTERACTIVE MODEL OF INSTITUTIONAL FINANCIAL CONTROL FRAUD

This model, at the "institutional" or macro-level of interaction, links "financial control fraud," "governing corruption," and "regulatory collusion." These are the critical forces that do not merely involve control trust or theft by an organization. In this case study of financial control fraud, the trust and theft has involved the Wall Street financial industry as a whole. Similarly, governing corruption in the case of Wall Street banking has gone further than Influence Market corruption. Governing corruption not only influences regulatory statutes, enforcement or judicial appointments, and elected representatives to Congress.

Governing corruption entails the ability to influence Congress' behavior and regulatory behavior more generally, from the financial industry's billion-dollar lobbying and political campaign contributions to the revolving doors between Wall Street and Washington, DC. In the case of revolving doors, Wall Street bankers and lawyers move back and forth between key positions in the regulatory, legal, and justice bureaucracies as well as in the White House. Having penetrated the three branches of government, Wall Street has in effect established an apparatus of regulatory collusion where criminal prosecutions of securities fraud are out of bounds.

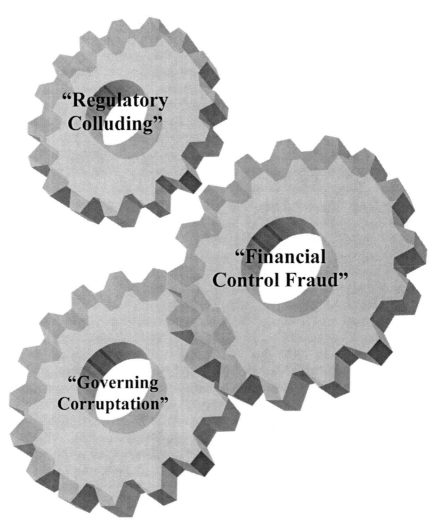

Figure 4.3.   Interactive Model of Institutional Fraud

At this level, these illegalities embody those institutionalized defrauding arrangements that envelop an entire industry, such as those financial activities involved in investment banking and mortgage lending at the beginning of the twenty-first century. In a post-industrial service economy, finance capitalism has become the dominant form of U.S. capitalism. Accordingly, in this economic world of finance capital, the systemic occurrences of securities fraud revolved around the same speculative instruments, devices, and strategies that are inseparable from a century-long history of endless negotiations over regulatory laws and their enforcement.

This interactive model of institutional financial control is employed to construct a working image of "crimes of capitalist control" that are beyond incrimination like high-stakes securities frauds. In the case of the non-criminal prosecutions of the illegalities of Wall Street, these are composed of those bailed-out firms that were deemed too big to fail or jail because of the contradictions of bourgeois legality that have necessitated that the concern for the control of these financial crimes be subordinated to the concern over the damage control in the faith and legitimation of Wall Street financial capitalism. This model of financial fraud control operates institutionally and incorporates those control frauds operating organizationally from one Wall Street megabank to the next Wall Street megabank. While these two models of high-powered fraud are mutually reinforcing, institutional financial control fraud has a systemic reach across the political, economic, and legal bodies of U.S. society and well beyond. These structural social arrangements, for example, explain the contradictory rhetoric and reality of fighting upper-world financial abuse thematically reviewed in chapter 1.

The differences between control fraud and financial control fraud are matters of degree rather than kind. For example, a control fraud on behalf of one corporate entity like Enron or even the pandemic of control frauds during the S&L crisis of the 1980s may have been able to find attorneys, accountants, and raters to help them turn actual losses and delinquencies into unreal profits. In the case of one powerful corporation or a group of non-dominant corporations, poorly regulated industries may be targeted for exploitation and regulatory environments lobbied for transformation. These corporate organizations may be able to disguise their criminogenic activities, appearing healthy, sound, and legitimate when they are not. However, this type of control fraud in general falls short of financial control fraud because of the latter's power to formally and/or informally neutralize and decriminalize the crimes of capitalist control. Hence, the concern here is not those fraudulent businesses within an industry masquerading as legitimate, but rather with an entire financial industry transforming its fraudulent activities into non-criminal and legitimate business practices as usual.

Similarly, the differences between influence market corruption and governing corruption are also matters of degree of escalation of influence across the political-legal-economic spectrum. For example, as the costs and benefits of electoral politics and spoils increasingly raise the value/cost of both, governing corruption is about capturing the ideological hearts and minds of both political parties and filling the campaign re-election coffers of each, to cover their bipartisan bets so to speak. The ante is raised from system

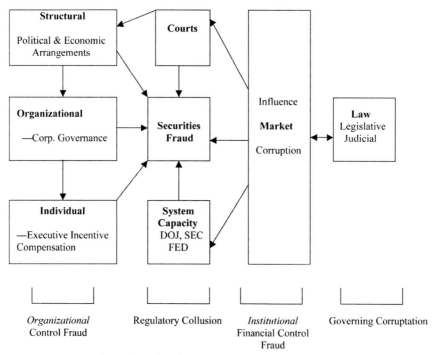

Figure 4.4. A Reciprocal Model of Wall Street Fraud

capacity to regulatory colluding when "revolving doors" of private and public positions of power make it difficult to distinguish between those running Wall Street and those running the Federal Reserve, the Treasury, the Security and Exchange Commission, or the Department of Justice.

The reciprocal model in Figure 4.4 is inclusive of the organizational and institutional relations across the financial landscape connecting Wall Street and Washington, DC. Finally, these interactive approaches stress the roles played in the "financial crisis by the breakdown of law and the failure of governance and regulation," which allowed Wall Street and company to escape criminal prosecution for their nefarious deeds.[57]

WALL STREET LOOTING:
A CRIME OF CAPITALIST CONTROL

The reciprocal approach to the political economy of Wall Street looting and the anatomy of the financial meltdown (see figure 4.5) revolve around the

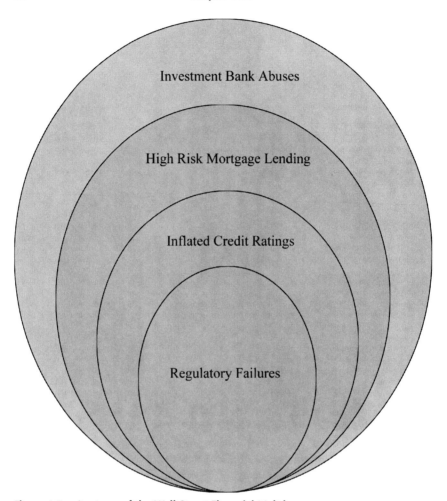

Figure 4.5.   Anatomy of the Wall Street Financial Meltdown

institutionalized interactions connecting "investment bank abuses," "high risk mortgage lending," "inflated credit ratings," and "regulatory failures."[58] As the U.S. Senate's *Anatomy of a Financial Collapse* (*AFC*) emphasized, the evidence gathered by the subcommittee demonstrates that:

• "Investment banks were the driving force behind the structured finance products that provided a steady stream of funding for lenders originating high risk, poor quality loans and that magnified risk throughout the U.S. financial system. The investment banks that engineered, sold, trade, and profited from mortgage related structured finance products were a major cause of the financial crisis."[59]

- "Unacceptable lending and securitization practices were present at a host of financial institutions that originated, sold, and securitized billions of dollars in high risk, poor quality home loans. . . . These lenders were not the victims of the financial crisis; the high risk loans they issued were the fuel that ignited the financial crisis."[60]
- "Credit rating agencies were aware of problems in the mortgage market, including an unsustainable rise in housing prices, the high risk nature of the loans being issued, lax lending standards, and rampant mortgage fraud." Nevertheless, agencies inflated their credit ratings as they "weakened their standards as each competed to provide the most favorable ratings to win business and greater market share."[61]
- "Regulatory failures were a proximate cause of the financial crisis" and "allowed high risk loans . . . to proliferate, negatively impacting investors across the United States and around the world." The failure to restrict "unsafe lending practices" resulted in a record number of defaulted loans and "financial institutions around the globe suffered hundreds of billions in losses, triggering an economic disaster."[62]

Investment Banking Fraud: The "Abuses" of Goldman Sachs

In the "years leading up to the financial crisis, large investment banks designed and promoted complex financial instruments, often referred to as structured finance products, which were at the heart of the crisis."[63] These included residential mortgage-backed securities (RMBS), CDO securities, credit default swaps (CDS), and CDS contracts linked to the asset-backed securities index (ABX). From 2004 to 2008, financial institutions in the United States issued nearly $2.5 trillion in RMBS and over $1.4 trillion in CDO securities, backed mostly by mortgage-related products. As the underwriter of residential mortgage-backed securitizations, banks typically charged $1 to $8 million each. To act as placement agents for a CDO securitization, their fees ranged from $5 to $10 million. Those fees "contributed substantial revenues to the investment banks, which established internal structured finance groups, as well as a variety of RMBS and CDO origination and trading desks within these groups, to handle mortgage related securitizations."[64]

In turn, the trading desks of these investment banks participated in those secondary markets, buying and selling RMBS and CDO securities either on behalf of their clients or in connection with their own proprietary transactions. These types of financial products allowed investors to profit off of both the successes and failures of RMBS and CDO securitization. Similarly, the establishment of the ABX Index allowed counterparties to wager on the rise or fall in the value of a basket of subprime RMBS securities. Sometimes, the investment banks

> matched up parties who wanted to take opposite sides in a transaction and other times took one or the other side of a transaction to accommodate a client. At still other times, investment banks used these financial instruments to make their own proprietary wagers. In extreme cases, some investment banks set up structured finance transactions which enabled them to profit at the expense of their clients.[65]

Among an array of structured financial products, Goldman Sachs (GS), for example, specialized in "short selling" that allowed them to benefit from the downturn in the mortgage market.[66] In the same way, GS designed, marketed, and sold CDOs "that created conflicts of interest with the firm's clients and at times led to the bank's profiting from the same products that caused substantial losses for its clients."[67]

Running up to the meltdown (2004–8), GS was a major player in the U.S. mortgage market, buying and selling RMBS and CDO securities on behalf of its clients while amassing its own multibillion-dollar proprietary mortgage holdings. In 2006 and 2007, GS designed and underwrote ninety-three RMBS and twenty-seven mortgage-related CDO securitizations totaling about $100 billion. Beginning in December 2006 when

> it saw evidence that the high risk mortgages underlying many RMBS and CDO securities were incurring accelerated rates of delinquency and default, Goldman quietly and abruptly reversed course. Over the next two months, it rapidly sold off or wrote down the bulk of its existing subprime RMBS and CDO inventory, and began building a short position that would allow it to profit from the decline of the mortgage market.[68]

In 2007, it twice built up and cashed in sizable mortgage-related short positions, reaching a peak of short selling totaling $13.9 billion. By year's end, Goldman's Structured Products Group had produced record profits totaling $3.7 billion. Goldman's short positions were "in direct opposition to the clients to whom it was selling CDO securities, yet it failed to disclose the size and nature of its short position while marketing the securities."[69] Four of those CDO securities for 2007 were sold as Hudson 1, Anderson, Timberwolf, and Abacus. These investors virtually lost everything; three investors together lost about $1 billion from their Abacus investments.

During the summer of 2008, the SEC started investigating Goldman's marketing of the subprime mortgage deal with Abacus. One year later in July

2009, the SEC sent GS a Wells notice informing the firm of its intention to file a lawsuit against the company. On the first occasion, GS failed to disclose in its financial reports that it was under investigation by the SEC for failing to disclose material information to investors in violation of SEC Rule 10b-5. On the second occasion, Goldman chose not to disclose the SEC's pending enforcement action on its financial statements.

In sum, leading up to the Wall Street meltdown Goldman Sachs, like other investment banks using loans from subprime lenders known for issuing high risk and poor quality mortgages, underwrote and sold risky securities across the United States and around the world. On top of this, GS enabled lenders to acquire new funds to originate still more high risk, poor quality loans not as the toxic or junk loans that they were but as triple-A rated. Also, without full disclosure Goldman failed to reveal the shorting of the very CDO securities that it was marketing. If this risk was not enough, GS came up with some very complex structured finance products, such as synthetic CDOs[70] and naked credit default swaps in which the buyer does not own the underlying debt. These instruments only amplified market risk by allowing investors without any ownership interests to place unlimited side bets on their performance. To have stopped the flow of these high-risk investment strategies in general or the "CDO machine" in particular would have meant "less income for structured finance units, smaller executive bonuses, and even the disappearance of CDO desks and personnel, which is finally what happened."[71]

Recall that securities fraud refers to when a stockbroker, brokerage firm, corporation, or investment bank misrepresents information that investors use to make decisions. More specifically, the "types of misrepresentation involved in this crime include providing false information, withholding key information, offering bad advice, and offering or acting on inside information."[72] So what have been the legal consequences for Goldman Sachs and/or any of its employees who were involved in any of these fraudulent transactions? By the spring of 2012, there had not been a single criminal prosecution against either Goldman Sachs or one of its employees. One relatively young twenty-eight-year-old trader and executive, Fabrice Tourre, who had a civil suit still pending against him, filed in 2010 by the SEC, was working in the GS London office.

On July 15, 2010, Goldman Sachs settled a civil case with the SEC, and agreed to the largest penalty ever assessed against a financial services firm—$550 million. As with most of the financial settlements between other bailed-out institutions like AIG or Bank of America and the federal government, GS did not have to "admit to any wrongdoing" with respect to its fraudulent or criminal conduct. It did acknowledge that it should have been more forthcoming in disclosing some information and in the marketing of some of their products. GS also agreed to tighten its internal controls and to monitor its personnel to ensure that disclosures in future offerings of mortgage and CDO products are full and accurate. Strangely, while the judge ruled that there was no finding of willful wrongdoing, he nevertheless issued a permanent injunction from violations of the anti-fraud provisions of The Securities Act of 1933. Does that mean that the next time Goldman commits fraud, that federal prosecutors will file criminal charges? It certainly should mean that; however, as repeat offenders, this has not been the case in the past. Such are the structural contradictions of bourgeois legality.

In any event, although Goldman et al. have been able to remain beyond incrimination with the U.S. DOJ, this does not mean that GS has escaped lawsuits from its investors and/or shareholders. In fact, several investor lawsuits have been brought forth, including three pension funds as co-lead plaintiffs in an investor lawsuit against Goldman. District Judge Paul Crotty in February 2011 designated the Arkansas Retirement System, the West Virginia Investment Management Board, and the Plumbers and Pipefitters National Pension Group in Alexandria, Virginia, to lead six consolidated lawsuits against Goldman and various of its officers and directors. Finally, on June 2, 2011, it was reported that Goldman Sachs had been served a subpoena by the Manhattan district attorney and New York State, who were investigating several derivative trades that Goldman had executed in 2006 and 2007. Criminal lawsuits, however, from state prosecutors are now out of the question because of the deal reached between the megabanks, the DOJ, and the 50 state attorney generals in February 2012.

Mortgage Lending Fraud: The "High Risks" of Washington Mutual Bank

How did the nation's largest thrift and sixth largest bank, with $300 billion in assets, $188 billion in deposits, 2,300 branches in 15 states, and over 43,000 employees at the time of its failure on September 23, 2008, find itself seized by its regulator, placed into receivership with the FDIC, and shortly thereafter sold to JP Morgan Chase for $1.9 billion? The short answer is that beginning in 2004 Washington Mutual Bank (WaMu) changed its lending strategies to pursue higher profits by securing high-risk loans. A longer answer based on documents obtained by the Anatomy inquiry reveal that WaMu launched its high-risk strategy because

> higher risk loans and mortgage-backed securities could be sold for higher prices on Wall Street. They garnered higher prices, because higher risk meant the securities paid a higher coupon rate than other comparably rated securities, and investors paid a higher price to buy them. Selling or securitizing the loans also removed them from WaMu's books and appeared to insulate the bank from risk.[73]

At the same time, WaMu and its subsidiary Long Beach Mortgage Corporation started to engage "in a host of shoddy lending practices that produced billions of dollars in high risk, poor quality mortgages and mortgage-backed securities."[74] These fraudulent practices included

- qualifying high-risk borrowers for larger loans than they could afford;
- steering borrowers from conventional mortgages to higher risk loan products;
- accepting loan applications without verifying borrowers' income;
- using loans with low, short-term "teaser" rates that could lead to payment shock when higher interest rates took effect later on;
- promoting negatively amortizing loans in which many borrowers increased rather than paid down their debt; and
- authorizing loans with multiple layers of risk.

In addition, WaMu and Long Beach "failed to enforce compliance with their own lending standards; allowed excessive loan error and exception rates; exercised weak oversight over the third party mortgage brokers who supplied half or more of their loans; and tolerated the issuance of loans with fraudulent or erroneous borrower information."[75] Finally, the "icing on the cake" was that they designed compensation incentives that rewarded those loan personnel who issued more of the higher risk loans.

What were the consequences of this "race to the bottom" in high-risk mortgage lending? On the way to the implosion, several things occurred: First, by 2007, WaMu and Long Beach together had securitized more than $77 billion in subprime loans. Second, from 2003 to 2006, the higher risk loans grew from 19 percent of WaMu's loan originations to 55 percent in 2006; at the same time, the lower risk and fixed-rate loans fell from 64 percent to 25 percent of its originations. Third, during the same period, WaMu increased its securitization of subprime loans sixfold, increasing such loans from nearly $4.5 billion in 2003 to $29 billion in 2006. Fourth, WaMu also increased its flagship product, Adjustable Rate Mortgages (Option ARMs). These loans, in effect, created high-risk, negatively amortizing mortgage loans. When the housing market crashed in 2006 and the foreclosure "boom" kicked off, most of these home loan borrowers would find their homes "underwater." From 2003 to 2007, these types of ARM loans represented half of all of WaMu's loans. In 2006, Washington Mutual originated more than $42.6 billion in Option ARMs and sold or securitized at least $115 billion to investors, including sales to Fannie Mae (Federal National Mortgage Association) and Freddie Mac (Federal Home Loan Mortgage Corporation). Fifth, by 2007 high-risk home equity loan products made up $63.5 billion or 27 percent of its loan portfolio, an increase of 130 percent from 2003.

By 2006, as WaMu's high-risk loans were beginning to incur high rates of delinquency, signs of the "perfect storm" were starting to form. In 2007, its mortgage-backed securities began incurring losses and ratings downgrades. Also in 2007, "the bank itself began incurring losses due to a portfolio that contained poor quality and fraudulent loans and securities. Its stock price dropped as shareholders lost confidence, and depositors began withdrawing funds, eventually causing a liquidity crisis at the bank."[76] When WaMu finally went belly-up in 2008 and went into receivership with the Federal Deposit Insurance Corporation, had it not been for the sale to JP Morgan Chase for a mere $1.9 billion, the failure of WaMu might have exhausted the entire $45 billion insurance fund of the FDIC.

It is interesting to note that in addition to all of the designed or institutionalized fraud strategies at WaMu, e-mails, memos, audit reports, and reviews reveal that the company's internal attempts to stop the sale of fraudulent loans to investors and to control other unsanctioned forms of "extensive fraud" where employees "willfully" circumvent bank policies were described as "ineffective." None of this was news to Washington Mutual's president, Steve Rotella, who had described their subsidiary Long Beach with such words as "terrible" and "a mess," with default rates that were "ugly." Rotella also referred to WaMu's prime home loan business as the "worst managed business" he had seen in his career.[77]

Once again, in the Land of Fraud, inquiring minds would like to know: How have WaMu and its executives managed their liability when it comes to criminal prosecutions? In the case of this fraudulent giant, on August 5, 2011, the U.S. attorney's office in Seattle announced that it was closing down its criminal investigation and would not be filing any criminal charges.[78] In fairness to WaMu and mortgage lending fraud, however, there really was a whole lot of illegal competition for the feds to investigate, including from the likes of Countrywide Financial Corp, IndyMac Bancorp, New Century Financial, and many others.

By the end of summer 2011, it seemed as though the federal investigations were all stalling and that no formal criminal charges against the major mortgage fraudsters would result. Then again, as U.S. attorneys in Los Angeles were winding down their criminal investigations of IndyMac; for example, U.S. attorneys in Brooklyn, New York, were opening up their own investigation of the company. As a spokeswoman for the DOJ stated, "The Justice Department has and will continue to investigate financial fraud, whether it occurs on Wall Street or Main Street."[79] Unfortunately, the DOJ will not file its first criminal prosecution against any of the major Wall Street financial firms whose securities violations caused the collapse of the economy in 2008.

Early in 2011, a criminal probe of Angelo Mozilo, former CEO of subprime lender giant Countrywide Financial, now owned by the Bank of America, was closed without any criminal charges being filed. One of the few successful criminal prosecutions related to the housing crisis ended in June 2011 when the former chairman of Taylor, Bean & Whitaker Mortgage Corporation was sentenced to thirty years in prison. Six other executives at the government-sponsored Fannie Mae entity had previously been sentenced to prison for their roles in the $3 billion mortgage fraud scheme that led to the collapse of an Ocala, Florida, company as well as the regional bank Colonial BancGroup of Montgomery, Alabama.[80]

In comparison, the SEC has had a bit more success with civil enforcement actions of major mortgage fraudsters than the feds have. In 2010, for example, Mr. Mozilo agreed to pay $67.5 million to settle civil-fraud charges, and three executives at New Century paid a total of a little more than a paltry $1.5 million to settle civil-fraud charges.[81] According to SEC Director Robert Khuzami, since 2008 the agency had filed thirty-eight financial-crisis-related cases and had collected some $2.8 billion in penalties and disgorgements for harmed investors by the end of 2011.[82] True to all of these civil cash settlements, none of these executives had to admit or to deny any wrongdoing. Again, such are the contradictions of bourgeois legality.

Inflated Credit Ratings: The Masking of Fraud by Moody's and Standard & Poor's

Historically, investments holding triple-A ratings have had less than 1 percent probability of incurring defaults. In 2007 the vast majority of RMBS and CDO securities with AAA ratings incurred substantial losses, some failing outright. Moreover, over 90 percent of the AAA ratings given to subprime RMBS securities issued in 2006 and 2007 were later downgraded by the credit agencies to junk status. In the case of Long Beach, seventy-five out of seventy-five of their AAA-rated securities issued in 2006 were later downgraded to junk status, defaulted, or withdrawn.

Between 2004 and 2007, Moody's and Standard & Poor's issued credit ratings for tens of thousands of RMBS and CDO securities. Even though many of these consisted of high-risk loans, most of these received AAA ratings deeming them safe investments. In late 2006, those high-risk mortgage loans began incurring delinquencies and defaults at an alarming rate. Nevertheless, for the next six months Moody's and S&P continued to rate these securities AAA. Then, in July 2007,

> as mortgage delinquencies intensified and RMBS and CDO securities began incurring losses, both companies abruptly reversed course and began downgrading at record numbers hundreds and then thousands of their RMBS and CDO ratings, some less than a year old. Investors like banks, pension funds, and insurance companies, who are by rule barred from owning low rated securities, were forced to sell off their downgraded RMBS and CDO holdings, because they had lost their investment grade status.[83]

Of course, the inevitable happened rather quickly. Because of the downgraded ratings, the RMBS and CDO securities held by financial firms lost much of their value, and new securitizations were unable to find investors. Initially these markets froze and then collapsed, leaving investors and financial firms around the world holding unmarketable subprime securities. The Senate's inquiry uncovered several factors that contributed to the erroneous ratings handed out by Moody's and S&P.

Most significantly, there was the inherent conflict of interest in the system used to pay for credit ratings. Amazingly, the Wall Street firms that sought their ratings and profited from the financial products being rated paid credit-rating agencies for their ratings. "Under this 'issuer pays' model, the rating agencies were dependent upon those Wall Street firms to bring them business, and were vulnerable to threats that the firms would take their business elsewhere if they did not get the ratings they wanted. The ratings agencies weakened their standards as each competed to provide the most favorable rating to win business and greater market share."[84] To put it simply, it was not in the short-run interest of these credit-rating agencies to provide accurate credit ratings for high-risk RMBS and CDO securities, because doing so would have hurt their own revenue streams.

Additional factors that the inquiry identified included: (1) failures to include relevant mortgage performance data and to apply updated rating models to the new types of transactions; (2) unclear and subjective criteria used to produce ratings; and (3) despite record revenues, inadequate staff to perform various rating and surveillance services. One could argue that the business of Moody's and S&P during the run-up to the financial crisis was that of defrauding or of masking the fraudulent mortgage lending industry as a whole. In any case, there certainly was a lot of fraud going around to share among these different groups of fraudsters.

Nevertheless, on April 1, 2011, U.S. District Judge Jed Rakoff of Manhattan, New York, threw out a class-action lawsuit accusing Moody's Investor Services and Standard & Poor's of defrauding investors about the safety of

$63.4 billion of mortgage debt. "Plaintiffs led by the Public Employees' Retirement System of Mississippi accused rating agencies and banks of misleading them about the safety of 84 mostly investment-grade offerings of residential mortgage-backed securities."[85] Judge Rakoff, who has presided over three of the SEC's biggest cases, is also an outspoken critic who has excoriated the agency for an enforcement strategy that he believes has not done enough to punish banks for their bad practices. He has also questioned whether or not the language of "neither admit nor deny" is in the public interest. In late 2011 he rejected "a $285 million settlement with Citicorp over charges that it sold risky mortgage-backed securities without telling investors that it was also betting against the debt."[86] Rakoff stated that the "deal would allow Citigroup to settle a four-year investment at only a very minimal cost to the financial institution and without agreeing to the facts alleged by the SEC."[87] Once again, such are the contradictions of bourgeois legality.

Regulatory Failures: The Office of Thrift Supervision as "Fraudster"

With the abundance of all kinds of fraud moving throughout the securities industry during the run-up to the financial meltdown, what were the regulators in the Land of Fraud doing about it? In the case of the unsafe and unsound practices that led to the demise of Washington Mutual, the Office of Thrift Supervision (OTS) over a five-year period from 2004 to 2008 identified more than "500 serious deficiencies . . . yet failed to take action to force the bank to improve its lending operations and even impeded oversight by the bank's backup regulator, the FDIC."[88] Despite the fact that OTS examiners had repeatedly informed WaMu that the institution had many significant problems with its lending practices, risk management, asset quality, and appraisal practices, not once did the regulator take a public enforcement action to correct the situation, nor did it downgrade the bank's rating for safety and soundness.

OTS also had other regulatory options at its disposal to enforce conformity with sound and expected lending practices, such as requiring a public plan with deadlines for corrective actions or imposing civil fines for inaction. However, the OTS chose to ignore these options as well. Meanwhile, over the same period of time, OTS officials were resisting calls from the FDIC "for stronger measures" and even impeded FDIC oversight efforts at times by "denying FDIC examiners office space and access to bank records."[89] Not until 2008, as WaMu was incurring mounting losses from what was then almost two years of rising rates of delinquency and default, did OTS finally take two informal, non-public enforcement actions. One required that Washington Mutual agree to a "Board

Resolution" in March and to a "Memorandum of Understanding" in September. Neither of these imposed sufficient changes to prevent the bank's failure.

And just two weeks before WaMu was seized in the fall of 2008, the OTS was still fighting with the FDIC over the downgrading of the bank's safety and soundness rating. Seems as though, even if the Office of Thrift Supervision was not formally in collusion with this financial institution that it was responsible for regulating, then OTS was either, at best, an incompetent enforcer or, at worst, a regulating fraudster. In any event, these regulatory relations between the OTS and WaMu exemplify the meaning of regulatory colluding. The Senate inquiry has other names or explanations for these enforcement failures, such as "a regulatory culture of deference to management." A culture where the OTS viewed their thrifts as "constituents" and relied on those in charge "to police" their own operations. Even when, in the case of Washington Mutual, there were clear incentives in place to encourage insider fraud by their employees. Such are the contradictions of bourgeois legality.

Chapter Five

Financial Looting, Victimization, and Legal Intervention

On Criminal Prosecution and Civil Law Enforcement

Throughout U.S. history the illegal use of public money by economic and political elites for personal gain without any penal sanctions has been the most common sanction, if and when, the state decides to intervene. The fraudulent use of public money can be traced back to an "insider trading" arrangement that involved the nation's first Secretary of the Treasury, Alexander Hamilton. This financial corruption revolved around the use of federal funds that enriched politicians and close friends of Hamilton. The non-prosecution of the facts against Hamilton and his associates may have established a precedent of sorts. That is, crimes committed by the financially powerful may not really be crimes even when they obviously are crimes.

At the time of the Constitutional Convention in 1787, national and state governmental debts totaled $80 million. Forty of the fifty-five delegates held debt certificates issued by the federal and state governments during and following the Revolutionary War. When issued these certificates were worth $5,000 or more, but their value had steadily declined as the new nation became embroiled in financial chaos under the Articles of Confederation.[1] Other delegates like Benjamin Franklin who had "loaned the national government $3,000 at 6 percent interest, noted that such loan certificates had fallen drastically in value and hoped and believed that their value would 'mend when our new Constitution is adopted.'"[2]

Under the circumstances, Hamilton decided that the new federal government would honor its debt and make good on what had become essentially worthless paper. The secretary of the Treasury had also agreed "to pay in full people owning the certificates at the time of redemption, not necessarily the original owners. Word of this policy was leaked to Hamilton's friends and in-laws, all of who began buying up certificates at a record pace."[3] By the time the policy was officially announced on January 14, 1790, the certificates were almost totally owned by speculators. As white-collar criminologist David Simon underscores:

> Hamilton's assistant, William Duer, ignored all charges of conflict of interest and engaged in numerous shady schemes. Besides benefitting from insider information about the debt certificates (he bought as many as he could with borrowed money), Duer demanded kickbacks on government contracts. An outraged public finally forced Hamilton to request Duer's resignation. But Hamilton's relatives and associates were guilty of some of the same conflicts of interest, and their punishment was merely to have their fortunes greatly increased.[4]

The treatment of Hamilton's associates at the end of the seventeenth century as "beyond incrimination" is consistent with the history of large-scale fraud and looting throughout nineteenth- and twentieth-century America. As reviewed in chapter 1 of this book, the non-criminal reactions to securities fraud and financial looting represent a constant, dependable, and unswerving pattern of non-enforcement of the criminal sanction for society's most powerful wrongdoers of the public trust. The sociological theory of law first articulated by Donald Black in *The Behavior of Law* (1976) helps to explain these non-criminal outcomes. When applied to the Reciprocal Model of Wall Street Fraud (see figure 4.4), which takes into account the behavioral interests of offenders, regulators, and finance capitalism, Black's theory of the "law in action" complements the contradictions or the dialectics of bourgeois legality.

CONTRADICTORY LEGAL RESPONSES TO WALL STREET LOOTING AND VICTIMIZATION

As articulated at the beginning of the framing of this inquiry, state-legal criminalization of security fraud hangs in the balance of the contradictory forces of free-market capitalism. For example, when similarly dominant interests and behaviors of the political economy are both illegal and controlling, as numerous financial transactions were in the run-up to the Wall Street meltdown, such as credit swap defaults, then bourgeois legality finds itself in the contradictory position of both trying to chastise and to excuse these violations. In practice, how have these contradictions in "legal relativism" been accommodated? Pragmatically, through the differential application and selective enforcement of civil, criminal, and regulatory law. Cognitively, through the cultural and social denial of the mass victimization of the American people and the corresponding lack of moral accountability for those responsible. These denials have been reinforced by a U.S. mass media that has failed to examine the obvious state-legal contradictions in the control, discipline, justice, or punishment of those securities frauds that caused the financial crisis of 2007–8 and the ensuing Great Recession that followed.

Like the omissions from civic discourse, there has also been a general capitulation in academic studies of law, crime, and society. For example, whether one is examining the Wall Street fiasco from the dominant lens of criminology, economics, or jurisprudence, the traditional epistemological orientations have been ideologically disconnected from the socio-legal realities of high-stakes securities fraud. In the case of mainstream criminology, more than forty years ago deviance theorist David Matza underscored that among "their most notable accomplishments, the criminological positivists [had] succeeded in what would seem the impossible. They separated the study of crime from the workings and the theory of the state."[5]

Similarly, mainstream economists and jurisprudents have respectively separated their studies of the economy and the law from any analysis of the state. Matza was careful to point out that this separation was not necessarily a conscious or a deliberate action. Rather, he contended that these scholars or scientists' partial blindness was due to the fact that these fields structured their studies "in such a way as to obscure obvious connections or to take the connections for granted and leave the matter at that."[6] As both an iconoclast among sociological positivists and an integrationist among legal scholars, Donald Black's holistic method for the study of legal behavior stands apart from most mainstream theorists. First and foremost, Black's formulations imply that

> equality before the law does not exist. The reality is legal relativity, not legal universalism: Law varies with its social geometry—its location and direction in social space. Such a theory completely flies in the face of the conventional conceptions of law and justice found among lawyers, judges, legal scholars, and members of the general public.[7]

More precisely, Black provided "a set of theoretical formulations that predict and explain variation in the quantity and style of law," or what he also referred to as "governmental social control."[8] Not without controversy and disagreement among sociologists, criminologists, and legal scholars are Black's twenty-eight principles of the law in action. Debate still exists about whether these legal principles are actually theorems, hypotheses, or propositions that may be adequately tested or not. One early reviewer from the *American Journal of Sociology* (1978) had this to say: Black presents "a host of new hypotheses derived from the general theorems that made the integration possible."[9] Today, many would agree with Mark Cooney, who recently concluded in his foreword to the special 2010 edition that *The Behavior of Law* "contains a valid and general scientific theory."[10]

Black's comprehensive theory of law links governmental social control to stratification, differentiation, social distance, location in the center/periphery of society, symbolic culture, organization, and non-legal social control. As Cooney points out, the "variations in the incidence and in the direction of legal social control are explained in terms of variations in these fundamental 'aspects' of social life."[11] Furthermore, Black's epistemology of pure sociology dispenses not only with human psychology and the focus on the individual as the unit of motivation, but also with the normative aspirations of jurisprudence.[12] As a quantifiable variable, law may increase or decrease and different legal settings have more or less of it. The quantity of law may be measured, for example, by such things as the number of complaints filed, the number of these that are prosecuted, the outcomes for the plaintiffs or for the defendants, the convictions or acquittals, the incarcerations or the compensations. More generally, "The quantity of law is known by the number and scope of prohibitions, obligations, and other standards to which people are subject, and by the rate of legislation, litigation, and adjudication."[13]

Taken as a whole, Black's formulations predict such things as "when people are more likely to call the police or contact a lawyer, when the police are more likely to make an arrest or a lawyer to file a complaint in court, when a case is more likely to succeed in court, attract more punishment, require a greater payment of damages, and so on."[14] Each of these formulations predict and explain "the quantity of law when other facts about a case are constant, such as the other features of its social geometry and the specific nature of an alleged crime or other form of illegality."[15] For the purposes of prosecuting Wall Street looting and victimization, one of the simplest formulations is that "downward law (from social superiors against inferiors) is greater than upward law (from social inferiors against superiors)."[16] In short, legal-criminal social control "is greater in a downward direction within a stratification system than vice versa, and it varies with the vertical distance between the parties—in a downward direction distance makes for more law, in an upward, for less."[17] In the case of wealthy financial fraudsters throughout U.S. history, they have generally received little, if any, criminal law for which they were legally eligible. Conversely, they have received more than their fair share of non-criminal alternatives.

Black also stresses that the socioeconomic statuses (SES) of the offenders or of the victims are less important than the relative SES of the social groups to which the perpetrators and victims belong. The relative positions of these groups' interests structure the contradictory ways in which the rest of society defines and interprets "criminal" events.[18] In short, the stratified positions of these potential offenders and victims in relation to third parties—from bystanders to agents of social control, from judges to jurors, and from legislators to the mass media—structures whether the reality of Wall Street looting becomes either a "securities fraud" or a "securities bailout."

Conceptually, Black discusses and identifies four styles of law or governmental social control: (1) penal, (2) compensatory, (3) therapeutic, and (4) conciliatory. All but the therapeutic mode, which aspires toward achieving normality for the deviant violator, are applicable to Wall Street looting. Penal control in its purest form involves the state taking the initiative against the offender. The question becomes the guilt or innocence of a criminal defendant. By contrast, in the case of compensatory control, the victim takes the initiative without the assistance of the state. As the plaintiff, his complaint "alleges that someone is his debtor, with an unfulfilled obligation. He demands payment."[19] Both of these legal forms of governmental control are adversarial. They have contestants—complainants and defendants—winners and losers. In the case of criminal-penal control, the conflicts are between self-determination versus punishment. In the case of compensatory-civil control, the conflicts are between self-determination versus payment.

Both the therapeutic and conciliatory styles of law are remedial. They involve methods of social repair and maintenance, or of providing assistance to people in trouble. In "these styles of social control the question is what is necessary to ameliorate a bad situation."[20] In the case of conciliation, the goal is about re-establishing social harmony. In the pure case, "the parties to a dispute initiate a meeting and seek to restore their relationship to its former condition. They may include a mediator or other third party in their discussion, together working out a compromise or other mutually acceptable resolution."[21] Finally, Black carefully emphasized that "social control may deviate from these styles in their pure form, combining one with another in various ways."[22]

In the case of Wall Street looting and federal regulatory colluding, there have been multiple expressions or overlapping exercises in both compensation and conciliation. Predictably, at the very height of the Wall Street pyramid securities fraudsters have not been subject to any criminal or penal control. Further down the financial market food chain, a relatively small number or handful of "inside traders" have been subjected to criminal arrests, indictments, and convictions. Further down the network of financial illegalities, a few thousand petty mortgage fraudsters have been criminally prosecuted and sanctioned. Most of these fraudsters were caught up in the sweeps carried out by the FBI's Operation Stolen Dreams in the spring of 2010.

TRACKING DOJ AND SEC FINANCIAL FRAUD CASES

By the spring of 2012, some four years after the Wall Street debacle, no senior executives from any of the major financial institutions had been criminally charged, prosecuted, or imprisoned for any type of securities fraud. This is in stark contrast to the savings and loan scandals of the 1980s, when special governmental task forces referred some eleven hundred cases to prosecutors, resulting in more than eight hundred bank officials going to prison. Comparatively, some critics have argued that there has been a lack of collective governmental resolve to criminally pursue these offenses. Other critics have argued that a collective governmental resolve not to hold these offenders accountable has all but succeeded. Both of these claims are sustained by an examination of the available evidence.

According to the Securities and Exchange Act of 1934, "A private right of action that involves a claim of fraud, deceit, manipulation, or contrivance of a regulatory requirement concerning the securities law" and as amended by the Sarbanes-Oxley Act of 2002, "may be brought not later than the earlier of '(1) 2 years after the discovery of the facts constituting the violation; or (2) 5 years after such violation.'"[23] Hence, it is not very likely that too many more claims will be filed and accepted by a court of law. Moreover, whether the Obama administration had been able or not to "pull off" its desired foreclosure settlement with the largest banking institutions and the fifty attorney generals, effectively protecting the banks from any future civil and criminal enforcement actions, the statutes of limitations for most of these frauds was already coming into play.[24]

Non-prosecution of securities fraud is precisely what the economic elites of Wall Street and the political elites from the Bush II and Obama administrations as well as from the majorities of both the U.S. Senate and House of Representatives have desired since the collapse of Wall Street. The outcome of no criminal prosecutions is neither by accident nor conspiracy but mostly by consensus or collusion. A concerted effort more generally not to prosecute "big time" financial fraud had begun in 2003, picking up momentum in 2005–6 with the successful overturning of the criminal fraud conviction of Arthur Andersen by the U.S. Supreme Court. From that point on, instead of strategies to "better" control these financial crimes, strategies have been developing to control the damage done to the faith of Wall Street investors in the financial system. The outcomes of this non-penal strategy of controlling financial fraud have resulted in (1) conciliatory efforts by the government, namely the SEC and the DOJ, to restore institutionalized business as usual (see tables 5.1 and 5.2);[25] and (2) compensatory efforts by private investors, individual or corporate, to seek damages for their losses (see chapter 6).

Conciliatory Collusion

For an example of "conciliatory collusion," take the case of criminal prosecution versus conciliatory compensation and investment faith in Goldman Sachs (table 5.2, third case down). As far back as April 2010 when the SEC accused

Goldman in a civil complaint of "duping clients by selling mortgage securities that were secretly created by a hedge fund firm to cash in on the housing market's collapse," and at a time when GS shares were trading near $180, "Goldman investors ha[d] been on a roller-coaster ride."[26] Three months later, on July 15th, the Securities and Exchange Commission announced that Goldman would "pay $550 million and reform its business practices to settle SEC charges that Goldman misled investors in a subprime mortgage product just as the U.S. housing market was starting to collapse."[27] Of the monies paid by Goldman, "$250 million [were] returned to harmed investors through a Fair Fund distribution and $300 million [were] paid to the U.S. Treasury."[28]

The fine represented 4 percent of GS's record-setting $13.4 billion in profits in 2009. For perspective, back in 1989 the investment banking firm Drexel Burnham was fined $650 million, putting it out of business. A year later its CEO, junk bond king Michael Milken, paid a $600 million settlement fine and served a stretch in prison.[29] Remarking on the case's quick resolution, Robert Khuzami, director of the SEC's Division of Enforcement, had this say: "This settlement is a stark lesson to Wall Street firms that no product is too complex and no investor too sophisticated, to avoid a heavy price if a firm violates the fundamental principle of honest treatment and fair dealing."[30] Echoing the message of his boss, Deputy Director Lorin Reisner added that the "unmistakable message of this lawsuit and today's settlement is that half-truths and deception cannot be tolerated and that the integrity of the securities markets depends on all market participants acting with uncompromising adherence to the requirements of truthfulness and honesty."[31] All rhetoric aside, the material compensation amounted to a "slap on the wrist."

In agreeing to the SEC's largest-ever penalty paid by a Wall Street firm, GS recognized in settlement papers submitted to the U.S. District Court for the Southern District of New York that

> Goldman acknowledges that the marketing materials for the ABACUS 2007-AC1 transaction contained incomplete information. In particular, it was a mistake for the Goldman marketing materials to state that the reference portfolio was "selected by" ACA Management LLC without disclosing the role of Paulson & Co. Inc. in the portfolio selection process and that Paulson's economic interests were adverse to CDO investors. Goldman regrets that the marketing materials did not contain that disclosure.[32]

In connection with the settlement, the SEC took into consideration the fact that Goldman had begun conducting a comprehensive, firm-wide review of its business standards. It is further worth underscoring that the reforms called for in the settlement required "remedial action" by Goldman in its review and approval of offerings of certain mortgage securities. Those involving, for example, "the role and responsibilities of internal legal counsel, compliance personnel, and outside counsel in review of written marketing materials for such offerings."[33] The settlement also required "additional education and training of Goldman employees in this area of the firm's business."[34] Convolutedly to this criminologist's understanding of the law, Goldman and the SEC had agreed to settle the case without GS "admitting or denying the allegations" and yet "consenting to the entry of a final judgment that provides for a permanent injunction from [any future] violations of the antifraud provisions of the Securities Act of 1933."[35]

Contradictorily, if the past is an indicator of the future, then the next time Goldman commits securities fraud it is more than reasonable to assume that this new "solitary" violation will not result in anything more than another fine, more education, and promises not to do once again what they have never admitted to doing in the first place, let alone ever being subject to criminal arrest or imprisonment. Either way—conciliatory compensation or conciliatory collusion—Wall Street investors may not be too confident about their investments knowing that finance capital is back to business as usual. Without any serious penalties, investors may not be very comfortable knowing that Goldman deliberately misled its clients. Nor can these investors know for sure that fraudulent securities practices as usual have stopped at GS. After all, seven months later in the winter of 2011 came the Senate report, *Anatomy of a Financial Collapse*. This prompted a Justice Department inquiry, and Goldman received a subpoena from the office of the Manhattan district attorney in June of that year. Then, when confirmation occurred on Monday morning, August 22, that the firm's chief executive officer, Lloyd Blankfein, had hired a prominent criminal defense lawyer, Reid Weingarten, by late afternoon the trading of Goldman shares had "tumbled nearly 5 percent, knocking $2.7 billion off the firm's market value."[36]

Although a person close to GS stated that neither Mr. Blankfein nor any other Goldman executive had received an individual subpoena, investors apparently still feared the worst. The person also emphasized that Goldman was cooperating with the Justice Department investigation. The point is that the sudden fall in Goldman's stock price in response to ongoing criminal investigations not only underscores GS's vulnerability, but also the government's necessity to put all of the messy fraud business "behind them." As Michael Mayo, an analyst with Crédit Agricole Securities, has stated, "Until Goldman resolves its legal issues, the company and the stock are vulnerable to all sorts of perceptions," real or imaginary.[37]

When the financial storm was brewing in the summer of 2008, official collusion was informal policy between the DOJ and Wall Street. Just as some of the biggest institutions on Wall Street had been fearing for their very survival, "a bit of good news bubbled through large banks and the law firms that defend them."[38] U.S. federal prosecutors had adopted new guidelines about charging corporations with crime. From now on, they would be taking a softer approach involving high-stakes financial crimes. In a September memo from the powerful East Coast law firm Sullivan and Cromwell to its Wall Street clients, the Department of Justice's new directive, adopting a process known as "deferred prosecutions," was revealed as a means of avoiding criminal charges in the first place. This signaled "an important step away from the more aggressive prosecutions" that had occurred earlier in the decade.[39] The memo had referred to some of the forceful prosecutions of corporate wrongdoing during the first Bush II administration, involving senior executives at Enron, WorldCom, Tyco, Adelphia, and Rite Aid that were all convicted and imprisoned for their control fraud schemes. As discussed in the opening chapters of this book, following the re-election of Bush in 2004, criminal prosecutions of corporate crime fell precipitously.

These deferred policies were not altogether new at the time of their official adoption by the DOJ and the SEC in 2008. As far back as a 2003 Justice Department memo, companies were given "more credit for cooperating than in the past. This message was reinforced in another memo in 2006," which read in part, "It is entirely proper in many investigations for a prosecutor to consider the corporation's pre-indictment conduct, e.g., voluntary disclosure, cooperation, remediation or restitution, in determining whether to seek an indictment."[40] During the same period that the DOJ was taking a "gentler" approach to financial fraud, increasing its numbers of deferred prosecutions, the "non-prosecution" agreement was also born. These policies provided new possibilities besides guilty or not guilty, often providing leniency if companies agreed to investigate themselves and report their own wrongdoing. In exchange for this cooperation, "the government could enter into agreements to delay or cancel the prosecution if the companies promised to change their behavior."[41]

For example, at the time of the Arthur Andersen appeal to overturn its fraud conviction, there was a debate going on at the Justice Department over "aggressive prosecution" or what many business leaders had been critiquing as an overzealous and dangerous enforcement of the law. In May 2005, DOJ officials met ahead of a session with a cross-agency group, the Corporate Fraud Task Force. In the meeting, the deputy attorney general at the time, James Comey, "posed questions that surprised some attendees," as these focused attention on whether or not American businesses were being hurt by the Justice Department's investigations of fraud.[42]

These same kinds of legal contradictions were also discussed in a mid-October 2008 meeting between Timothy Geithner, then-president of the

Federal Reserve Bank of New York, and Andrew Cuomo, New York's attorney general at the time. Mr. Geithner's expressed concern was over the fragility of the financial system. According to three people who were briefed at the time of the meeting, the now-secretary of the Treasury's worry "sprang from a desire to calm markets, a goal that could be complicated by a hard-charging attorney general."[43]

Asked whether the unusual meeting between Geithner and Cuomo had changed the latter's approach, a spokesman for the now-governor of New York stated on April 13, 2011, that "Mr. Geithner never suggested that there be any lack of diligence or any slowdown."[44] Moreover, Cuomo's office said, "The attorney general went on to lead the most aggressive investigation of A.I.G. and other financial institutions in the nation."[45] From their meeting until the time that he left to become governor, Cuomo focused on the financial crisis, with mixed success. While Cuomo sued the accounting firm Ernst & Young, accusing the company of helping its client Lehman Brothers "engage in massive accounting fraud," no arm of government has ever "sued Lehman or any of its executives on the same accounting tactic" (see table 5.2, seventh case down).[46]

Similarly, when investigating the 2008 bonuses that were paid out to the megabanks after the bailouts, Cuomo decided against bringing a lawsuit to "claw back" some of that money, instead choosing "to publicly shame the companies by releasing their bonus figures."[47] More significantly, after issuing mortgage-related subpoenas to eight large banks in the spring of 2010, to discover whether or not the banks had "misled the ratings agencies about the quality of the loans they were bundling," Cuomo did not before leaving office as attorney general bring a case against the banks and neither had his replacement by fall of 2011. To his credit, however, while the SEC settled its case with Bank of America "without charging any executives with wrongdoing, Mr. Cuomo filed a civil fraud lawsuit against Kenneth D. Lewis, the former chief executive, and the bank's former financial officer."[48] The case is still pending.

Eighteen months later the Obama Justice Department was going all out to "forge a consensus among governmental officials seeking to negotiate a foreclosure settlement with banks" and the state attorney generals over the objections of a few AGs led by New York Attorney General Eric Schneiderman, who took over in January 2011 after Cuomo left the office to be sworn in as governor.[49] By late August 2011, a fifty-state deal with JP Morgan Chase, Bank of America, Wells Fargo, Citigroup, and Ally Financial looked almost certain to go down to defeat as Schneiderman from New York and other top law enforcement officers from Massachusetts, Delaware, and Nevada were taking issue with the plan to scuttle the state and federal investigations into financial wrongdoings in exchange for a \$26 billion settlement.[50] This figure would certainly have been smaller had these banks not been secured against future criminal and civil liabilities. The figure to begin with represented a tiny portion of the losses incurred by investors. For example, in 2008, one state pension fund from Florida lost \$62 billion alone. Schneiderman had also sued to block an individual \$8.5 billion settlement with Countrywide investors because he claimed the agreement could "compromise investors' claims in exchange for a payment representing a fraction of the losses."[51]

Since Obama's fraud investigations began in the fall of 2010, the federal government has limited its investigations to the epidemic of "foreclosure irregularities" such as "robo-signing" and to the illegal home seizures by banks. By contrast, Schneiderman and other state attorney generals were also investigating more serious securities fraud and believed that any settlement with the banks should not preclude New York and other states from pursuing legal claims brought from investors related to the packaging of mortgages into fraudulent securities. The point is that the financial crimes that caused the Wall Street meltdown of 2007–8 go beyond fraudulent "paperwork" offenses like mass tax evasion (e.g., failing to pay fees associated with mortgage registrations and deed transfers) and mass perjury (e.g., robo-signing practices) to include a securitization process that resulted in market schemes where junk subprime loans were disguised as AAA-rated investments.

In essence, these banks had created *quid pro quo* market relations where they lent money to criminally corrupt enterprises like Countrywide and New Century who, in turn, made hundreds of thousands of bad loans, and then immediately sold them back to the banks who turned them into their deadly mortgage-backed securities that cost investors hundreds of billions dollars. One can call these financial operations a "criminal cartel" or an "enterprise crime" as Friedrichs prefers. Regardless of the terms used to describe these illegal activities, reference is made to "the interrelated dealings of legitimate businesspeople, political officials, and syndicated racketeers."[52]

Whatever criminological terms are used to label these crimes, the Obama administration, the banks, and most attorney generals were doing their best to ignore these fraudulent securities activities as their predecessors before them had also done. In the present, the objective has been to return back to business as usual with some minimal relief for mortgages destined for foreclosure without refinancing, but at a fraction of the costs to the banks that were responsible for the losses suffered by millions of investors and homeowners. As an official for the administration stated, "We are very far down the road for a settlement that will create servicing standards and will also result in a significant financial contribution towards helping homeowners and the housing market more generally."[53] Adding investor claims could delay a settlement by as much as two years, said another state official in favor of the deal. Kathryn Wylde, a Fed board member who is supposed to be representing the public, gave a most telling statement when she was quoted in the *New York Times* as saying to Schneiderman,

> It is of concern to the industry that instead of trying to facilitate resolving these issues, you seem to be throwing a wrench into it. Wall Street is our Main Street—love 'em or hate 'em. They are important and we have to make sure we are doing everything we can to support them unless they are doing something indefensible.[54]

In sum, the softer, less adversarial approach to financial control fraud has resulted not only in companies cooperating with the government, but also with one another, creating institutional financial strategies in response to investigations. For example, "legal representatives for Goldman Sachs, Morgan Stanley, JPMorgan Chase and others talk regularly about what they hear from the government."[55] Known as "joint-defense calls," these conversations have become even more important as lawyers can exchange more information due to the increased cooperation of government and financial firms. For example, Goldman's $550 million settlement with the SEC was helpful to other banks as they were more prepared when they had to engage prosecutors to refute any potential allegations or to negotiate their own non-criminal settlements.

Criminal Violations

In the world of big-time securities fraud the three criminal cases represented by the defendants in table 5.1 were pretty far down the financial food chain. In the first case, two former executives from the defunct Bear Stearns were found not guilty in 2009. The two former brokers from Crédit Suisse were indicted in 2008, the same year that "auction rate" securities failed and the auction market was frozen. It is hard to imagine that other financial institutions like Lehman Brothers, who came up with this security in 1984, or Goldman Sachs, who created the first auction rate security for tax-exempt markets in 1988, were not "guilty" of misleading clients about these purchases as they were about many of their other derivative instruments during the same period that led up to the meltdown.

In the biggest of these cases, involving a $2.9 billion fraud by Taylor, Bean & Whitaker Mortgage Corp, six executives pleaded guilty to mortgage fraud in 2010 after they had filed for bankruptcy a year earlier. In addition, after a ten-day trial in April 2011, a federal jury in Virginia found Lee Farkas, the former chairman, guilty on fourteen counts of securities, bank, and wire fraud as well as conspiracy to commit fraud. Among these felony convictions, one

Table 5.1. Criminal Cases

Agency	Defendants	Charges	Status
Justice Department (Eastern District of New York)	Two former executives at Bear Stearns, the failed investment bank: Ralph R. Cioffi and Matthew M. Tannin	Filed in June 2008. The executives were accused of misleading investors in two hedge funds managed by Bear Stearns about the quality of mortgage assets held in those funds, which collapsed.	The defendants were found not guilty in November 2009.
Justice Department (Eastern District of New York) and SEC	Two former brokers at Credit Suisse: Eric Butler and Julian Tzolov (Credit Suisse was not named)	Filed in September 2008. The brokers were accused of committing securities fraud by misleading clients about their purchases in the auction-rate securities market, thereby gaining higher sales commissions.	Mr. Butler was found guilty in August 2009. In January 2010, he was sentenced to five years in prison and a $5.25 million fine and disgorgement. Mr. Tzolov pleaded guilty in July 2009; in June 2011, he was sentenced to five years in prison.
Justice Department (Eastern District of Virginia) and SEC	Several former executives at Taylor, Bean & Whitaker, a mortgage company, or its banking partner, Colonial Bank: Lee B. Farkas, the former chairman of Taylor, Bean, was the most prominent	Filed in June 2010. Mr. Farkas and other executives were accused of fraud in what became a $2.9 billion scheme to issue false mortgages to obtain money from government-related entities like Freddie Mac and later to help Colonial Bank commit fraud to receive federal bailout funds.	Six executives at Taylor, Bean or Colonial Bank have pleaded guilty in the scheme. Mr. Farkas was found guilty of fourteen counts of fraud in April 2011 and was sentenced in June to thirty years in prison.

included a failed attempt to defraud regulators during the height of the financial crisis and to steal over $550 million through the TARP bailouts on the
condition that Colonial Bank would also raise $300 million in private money.
Among other fraudulent schemes, one included the creation of fake mortgages
that Fannie Mae was aware of since 2002 and that the DOJ decided not to
indict in 2004 for failure to report the fraud.

It seems at times as though prosecutions involving mortgage frauds stemming from Operation Stolen Dreams or the relatively aggressive prosecutions
of insider trading have served as distracters from the Wall Street looting
and/or evidence that the DOJ is not hard at work pursuing securities fraud.
Certainly the most celebrated governmental insider trading case involved
the Galleon Group founder and hedge fund billionaire, Raj Rajaratnam, convicted on all fourteen counts of securities fraud and conspiracy in May 2011,
sentenced in October to eleven years in prison, and who remains "free" while
his lawyers prepare his case for an appeal. In the government's inside trading
investigation that centered on Rajaratnam, all totaled, there were twenty-six
defendants criminally charged.

By the end of summer 2011 only one of them had not been convicted or
pleaded guilty. That was Deep Shah, a fugitive Moody's analyst who was
ordered to pay $35 million to the SEC for leaking the news of impending
private equity takeovers to hedge fund traders. In the judgment signed by
federal district court judge Jed Rakoff, Shah was ordered to "pay a $24.6
million civil fine, $1.76 million in interest and forfeit $8.2 million of illegal
profits."[56] However, unless the authorities can track down the young man,
rumored to be somewhere in Mumbai, they do not stand much of a chance of
getting their money. Nevertheless, compared to the non-criminal prosecution
of mortgage-backed securities fraud engaged in by the biggest financial firms
on and off Wall Street, it can be argued that the U.S. campaign against insider
trading has been a "success," and at least some kind of message has been sent
that this type of financial fraud might be taken seriously. With respect to Wall
Street looting, the same type of message has been totally missing.

Civil Violations

Keep in mind, when reading through table 5.2 on non-criminal civil suits, that
at the height of the housing boom "mortgage central" was headquartered at
Goldman Sachs' fast-growing mortgage trading desk. At the time, "hundreds
of employees worked closely in teams, devising mortgage-based securities—
billions of dollars' worth—that were examined by lawyers, approved by
management, then sold to investors like hedge funds, commercial banks and
insurance companies."[57] Yet, the one person, Fabrice Tourre, a twenty-eight-
year-old mid-level executive, is the sole individual across Wall Street and at

Table 5.2. Civil Cases

Agency	Defendants	Charges	Status
SEC	Three former executives at American Home Mortgage: Michael Strauss, chairman and chief executive; Stephen Hozie, chief financial officer; and Robert Bernstein, controller	Filed in April 2009. Executives were accused of accounting fraud and of making materially misleading statements about the company's liquidity. American Home filed for bankruptcy in August 2007.	Settled in April 2009 with Mr. Strauss for $2.45 million and a five-year ban from serving as an official at a public company. Settled in June 2010 with Mr. Hozie for $1.23 million and a five-year ban from acting as an accountant before the SEC. Settled in November 2009 with Mr. Bernstein for $125,000 and a suspension for at least three years from acting as an accountant before the SEC.
SEC	Three former executives at Countrywide Financial, the mortgage giant: Angelo R. Mozilo, chairman and chief executive; David E. Sambol, president; and Eric P. Sieracki, chief financial officer	Filed in June 2009. Executives were accused of disclosure fraud for falsely describing the company's underwriter guidelines to investors and for claiming that it made mainly prime, good-quality loans when it was expanding its subprime business. The SEC also accused Mr. Mozilo of insider trading because he wrote in private e-mails that he knew many of the company's loans were "toxic" even as he exercised stock options for personal gain.	Settled in October 2010 for $67.5 million from Mr. Mozilo, who also agreed to a lifetime ban from working as an officer of a public company. Mr. Sambol settled for $5.52 million and a three-year ban from serving as a public company officer. And Mr. Sieracki paid $130,000 to settle. (Bank of America, which now owns Countrywide, paid $20 million of Mr. Mozilo's settlement and $5 million of Mr. Sambol's.)

(continued)

Table 5.2. *(Continued)*

Agency	Defendants	Charges	Status
SEC	Goldman Sachs and one of its mortgage workers, Fabrice P. Tourre	Filed in April 2010. Goldman and Mr. Tourre were accused of making materially misleading statements and omissions related to the creation of a mortgage security called Abacus. The SEC said the company and Mr. Tourre did not disclose that an investor betting on a decline in the housing market had helped design that security.	In July 2010, Goldman settled for $550 million. The case against Mr. Tourre is still pending.
SEC	Morgan Keegan, a brokerage firm, and Morgan Asset Management, an investment advisor, both owned by Regions Financial, a big Alabama-based bank; James C. Kelsoe Jr., senior portfolio manager for Morgan Asset; and Joseph T. Weller, controller of Morgan Keegan	Filed in April 2010. The firms and executives were accused of defrauding investors by inflating the value of mortgage-backed securities in its bond funds. Investors in the five funds, marketed as relatively safe, are said to have lost about $1.5 billion when the market for mortgage securities seized up in 2007. Regulators said that Mr. Kelsoe betrayed the funds' marketing materials by investing in risky products, and that Mr. Weller did not fulfill responsibilities to price the securities fairly.	Settled in June 2011. The company agreed to pay $200 million. Mr. Kelsoe agreed to pay a $500,000 penalty and to be barred permanently from the securities industry. Mr. Weller agreed to a $50,000 fine.

SEC	ICP Asset Management, a private firm, and Thomas C. Priore, the owner and president	Filed in June 2010. ICP and Mr. Priore were accused of defrauding investors in four complex mortgage securities by overpaying for some assets placed in the securities and failing to obtain approval from investors for certain trades, among other things.	The case is still pending.
SEC	Citigroup and two former executives: Gary L. Crittenden, the chief financial officer; and Arthur Tildesley Jr., the head of investor relations	Filed in July 2010. Citigroup and the two executives were accused of making materially misleading statements about the bank's subprime mortgage exposure to the company's investors, leaving out $39 billion of securities that the bank held just as the financial crisis was beginning.	In July 2010, Citigroup settled for $75 million. Mr. Crittenden agreed to a $100,000 fine; Mr. Tildesley, an $80,000 fine, while keeping a job at Citigroup.
New York Attorney General	Ernst & Young	Filed in December 2010. The accounting firm was accused of helping Lehman Brothers engage in "massive accounting fraud" by condoning a practice known as Repo 105 in which the investment bank shifted tens of billions of dollars in assets off its balance sheet before the end of several quarters leading up to its collapse in 2008.	The case is still pending. It was filed by Andrew M. Cuomo at the end of his term as attorney general, and is now being handled by his successor, Eric Schneiderman.

(continued)

Table 5.2. *(Continued)*

Agency	Defendants	Charges	Status
SEC	Three former executives at IndyMac, a failed bank in California: Michael W. Perry, chief executive; A. Scott Keys, chief financial officer; and S. Blair Abernathy, a later chief financial officer	Filed in February 2011. The executives were accused of making false and misleading statements about the bank's financial condition in quarterly filings and in raising capital months before the bank failed.	In February 2011, Mr. Abernathy settled, agreeing to a $100,000 penalty and forfeiting $25,000 in earnings. The cases against Mr. Perry and Mr. Keys are still pending.
FDIC	Three former executives at Washington Mutual, a failed bank: Kerry K. Killinger, chief executive; David C. Schneider, president of home lending; and Stephen J. Rotella, chief operating officer	Filed in March 2011. The executives were accused of knowingly pushing the bank into making lots of high-risk mortgage loans, simply to help their own short-term compensation at the bank.	The case is still pending.
SEC	Wells Fargo	Filed in April 2011. Wachovia Capital Markets, now owned by Wells Fargo, was accused of fraud for selling complex mortgage securities to an Indian tribe for more than the bank believed they were worth.	Settled in April 2011 for $11 million.

Justice Department (Southern District of New York)	Deutsche Bank and its MortgageIT unit.	Filed in May 2011. The bank was accused of fraud involving mortgages that were guaranteed by the Federal Housing Administration but were of shoddy quality. The bank and its MortgageIT unit were accused of breaching fiduciary duty to the government to ensure that loans were of a high enough standard to receive the government guarantee.	The case is still pending.
SEC	JP Morgan Securities and Edward S. Steffelin, an executive of GSC Capital Corporation, a separate company that did business with JP Morgan	Filed in June 2011. J.P. Morgan was accused of misleading investors in structuring and marketing a security known as a synthetic collateralized debt obligation in which a hedge fund that helped select the assets stood to gain if the investments lost value. Mr. Steffelin was accused of leading investors to believe that his firm, not the hedge fund, put the investment together.	Settled in June 2011 with JP Morgan for $153.6 million, of which more than $125 million is to go to the investors. JP Morgan also voluntarily paid $56.7 million to investors in a similar transaction. The case against Mr. Steffelin is pending.

Goldman Sachs sued by the SEC for mortgage-securities fraud. As a former New York attorney general and presently a New York City councilman, G. Oliver Koppell has commented about the exceptional indictment of one executive: "It's impossible that only one person was involved with fraudulent activities in connection to the sales of these mortgage securities."[58]

What can be taken away from these twelve civil cases? Two of these cases were filed in 2009, and five each were filed in 2010 and 2011. Regulatory agencies brought forward charges in ten (e.g., SEC = 9, FDIC = 1) of these cases, and criminal law enforcement agencies brought charges in two of these—both in New York—one by the U.S. attorney and the other by the state AG. Five of these cases were already settled at the same time as the charges were announced. As of June 2011, none of these cases had gone to trial; two cases were still pending from 2010 and two from 2011. These "non-adversarial" proceedings have involved charges against a total of fourteen former employees and only one present employee. The relatively few defendants and/or their companies charged span the entire financial industry, involving six banks, two mortgage companies, two brokerage firms, an asset management company, and one auditing company. The illegal charges have included: accounting frauds, breaching fiduciary duties, defrauding investors, disclosure fraud, stealing, misleading investors, misleading statements, and securities fraud.

In light of the epidemic of securities fraud throughout the collateralized mortgage-based financial markets of the U.S. leading up to the meltdown of 2007–8, what can be inferred from the paltry number of civil settlements and the two criminal fraud convictions for securities violations? Today's financial elite at the pinnacles of economic and political power, like their historical predecessors, whether in previously agriculturally based or industrially based economies, have all consistently gotten away with much more in the way of rewards than punishments for their illegal behaviors. When punishment comes, if it does at all, it comes with "conciliating" and "compensatory" fines typically representing a fraction of the actual loot absconded with. These punishments never come with imprisonment. In sum, these types of financial frauds have never been treated as the material crimes that they are. Instead, these crimes have been treated as pardonable offenses designed primarily to re-establish social harmony in the financial markets.[59]

Colluding, SEC Waivers, and the Big Banks

The repeated granting of nearly 350 exemptions to laws and regulations over the last decade that could have otherwise acted as a deterrent to securities fraud recidivism and as a protection for investors dwarfs the number of SEC cases in which the waivers have been denied. This form of colluding with big banks like JP Morgan, Bank of America, and Goldman Sachs has helped to keep them in business by providing them with market advantages that should have been reserved for the most dependable companies, not for those that are habitually settling fraud cases. For several years now, "wrangling over waivers" has been "an important part of the negotiations when companies accused of fraud discuss a settlement with the S.E.C., and some of it can involve a form of corporate plea bargaining to a lesser charge."[60]

An analysis by the *New York Times* counted 91 waivers since 2000 granting immunity from lawsuits and 204 waivers related to raising capital funds. The *Times* analysis also "found 11 instances where companies that had settled fraud cases had actually lost the special privilege for fast-track stock or bond offerings, versus 49 times that the S.E.C. granted waivers from the punishment to Wall Street firms since 2005."[61] For example, between 1999 and 2012, JP Morgan settled six fraud cases, including a $228 million settlement in summer 2011. While it had obtained at least twenty-two waivers since 2003, JP Morgan had received three waivers alone related to their biggest multimillion-dollar penalty with the SEC to settle civil and criminal charges that "it cheated cities and towns by rigging bids with other Wall Street firms to invest money raised by several municipalities for capital projects."[62] In seeking those reprieves, lawyers for JP Morgan had argued in letters to the SEC that their clients should be granted waivers because the company has "a strong record of compliance with the securities laws."[63]

During the same period, Bank of America had settled fifteen fraud cases and received at least thirty-nine waivers. Similarly, before losing most of its privileges in 2010, Citigroup had settled six fraud cases and received twenty-five waivers in the previous eleven years. By granting these waivers or exemptions from punishment, the SEC lets these Wall Street firms maintain powerful advantages over the competition. In effect, these agreements allow these banks "to continue to tap capital markets without delay (and government approval), to manage mutual funds," to help small firms raise money, and to "continue to get certain protections from class-action lawsuits."[64]

The SEC has defended these practices by stating that they do not have the necessary resources to take these cases to court rather than settle. The SEC also argues that without these waivers or exemptions to settle charges of securities fraud, the ramifications would be enormous for the firms, affecting their abilities to stay in business, according to David Ruder, a former SEC chairman. Similarly, when waivers are denied, the purpose of taking away the fast-track offering privileges to capitalize "is to protect investors, not to punish a company," stated Meredith Cross, the SEC's corporation finance director.[65] Meanwhile, Senator Charles Grassley, an Iowa Republican who

serves on committees that oversee the SEC, has been wondering why the
commission "isn't using all its weapons to deter fraud." He went on to say
that these practices make already weak punishments "even weaker by waiv-
ing the regulations that impose significant consequences on the companies
that settle fraud charges. No wonder recidivism is such a problem."[66] Such
are the contradictions of bourgeois legality.

FINANCIALLY RESPECTABLE "CRIMES" OF NON-CONTROL

In criminological and socio-legal circles alike, the absence of law or social
control as an explanation for a variety of crimes has a long tradition.[67] By contrast, sociologists and psychologists have used social control for more than
a century to explain the conduct of people in organizations, neighborhoods,
public spaces, and face-to-face encounters. Social control is ubiquitous and
can be found wherever and whenever "people hold each other to standards,
explicitly or implicitly, consciously or not; on the street, in prisons, at home,
at a party." Importantly, social control also "divides people into those who
are respectable and those who are not; it disgraces some, but protects the
reputations of other."[68] In the legal process of social control, criminality and
respectability are both defined at the same time. As Black contends, social
respectability helps to explain the behavior of the law. In addition, it is a
quantifiable variable, known by the type of social control (criminal vs. non-
criminal) to which a group or person has been subject. Accordingly, "To be
subject to law is, in general, more unrespectable than to be subject to other
kinds of social control. To be subject to criminal law is especially unrespectable."[69] As one of Black's legal principles argues, when all else is constant,
the amount of law varies inversely with the respectability of the offender's
socioeconomic standing.

These characteristics of the behavior of law and of social control beg a
couple of related questions, such as, "When it comes to financial control, who
exactly is regulating whom?" and "How far will agents of law enforcement
or academia go to 'whitewash' the financial crimes of Wall Street in order to
protect those fraud minimalist reputations of some of the most 'successful'
bankers in the world?"

After the whistle-blowing Congressional testimony of SEC attorney Darcy
Flynn in the summer of 2011, it became well known that "the nation's top financial police [had illegally] destroyed more than a decade's worth of intelli-
gence they had gathered on some of Wall Street's most egregious offenders,"
including insider trading and securities fraud investigations involving such

Wall Street heavies as Goldman Sachs, Lehman Brothers, AIG, Deutsche Bank, and many others.[70] All totaled there were the records of some nine thousand investigations of wrongdoing or "Matters Under Inquiry" (MUI) since 1993 that were "deep sixed." There were also a cozy number of cases involving high-profile firms that were never graduated into full-blown criminal investigations because of what has been referred to as an "obstruction of justice" by misbehaving attorneys caught up in the revolving personnel doors of regulation and Wall Street.

The problem goes beyond revolving personnel doors that are not really conflicts of interests per se. As Matt Taibbi of *Rolling Stone* wrote during summer 2011, the

> SEC could have placed federal agents on every corner of lower Manhattan throughout the past decade, and it might not have put a dent in the massive wave of corruption and fraud that left the economy in flames three years ago. And even if the SEC staffers from top to bottom had been fully committed to rooting out financial corruption, the agency would still have been seriously hampered by a lack of resources that often forces it to abandon promising cases due to a shortage of manpower.[71]

More interestingly perhaps, ponder some hypotheticals raised by Taibbi and what might never have been:

> Forget about what might have been if the SEC had followed up in earnest on *all* those lost MUIs. What if even a handful of them had turned into real cases? How many investors might have been saved from crushing losses if Lehman Brothers had been forced to reveal its shady accounting way back in 2002? Might the need for taxpayer bailouts have been lessened had fraud cases against Citigroup and Bank of America been pursued in 2005 and 2007? And would the U.S. government have doubled down on its bailouts of AIG if it had known that some of the firm's executives were suspected of insider trading in September 2008?[72]

Chapter Six

Consuming Victims and Victimless Identities

On the Social Construction of Victimization and the Re-emergence of Public Victims

Wall Street financial victimization of consumers is difficult to separate from the organizational or institutional forms of victimization as these are related to the emotional and material well-being of stratified victims. Take the anger, humiliation, or shame that are shared by confederacies of victims such as the underemployed or the foreclosed. Their victimization is less about individual-behavioral characteristics and more about social groupings and subcultural characteristics like class, race, gender, and age. More generally, variables of categorical power and other social indicators of value serve to differentiate the types of abuse that are constructed as acceptable or non-acceptable for investors, non-vestors, men, women, boys, girls, heterosexuals, homosexuals, whites, African Americans, Asian Americans, Hispanic Americans, the rich, the poor, immigrants, the mentally ill, and so forth.

For example, Arline Geronimus, a social epidemiologist and professor of health behavior, has developed a "weathering framework" to measure the rates of aging that link social inequality, racism, and biology to socioeconomic and racial/ethnic group victimization. Her approach based on studies of African Americans and whites living in Detroit has demonstrated that blacks are, bio-logically, older than whites of the same chronological age. Geronimus and her colleagues have shown that blacks are exposed to stressors ranging from environmental pollution to racism-induced anger that accumulate and feed on each other, altering the culture and behavior of a community. Moreover, repeated exposure and adaptation to these stressors can lead to higher rates of smoking, drinking, drug abuse, and violence. Even when these stressors did not lead to a rise in these behavioral patterns, blacks still experienced earlier health deterioration compared to whites. Such racial differences in victimization are not explained by poverty because "poor and nonpoor Black women had the highest probability of high [stress] scores, respectively, and the highest excess scores compared with their male or White counterparts."[1] In the same way, other focused research has "established that the health of Latino immigrants declines as they stay in America longer and improve their lots in life, and that South Asian Indian mothers, who have socioeconomic profiles comparable to whites, suffer from birth outcomes as poor as those of low-income blacks."[2]

The position here is that victims of stress as in the case of financial fraud experience victimization not unlike those experiences of the institutionalized victims of racist or sexist stress. What distinguishes institutionalized victims from individualized victims generally is that the former are often interwoven with the normative practices of socialization found in the home, at school, in the street, at the workplace, and even within in the criminal justice system.[3] In the case of Wall Street looting and federal regulatory colluding, the institutionalized forms of victimization attributed to systemic securities fraud and the lack of criminal punishment are carried out by the administration of financial justice in risk society. Financial justice is inseparable from the cultural attitudes, social identities, and contradictory relations of conflict and power that excuse, neutralize, or rationalize Wall Street fraud and victimization as risk-taking free-enterprise capitalism rather than as structured violations of securities laws and regulations.

As the previous two chapters have demonstrated, the vast majority if not all of these Wall Street financial frauds were not criminally pursued by state authority. These fraudulent crimes, when they are acknowledged through settlements, were regarded as exceptional events not worthy of criminal prosecution or deterrence. These financially criminal or fraudulent transactions are not viewed by capitalist regulatory control agents or by Wall Street banking representatives as normative illegal market behavior. Instead, throughout the financial industry the normative patterns of organized and structured fraud have been denied their social reality. Logically, many legal authorities have concluded that there were no fraudulent security transactions taking place. Ergo, there could not be too many injuries or victims for Wall Street to compensate. Most consumers or investors of the securities transactions that caused the financial collapse as well as millions of other Americans are of a contrary point of view. In fact, there have been numerous civil lawsuits seeking compensation from Wall Street firms for victimizing their investor clients, several of whom are discussed in the last section of this chapter. These lawsuits and their consistent awards for the plaintiffs testify loud and clear as to the correctness of Wall Street looting and fraud as normative.

Of course, victim status must be legally conferred and established in every case. As Kennedy and Sacco have concluded, "Although it would seem obvious to the casual observer that it is easy to define who is and who is not a victim of a crime," the "definition is often not easy to establish and can change as the event is examined and reconsidered in light of the harm done, the determination of what preceded the event, and the situation."[4] Stated differently, there is "much evidence that the process of determining who is a victim is laden with politics, socio-legal traditions, economics, and cultural values."[5] Importantly, the legitimation of victimization is also "affected by the interpretation of the media, which play an important role in constructing the role of the victim and in describing the responses needed to deal with the costs of victimization."[6]

In the case of Wall Street looting and victimization, the mass media—bloggers and alternative media aside—were rarely, if ever, heard discussing the crimes of Wall Street or the appropriate compensation for the victims on Main Street. In addition, the lobbying of claimsmakers and interest groups has influenced media coverage and the priorities assigned to responding to the different forms of victimization. Similarly, since the rediscovery of victims at the end of World War II, both the identities and rights of victims have grown and expanded. Not yet a part of the organized groups of collective victims, a significant number of direct victims of Wall Street are litigating their way to victimhood or victim identification. Many of the indirect victims of Wall Street began demonstrating and organizing in the fall of 2011 as part of the Occupy Wall Street movement. The protests that had begun in New York City in September had quickly spread across the country and around the globe.[7] Whether or not the OWS protests and tent cities, which were broken up by police forces and court orders in early 2012, would resurface in the fall as a significant force during the 2012 elections was still unknown as I completed this book in early 2012.

Historically, during the emergence of our criminal law tradition in the fourteenth and fifteenth centuries, victims "had an active participatory role in the criminal justice process and were responsible for not only initiating but also for prosecuting offenders."[8] Subsequently, victims in common-law countries were gradually marginalized from the criminal justice process, and by the twentieth century their role was primarily that of a prosecutorial witness for those crimes committed against the state. Over the last half-century or so, the exclusion of victims from the adjudicative process has seen a reinvigoration of public victims, in the form of spawning victim impact statements and legal compensation for certain crime victims as well as fueling initiatives in the areas of restorative justice. Together, these developments have provided selected recognition of victims and their rights.

In the contemporary United States, victims have some rights in all fifty states. These range "from the right to be notified of court and parole hearings, the right to be present and express opinions at sentencing hearings, the right to be consulted about plea agreements, the right to compensation and restitution, and the right to a speedy trial."[9] In the area of restorative justice, three approaches have been utilized more fully to involve victims of interpersonal crimes. These comprise efforts to have: (1) victims extricated from the traditional confines of the criminal justice system and to pursue conciliatory justice schemes in which victims are granted full recognition and respect for their dignity, (2) victim-offender mediation incorporated into the formal criminal justice process, and (3) victim participation and restorative values integrated throughout the criminal justice system.[10]

Despite the formal expansion of victims' legal rights and efforts to infuse restorative justice within and without the criminal justice system, research and audits have shown that many victims are not given the chance to exercise these rights,[11] or to participate in restorative justice programs that make a difference.[12] In the cases of corporate crime in general and financial crimes like securities fraud in particular, victims have been essentially excluded from the formal processes of compensation, restitution, and social control, unless they have filed their own civil lawsuits. This is especially true in the case of Wall Street looting and the 2007–8 financial collapse.

VICTIMOLOGY, VICTIMIZATION, AND STATE-SANCTIONED VICTIMS

Victimology is the scientific study of victims and victimization. The field can be traced back to 1937 when Benjamin Mendelsohn began gathering information about victims for his law practice. He subsequently conducted research on victims, including a rape study in 1940. In addition to coining the term *victimology*, he also introduced other related concepts such as *victimity* to suggest the converse of *criminality*. Initially, Mendelsohn and others "formulated a broad-based victimology that considered not merely crime victims, but all victims, including those produced by politics, by technology, by accidents, as well as by crime."[13]

In 1948, Hans von Hentig provided the first landmark victimological study, *The Criminal and His Victim*, followed in 1954 by Henri Ellenberger's "Psychological Relations between Criminals and Victims." The field, research, and applications of victimology have continued to unevenly develop, as evidenced by numerous victimization studies, typologies, international conferences, the emergence of *Victimology: An International Journal* in 1976, the creation of the World Society of Victimology in 1979, and the establishment of victim compensation programs in the United States and most of the developed nations. Nevertheless, the political struggle to sustain a broader perspective of victimology and victimization as envisioned by Mendelsohn has been difficult to pursue. Indeed, much of the field of victimology and virtually all of the policies involving victims and victimization have been limited to formally adjudicated victims of domestic or street crime, leaving victims of suite crime to fend for themselves.

As for typologies, there are essentially those that classify types of victims and those that classify events of victimization.[14] As Marilyn McShane and Traqina Emeka point out:

> Dictionaries often restrict our thinking about this topic by defining victims narrowly as persons. . . . In criminal justice textbooks, victims are defined in terms of having experienced injury or loss, having suffered. . . . There is the implication that victims have been exposed to circumstances of abuse, exploitation, harm, destruction, unfairness or a violation of law. Still, in most of these writings, traits are ascribed to a human, to a person. While this apparent consensus seems to provide a way to standardize victimology and define the boundaries of the subject matter, it also limits our consideration of the victimization experience.[15]

For the most part, victim typologies revolve around the psychological traits of the victims. These typologies are usually skewed toward vulnerable populations, such as the young, old, intoxicated, immigrant, minority group members, and so on. In fact, there are no typologies dealing with white-collar victims.

By contrast, victimization typologies are more useful because they do not limit themselves to individual victims of specific crimes, nor do they ignore victims of corporate or financial crime. For example, nearly a half-century ago Thorsten Sellin and Marvin Wolfgang utilized one such victimization typology.[16] Their typology consisted of four types of victimization: "primary," "secondary," "tertiary," and "mutual." Primary victimization refers to any direct personal harm, such as being assaulted or robbed at gunpoint. Secondary victimization refers to non-human victims including businesses, groups, or other organizations. Tertiary victimization refers to wrongs against society as a whole or to general social harms, including when corporations pollute the environment or public officials embezzle from the state. Mutual victimization refers to "the sharing of the offender/victim experience where there is mutual consent and participation, as in vice activities or conspiracies that backfire on one or more of the participants."[17] This was certainly true of the Wall Street financial collapse and the roles played by collateralized mortgage obligations, subprime loans, and credit default swaps.

Unfortunately, the field of victimology has followed the leads of Hentig and Ellenberger, narrowly focusing on criminal personal victimization, limited victim-offender relations, and victim precipitation (or the role/contribution that the victim brings to his/her own victimization). The field of victimology, for the most part, has not paid enough attention to the larger social, cultural, and economic relations that shape the geometry and politics of victimization. Accordingly, most victimology has been restricted to studying victims based on existing criminal law practices. As a consequence, there is no way to provide even a rough estimate, let alone to gauge the extent of white-collar victimization in general or of business and financial crime in particular. This is because none of the governmental victimization surveys, such as the National Crime Victimization Survey, collect any data on these offenses. Instead, their attention focuses exclusively on interpersonal crimes and victims at home and in the street. These types of individual, interpersonal, and micro-level analyses of crime victims deemphasize or exclude altogether the organizational and institutional sources of victimization. These treatments of victimization also ignore the structural or macro-level analyses of victims that move well beyond the formal constraints of the criminal law to include civil and regulatory laws as well as torts.

Because criminal justice officials, policymakers, and researchers have overlooked victims of white-collar crime, they have been referred to as "neglected victims."[18] Their neglect has been attributed to beliefs that their victimization is non-violent and trivial in nature. However, existing research on white-collar victimization suggests that these victims suffer from the same kinds of symptoms as victims of street crime, including feelings of anxiety and depression. Like victims of street crime, victims of suite crime also lose their basic faith or trust in the system.[19] In the areas of financial fraud, victims also garner less assistance and sympathy because they are often believed to be responsible for their sour investments, able to absorb their losses, and equipped to recover from their victimization.

At the same time, there do seem to be some differences between victims of the latter and former offenses. One research study exploring white-collar crime relationships of trust and distrust between offenders, victims, regulators, and the wider financial system found that "becoming the victim of a financial crime may not necessarily lead individuals to avoiding the financial system in general, because an integral part of their trust may be acknowledging that as investors they run risks."[20] Interestingly, the generalized distrust of these victims of the system emphasized an erosion in faith with financial regulators rather than with financial perpetrators. Similarly, rather than blame themselves for their victimization, these victims blamed regulators.[21]

The criminal law in action also constricts the state boundaries of crime/victimization and the governmental scope of those who are considered victims. In turn, the practices of the administration of law help to provide a narrowing of consciousness about harms, injuries, and victimization. Furthermore, the penal code may create an official or social reality of victimization that "stresses acts mostly committed by less privileged people. Likewise, the penal code "de-emphasizes and softens the acts committed by more privileged people, and then excludes from its definition other, extensive, and (usually more) harmful acts altogether, such as corporate crimes, state crimes, and what human rights advocates would call 'crimes against humanity.'"[22]

In his classic treatise *The Politics of Victimization* (1986), Robert Elias captured the quandary of victimology that is subject to a limited vision of victimization:

> Americans are a frightened people. We anticipate victimization even more than we experience it, although much actual victimization does occur. We mostly fear being robbed, raped, or otherwise assaulted, or even killed. Yet, while these crimes have captured our imaginations, they comprise only part of the victimization we suffer. We face not only the danger of other crimes, but also countless other actions that we often have not defined or perceived as criminal despite their undeniable harm. We may have a limited social reality of crime and victimization that excludes harms such as consumer fraud, pollution, unnecessary drugs and surgery, food additives, workplace hazards and diseases, police violence, censorship, discrimination, poverty, exploitation, and war. We suffer victimization not only by other individuals, but also by governments and other social institutions, not to mention the psychological victimization bred by our own insecurities.[23]

Just as relevant today is Elias' suggestion from a quarter of a century ago that the pathway to a more comprehensive victimology lies in the wedding of the narrower view of criminal-victim rights with the broader view of human-victim rights. This blending of rights may help to "dissolve the 'mental prison' that often characterizes how we think about victimization" and it frees us to examine "not only individual criminals but also institutional wrongdoing."[24]

Elias' conception of harm and victims moves beyond the traditional confines of legally defined or state-sanctioned victimization to the parameters of globally defined human rights pursued through social, political, and economic justice for all. For example, the wording of Article 1 of the 1985 UN Declaration extends the meaning of victims beyond that of crime victims to include antisocial behavior and breaches of human rights in general: "'Victims' mean persons who, individually or collectively, have suffered harm, including physical or mental injury, emotional suffering, economic loss or substantial impairment of their fundamental rights, through acts or omissions that do not yet constitute violations of national criminal laws but of internationally recognized norms relating to human rights."[25] Similarly, "anti-social behaviour orders" were introduced in England and Wales in the 1998 Crime and Disorder Act, later enhanced by the Anti-social Behaviour

Act of 2003. The 1998 law defined this behavior as "likely to cause harassment, alarm or distress to one or more persons not of the same household [as the perpetrator]."[26] In a similar vein, all of those persons, investors and nonvestors alike—everybody except for the finance capitalists—who everywhere inhabit the impoverished environments of global capital find themselves to be victims more or less of Wall Street looting and federal regulatory colluding. Unfortunately, the meaning of victimhood in use in most of the legal jurisdictions throughout the world are much more narrow in scope.

According to the Victim and Witness Protection Act (VWPA) passed by the U.S. Congress in 1982, victims can be reimbursed for their losses through restitution from offenders. Under the Victims of Crime Act (VOCA) of 1984, victims are entitled to compensation for their losses or injuries. The major thrust of VWPA was "the emphasis placed on restoring to the victim his or her prior state of well-being."[27] The act includes the defendant's payment of victim's costs for psychological care, lost income or property, and other expenses. Restitution in the federal criminal justice system, however, is infrequently used and indifferently enforced. In one study of federal court-ordered restitution for a three-year period, the percentage of total criminal sentences involving such orders ranged from 9 to 16 percent. At the time, the most frequent orders "occurred in cases of embezzlement, burglary, and fraud and were less likely to be applied in sexual offenses and assault."[28] Notably, Congress passed the Violence Against Women Act as part of the Violent Crime Control and Law Enforcement Act of 1994. The intent of the law was to enhance the investigation and prosecution of violent crimes perpetrated against women. The law also imposed mandatory restitution for these victims of interpersonal violence.

VOCA monies come to the states through a transfer of funds received through fines, penalty assessments, and bond forfeitures from federal criminals. Limited primarily to victims of violent crime, these programs reimburse victims for expenses such as medical bills and lost wages. Although state compensation programs received more than $146 million in VOCA grant funds between 1986 and 1994, the percentage of victims who actually applied for compensation was quite low (6 percent) and only two-thirds of those received any compensation. Low participation was due to victims being unaware of these programs or not meeting eligibility requirements such as reporting the crime within a specified period of time or agreeing to assist in the prosecution of the offender.[29]

In 2004, the Crime Victims' Rights Act was passed as part of the Justice for All Act in order to strengthen compensation and restitution programs. The law enumerated the rights afforded to victims of federal criminal cases. These included the rights to protection from the accused; to notification; to attending proceedings; to speak at criminal justice proceedings; to consult with the prosecuting attorney; to a speedy trial; and to be treated with fairness, dignity, and respect.[30] Unfortunately, since the U.S. Department of Justice failed to criminally prosecute even one of the numerous Wall Street securities fraudsters, none of their victims have been able to avail themselves of their rights to criminal compensation and restitution for their losses suffered. At the same time, at least for those individuals and/or institutions that can afford the monetary outlay involved, civil litigation or tort actions may prove to be the most productive method for remedying the plights of the most direct victims of Wall Street's fraudulent behavior.

On the other hand, when addressing or challenging Wall Street looting, investment victimization, and state-sanctioned regulation, white-collar criminologist Friedrichs reminds us that "even though we depend on governmental entities and agencies to control white collar crime, the state, its agencies, and politicians generally are the sources of some of the most serious and harmful crime."[31] Finally, regarding the enduring expressions of a range of hybrid and marginal forms of white-collar crime, such as state-corporate crime, crimes of globalization, finance crime, or enterprise (organized-political) crime, Friedrichs wants us to appreciate that each of these crimes of the powerful require "responses tailored to the specific character of the type of crime, ranging from the strengthening of consumer protection laws to the transformation of global economic policy."[32]

EMERGING REMEDIES AND VICTIMS OF NON-TRADITIONAL FINANCIAL CRIMES

Most victims of non-traditional financial crimes like Wall Street looting, price-fixing, or state-corporate corruption are objects of cultivated trust and indirect victimization. In the case of investment bankers and others in the financial services industries, these perpetrators are able to develop impersonal trust with their clients as they recruit multiple victims by tapping into ongoing market-social networks. These networks may range from wealthy, skilled investors to middle-class novices.[33] Because of the impersonal nature of trust, these victims are less able to protect themselves from these financial criminals, especially when their life savings are invested institutionally as part of their pension or retirement accounts.

This impersonal trust facilitates fraudsters "steal[ing] without direct contact with victims or physical proximity to the property appropriated, reducing risk of discovery and apprehension."[34] These types of investing relations increase the amounts that can be stolen as fraudulent schemes "are restricted only by the imagination of the offender and the trust that the victim has in the offender's ability to make a return on the investment."[35] Moreover, because many of these financial transactions require discovering the true value or risk of these investments, such as those involving complex derivative instruments like credit default swaps, this means that investors must rely on third parties like credit raters or securities regulators to help secure their economic interests.

Underlying the contradictions in the inadequate practices and remedies of victimology in general and of victim rights in particular are those victimization policies that have traditionally been aimed at or limited to those individualized victims harmed by deliberate acts of predation to the relative exclusion of larger groups of structured and stratified victims. At the same time, the restricted concepts of "victimized" have gradually expanded to include selected classes of victims, including minorities, women, and other oppressed groups who have been viewed as abused, exploited, or persecuted. Those victims who have suffered from racism, heterosexism, sexism, and so forth have increasingly been recognized as legitimate victims who under certain circumstances are entitled to restitution, compensation, or reparations. However, remedies for victims belonging to larger classes of white-collar victimization have not been as forthcoming as the remedies for the more narrowly drawn classes of victim. These groups of victims still seeking victim status include (1) workers subject to hazardous and illegal conditions in the workplace or to managerial practices that illegally deprive employees of just compensation and other labor-related rights; (2) consumers subject to corporate price-fixing and the sale of unsafe products; (3) customers, clients, and patients subject to fraudulent practices of small businesses, entrepreneurs, and professionals; (4) citizens and local residents subject to industrial pollution and toxins; and (5) taxpayers subject to governmental corruption, including fraudulent defense contracts, frauds involving institutions with U.S. insured deposits, and other political boondoggles linking governmentally supported "bridges to nowhere."

State-based remedies have been all but non-existent with respect to the Wall Street looting and federal regulatory colluding where the largest classes of American victims exist. Among the many classes of financial victims are various competitors, partners, shareholders, investors, pensioners, taxpayers, governmental entities, private corporations, and global markets. Since these injured parties are without access to victim compensation, legal restitution, or insurance returns due to the lack of any prosecutions, let alone criminal convictions, the only option left to those victims with direct investments to recoup any of their monetary losses is to pursue civil litigation (see figure 6.1).[36] The rest of this chapter focuses on some of the direct victims of Wall

Categories of Securities Fraud   **Legal Responses**

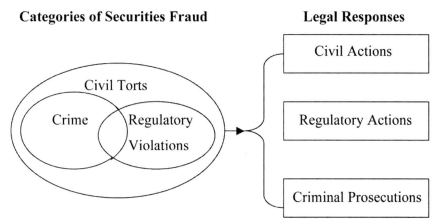

Figure 6.1. Categories of Securities Fraud and Legal Responses. Adapted from Ke Wang, *Securities Fraud, 1996–2001: Incentive Pay, Governance, and Class Action Lawsuits* (El Paso, TX: LFB Scholarly, 2010), 8.

Street securities fraud and to a sampling of the civil lawsuits that have been filed in pursuit of just compensation for these victim-plaintiffs.

CIVIL LITIGATION AS REMEDY?

Civil lawsuits "are the modern version of retribution/restitution practices from the past. The victim or the victim's family has the right to take civil action against offenders to recoup losses and to exact punitive damages."[37] These lawsuits also known as tort actions refer to wrongful acts that defendants have allegedly committed against the victim-plaintiffs. In order for the plaintiff to recover monetary compensation from the defendant for any harm inflicted, these civil cases must show only "a preponderance of evidence" that the defendants' culpable actions produced some type of damages or losses—monetary, physical, or psychological. Besides the issues of liability that surround the defendants' culpability (or not), there are the issues of collectability or recovery of damages.[38] As one leading story in the Money & Investing section of the *Wall Street Journal* read: "Chasing Fraud, Then Chasing Cash." The smaller print between the headline and the article read: "Regulators Struggle to Collect Fines; 'We Need to Do Better.'"[39]

In this day and age, civil cases require that victim-plaintiffs are able to afford the costs of expensive attorneys who will normally take about one-third of any award, assuming there is one. For many working and middle-class victims, the costs of litigation bar them from the civil legal system unless "class action" status is granted by a court of law. Depending on the granting of class-action status, banks "including JP Morgan Chase & Co. (JPM) and Bank of America Corp. (BAC) [could] pay more to resolve claims over their alleged roles in the collapse of a $2.3 trillion mortgage-backed securities market if sophisticated investors are allowed to sue as a group along with less savvy ones."[40] As was noted in chapter 2 regarding the litigation claims surrounding Bernie Madoff's Ponzi scheme, sometimes it is not easy to sort out the perpetrators from the victims.

As former SEC lawyer Jacob Frenkel, now in private practice, commented about mortgage-backed securities litigation, it "is possible to be both an alleged perpetrator and victim at the same time."[41] In the case of the big Wall Street banks like JPM and BAC, he added, "It's unprecedented that you [now] have the most sophisticated institutions as victims, to be in the position where their losses are so great that they have sued."[42] Class-action status or certification raises the stakes as investors are allowed to pool financial and legal resources, giving them greater leverage and increasing their damage awards compared to a series of individual awards. As for the future of class-action suits in the area of financial fraud, by September 2011, U.S. district courts had sent mixed signals. Some court rulings barred banks from class status because these investors were too sophisticated. Some sided with investors, allowing them in the case of home-loan-backed securities to sue as a class of victims. Others denied class-action status to retirement account investors.[43]

For those that can afford civil litigation, there are several advantages: First, whether or not a defendant is found guilty or innocent in a criminal trial or when the prosecutors have elected not to file criminal charges at all as in the numerous missed opportunities involving Wall Street fraud, the victim-plaintiffs have a viable legal alternative. Second, once "the venue switches from the criminal court to a civil proceeding, the victim is no longer an outsider [or just a witness] in the case. Instead, the victim and his or her ensuing problems are the central concern of the court case."[44] Third, in addition to the lower legal burden of proof, a favorable outcome does not require a unanimous decision by the jury. Fourth, jurors tend to be sympathetic to victims in civil cases where monetary awards and not the risks of imprisonment are at stake. Five, and not least of all, defendants in civil cases must testify, as they are unable to invoke the Fifth Amendment privilege against self-incrimination as in criminal proceedings.

BlackRock, Pimco, the Federal Reserve Bank of New York, Plus 19 v. Bank of America

The proposed settlement between Bank of America (BAC) and a select group of investors in June 2011 "represents a major acknowledgement of just how flawed the mortgage process became in the giddy years leading up to the financial crisis."[45] These twenty-two investors claimed that Countrywide Financial, the subprime mortgage lender that BAC acquired in 2008, had "created securities from mortgages originated with little, if any proof of assets or income."[46] They argued further that BAC "did not properly service these mortgages, failed to heed pleas for help from homeowners teetering on the brink of foreclosure and frequently misplaced documents."[47]

Bank of America agreed to pay $20 billion to cover the cost of home loans that later defaulted, hoping to put much but not all of the fallout from the subprime bust behind the megabank. Of the $20 billion, $8.5 billion was earmarked for investors who bought the most troubled securities backed by Countrywide mortgages. Another $5.5 billion was set aside to cover future claims by Fannie Mae, Freddie Mac, and private investors who also bought troubled mortgage bonds from the bank.[48] Now that these heavyweight investors have prevailed on BAC, they have moved their sights on companies like JP Morgan Chase, Citigroup, and Wells Fargo, raising the prospect of more multibillion-dollar deals.

The Retiree Shareholders v. Lehman Brothers

A pending agreement filed in August 2011 between former Lehman Brothers Holdings Inc., CEO Richard Fuld, and other directors/officers and their shareholders was derailed in October 2011 when U.S. District Judge Lewis Kaplan dismissed the case. The agreement would have settled a potential multibillion-dollar class-action lawsuit filed against the failed investment bank back in June 2008, some three months before Lehman filed for Chapter 11 protection. The investors who sued on behalf of a class of persons included the Alameda County (California) Employees' Retirement Association, the Government of Guam Retirement Fund, and the Northern Ireland Local Governmental Officers Superannuation Committee. Under the suit, the retirees "who bought common stock or certain other securities in the investment bank from June 2007 until the bankruptcy filing were 'seeking billions of dollars in damages on behalf of the purported class,' court papers said."[49]

The suit claimed that the defendants, during the fifteen months leading up to its filing of bankruptcy with the U.S. Bankruptcy Court in Manhattan, supplied offering materials and other securities filings that contained misrepresentations and omissions regarding the company's financial conditions. The retirees' suit also relied on disclosures of accounting irregularities, the use of Repo 105 transactions, and Lehman's exposure to subprime mortgages. In reaction to the federal judge's rejection of the retirees' bid to sue the investment bank's executives and directors for squandering their retirement savings, Mark Rifkin, the lawyer representing the retirees, had this to say: "We believe the decision overlooked the facts and misapplied the law. But this is not the final word for these employees. We are in the process of preparing an appeal."[50]

Class-Action Investors v. Washington Mutual

As discussed in some detail in chapter 4, when the housing market began to crash at the end of 2007, Washington Mutual's loans started failing at an alarming rate early in 2008. Later in the year the Office of Thrift Supervision "seized the company's savings and loan business in the largest bank failure in the nation's history."[51] In June 2011, Washington Mutual's officers, directors, underwriters, and auditor agreed to a $208.8 million settlement to end the class-action securities fraud lawsuits. The civil complaints filed in U.S. District Court for the Western District of Washington, for example, "accused the defendants of concealing from investors poor loan underwriting and inflated appraisals that overstated earnings and inflated the company's stock price."[52] The settlement reached is among the largest stemming from the financial crisis, exceeded by a $624 million settlement by the Countrywide Financial Corporation and a $475 million settlement by Merrill Lynch & Company.

Deutsche Bank v. WaMu v. JP Morgan v. FDIC

One interesting series of litigation motions pitted the Deutsche Bank, Washington Mutual, JP Morgan, and the FDIC against one another. In August 2011, a federal judge ruled that JP Morgan had to face a $10 billion lawsuit tied to the failure of WaMu. At the time, the judge also ruled that the Federal Deposit Insurance Corporation had to remain a defendant in the same lawsuit. In the latter denial, federal judge Rosemary Collyer refused the request of the FDIC that the agency be dismissed from the lawsuit filed by the Deutsche Bank National Trust Company over bad mortgages that were securitized by Washington Mutual. For the record, after WaMu was seized and the FDIC was appointed receiver, WaMu was immediately sold to JP Morgan Chase for $1.9 billion. That was in late 2008. In early 2009, the Deutsche Bank unit filed suit against all three financial entities.

The FDIC argued that as a government corporation it should be dismissed from the lawsuit and that DB should bring its claims against JP Morgan. The FDIC contended that when JP Morgan bought WaMu, JPM assumed both their liabilities and their assets. Of course, JP Morgan had already denied that it had assumed any of WaMu's liabilities and argued accordingly that it should be dismissed from the lawsuit. Judge Collyer of the U.S. District Court for the District of Columbia denied the government agency's request, saying, "It would be 'improvident and premature' to dismiss the F.D.I.C. from the lawsuit after refusing a similar request by JPMorgan."[53]

AIG v. Bank of America

Adding to the swell of investors seeking compensation for problematic mortgages that led to the financial crisis, the American International Group sued Bank of America in August 2011. This mortgage-security-related action seeks more than $10 billion in losses on $28 billion in investments. At the time of its filing, AIG was also busy preparing similar lawsuits against Goldman Sachs, JPMorgan Chase, and Deutsche Bank. The suit claims that BAC and its Merrill Lynch and Countrywide Financial units misrepresented the quality of mortgages placed in securities and sold to investors, such as the ones bought using savings from its insurance subsidiaries. AIG has a lot of company, as many investors are making similar claims that banks misled them into buying risky securities during the housing boom. By late summer 2011, at least ninety private lawsuits related to mortgage bonds had been filed, seeking at least $197 billion in damages.[54]

AIG's civil lawsuit also contends that the purchase of those mortgage bonds relied to some degree on inflated ratings established by BAC, ML, and CF providing false information to the rating agencies. The suit, however, does not involve any collateralized mortgage obligations that the company had insured because their 2008 government bailout agreement required that AIG sign a waiver not to sue big banks over their insured mortgage bonds. Notably, AIG signed no such agreement about mortgage bonds that the company bought outright from the big banks, as in the $28 billion purchase of securities from BAC.

The 200-page complaint filed by the law firm of Quinn Emanuel Urquhart & Sullivan relied on more than 1,900 pages of exhibits, interviews with former Bank of America employees, and the forensic analysis of more than 262,000 loans inside of 349 deals. The suit claims that four out of ten mortgages, on average, "differed significantly from the descriptions of the loans in the marketing materials."[55] For example, "the number of loans said to cover owner-occupied properties was lower than investors were told, and the amount of the loans compared with the value of properties was often higher."[56] The complaint also described the loan files of one particular mortgage security, "where 82 percent of the loans did not comply with the underwriting guidelines as marketed to investors."[57]

Allstate v. the Other Securities Brokers and Goldman Sachs

Between December 2010 and August 2011, Allstate Corporation had filed lawsuits against BAC/Countrywide Financial Corp., Morgan Stanley, JP Morgan Chase, Bank of America's Merrill Lynch unit, units of Citigroup Inc., Credit Suisse Group AG, Deutsche Bank AG, and finally Goldman Sachs. In each of these lawsuits, Allstate claims that it was fraudulently sold millions of dollars in mortgage-backed securities. The largest complaint was for over $700 million against Countrywide. In the case of *Allstate Corp. v. Goldman Sachs Group Inc.*, filed in New York State Supreme Court by its subsidiary Allstate Insurance Company, the broker defendants are accused of fraudulently selling the plaintiffs more than $123 million in mortgage-backed securities in 2006 and 2007, just prior to the housing market collapse. "The lawsuit alleges that Goldman violated state laws against fraud and negligent misrepresentation, and it seeks unspecified damages from Goldman and certain affiliates."[58]

The insurer claims that the documents Goldman provided at the time of the purchases "'contained untrue statements and omitted material facts' about the mortgages underlying the investments. 'Goldman knew these types of securities were, to use Goldman's own word . . . junk, dogs, crap, and lemons.'"[59] The insurer's complaint used material from governmental investigations into Goldman's role in the market's collapse, such as the findings from the U.S. Senate's Financial Crisis Inquiry Commission. The complaint alleges that the New York–based bank claimed that the mortgages backing the securities they sold were low risk and followed strict underwriting criteria, when "Goldman knew that lenders had systematically abandoned the stated underwriting guidelines, producing loans without regard to the likelihood of repayment."[60]

Allstate stands a good chance to win this case. As was discussed in chapter 5, Goldman paid $550 million in 2010 to settle similar civil fraud charges brought by the Securities and Exchange Commission. As was pointed out before, that was the largest penalty against a Wall Street firm in SEC history for which GS did not have to admit or deny wrongdoing. Again, both the SEC case and the Senate investigation concurred: Goldman had steered investors toward complex mortgage investments without acknowledging the securities were crafted with input from at least one client who was betting that they would fail.

U.S. Bank, China Development Industrial Bank, and Cambridge Place Investment Management v. Morgan Stanley

U.S. Bank, units of US Bancorp, as well as China Development and Cambridge have each sued Morgan Stanley in separate lawsuits related to complex structured products. In the case of U.S. Bank, it had sued Morgan Stanley over a credit default swap agreement. In 2011, Morgan Stanley disclosed in its first quarterly report to the SEC that MS had "reached a settlement over its role in a collateralized debt obligation known as Tourmaline CDO I."[61] While terms of the settlement agreement are confidential, Morgan Stanley reported that it would incur a loss "substantially less" than the $274 million that it had earlier projected in a previous filing with the SEC.

In the same filing, Morgan Stanley also reported that it could face a loss of $240 million over a Taiwanese (China Development) bank's civil complaint about subprime mortgage investments. The lawsuit filed in July 2010 claims that Morgan Stanley "misrepresented the risks" of another CDO called Stack 2006-1 and "knew that the assets backing the CDO were of poor quality" when the firm entered into the credit swap agreement with CDIB.[62] The quarterly report also noted that a hedge-fund group, Cambridge Place Investment Management, had recently filed a complaint against the company related to the sale of mortgage products to its client. The complaint alleges that in the $102 million deal with Morgan Stanley and other defendants, they "made untrue statements and material omissions" in the sale of "certain mortgage pass through certificates backed by securitization trusts containing residential mortgage loans."[63]

Two Wealthy Investors v. Citigroup

Individual investors have prevailed "in three quarters of the roughly 20 claims against the Citigroup funds that arbitration panels have decided."[64] Arbitration procedures are mandatory in most Wall Street customer agreements, and the resulting decisions may be appealed in civil courts. In April 2011 Citigroup Inc. was ordered to pay a total of $54.1 million to Jerry Murdock, Jr., a venture capital investor, and Gerald Hosier, a retired patent attorney, "for losses they suffered on a series of risky municipal bond funds that lost 77% of their value in the midst of the financial crisis."[65] According to the Securities Arbitration Commentator, the award by an industry arbitration panel was the largest ever levied against a major Wall Street brokerage firm in favor of individual investors.

The largest previous award to individuals under arbitration had been $20.2 million awarded to a group of individuals against Ameriprise Financial Inc. in 2006 related to the sale of variable annuities and mutual funds. Under the auspices of the Financial Industry Regulatory Authority, the arbitrary panel did not have to explain its reasoning for the aggressive award, which included an order for Citi to pay $17 million in punitive damages, $3 million in legal fees, and all of the hearing costs of $21,600 that are typically divided between the parties. In a prepared statement, Citigroup said, "We are disappointed with the decision, which we believe is not supported by the facts or law."[66] Mega brokerage firms "have been ordered to pay out larger sums to corporate investors, such as a $406.6 million award in 2009 against Credit Suisse in favor of STMicroelectronics NV in a case involving losses on auction-rate securities."[67] Credit Suisse is appealing that award.

Class-Action Shareholders v. Bank of America

A group of shareholders backed by some of the biggest class-action law firms in the nation filed a $50 billion private lawsuit against Bank of America on September 28, 2011. The suit claims that the Charlotte bank and its top executives committed securities fraud related to BAC's purchase of Merrill Lynch in September 2008. In brief, the suit claims that at the time of the acquisition, BAC deliberately hid or failed to disclose $15.31 billion in losses. For the record, the SEC sued Bank of America over the very same issue. Presiding judge Jed Rakoff "rejected the initial $33 million settlement as inadequate, and reluctantly approved the sweetened $150 million deal, noting it didn't impose enough costs on the executives involved."[68]

Steven Davidoff, a former deal lawyer turned law professor who writes regularly for *DealBook*, has opined that if certain facts alleged in the lawsuit prove to be accurate, then this should constitute "a prima facie case of securities fraud" not to mention a "huge liability." His reasoning is as follows:

> Plaintiffs in this private case have the additional benefit that this claim is related to a shareholder vote. It is easier to prove securities fraud related to a shareholder vote than more typical securities fraud claims like accounting fraud. Shareholder vote claims do not require that the plaintiffs prove that the person committing securities fraud did so with awareness that the statement was wrong or otherwise recklessly made. You only need to show that the person should have acted with care. This case is not only easier to establish, but the potential damages could also be enormous. Damages in a claim like this are calculated by looking at the amount lost as a result of the securities fraud. A court will most likely calculate this by referencing the amount that Bank of America stock dropped after the loss was announced.[69]

Not only is BAC facing a huge $50 billion liability from this claim, but it is also facing additional liability for those who bought and sold stock during this period. A judge ruled, on July 29, 2011, that claimants could proceed against Bank of America, the former CFO Joseph Price, and the former CEO Ken Lewis. The judge had earlier ruled that the disclosure claim related to the proxy vote could proceed in that case. With regard to the $50 billion case, it has been placed on the fast track, with an October 2012 trial date. As Yves Smith has written on her blog *Naked Capitalism*, BAC "is expected to argue that the losses were consistent with what shareholders expected, given that a good will write off of $2 billion was already disclosed, and they didn't know the full extent of the damage at the time of the vote. My guess is that if that is the best defense they can mount, they are going to have to write a very large check."[70]

Chapter Seven

The Wall Street Financial Reform and Consumer Protection Act of 2010

A Synopsis of Dodd-Frank and the Re-regulation of Financial Abuse

Since the Wall Street crash of 1929 tensions have persevered between those favoring and disfavoring regulation/deregulation. After the recent collapse of Wall Street and the subsequent bailouts, issues and questions about "re-regulation" have added further to the strains over financial market intervention. In the debatable words of Thomas Hoenig, president of the Federal Reserve Bank of Kansas City: "It is ironic that in the name of preserving free market capitalism in this country, we have undermined it so deeply."[1] His point being that for the past seventy-five years, whether during heightened periods of regulation or deregulation, the economic reality of financial markets has always relied upon and consisted of "banking on the state" as the Bank of England's Andrew Haldane has termed the relationship. Historically, this is a relatively new development in the contradictions of free-market capitalism. For the previous eight centuries, trade between nation-state banking enterprises had swung mostly in the other direction: "The state was reliant on the deep pockets of the banks to finance periodic fiscal crises. But for at least the past century the pendulum has swung back, with the state often needing to dig deep to keep crisis-prone banks afloat."[2]

At the heart of the current financial collapse/debacle/crisis are those markets in which the largest commercial and investment banks in the nation were key players. For example, the five largest investment banks in the country failed, were forced into mergers, or had to convert to bank holding companies to stay buoyant. Bank of America and Citigroup both required extensive assistance and the largest insurance company in the country, AIG, required special assistance, as did Fannie Mae and Freddie Mac. During the meltdown,

public safety nets and assistance were stretched far beyond anything that we had done in past crises. Deposit insurance coverage was substantially expanded and public authorities went well beyond this with guarantees of bank debt instruments, asset guarantees at selected institutions, and many other forms of market support. Discount window lending sharply departed from previous practices in terms of nonbanks and special lending programs. Substantial public capital injections were further provided through TARP to the largest financial organizations in the United States and to several hundred other banks on a scale not seen since the Reconstruction Finance Corporation in the 1930s. These steps were similar to those that many other major countries took.[3]

Thus, one of the main questions asked in this examination of Dodd-Frank and re-regulation is whether or not these financial reforms will eventually do enough to alter the economic relations of banking on the state.

According to Hoenig, over an extended period of time "we have experienced a ratcheting process in which public authorities are pressured to widen and deepen their state safety nets after every financial crisis brought on by excessive bank risk taking. This expansion in safety nets then sets the stage for the next crisis by providing even greater incentives for risk taking and further expanding moral hazard."[4] As a consequence, he continues,

We have become trapped in a repeating game in which participants continue to seek ever higher and more risky returns while 'banking' on the State to fund any losses in a crisis. Large organizations, moreover, are the key players in this process as States become more immersed in the perception during a crisis that they protect any bank regarded as systemically important. We must stop this game if we are to create a more stable financial system and not condemn us to an escalating series of crises with rapidly rising costs.[5]

For these reasons, can Dodd-Frank—a 2,300-page set of regulations consisting of 243 new formal rules—be adopted and implemented by 11 regulatory agencies to effectively break up the familiar banking and regulatory habits that have been developing since the S&L debacle of the 1980s? On the one hand, Barney Frank, in a March 2011 television interview with Charlie Rose, said that he "got better than 90 percent" of what he wanted and that thanks to this legislation, "too big to fail" will be all but eliminated in the future.[6] On the other hand, when Gramm-Leach-Bliley was passed in 1999, the five largest U.S. banks controlled about 38 percent of all banking industry assets or $2.3 trillion in assets. By 2011, the top five banks controlled 52 percent of all banking assets or $7.8 trillion. As for the faltering giant, Bank of America, which needed bailing out in 2009 by TARP and a $5 billion infusion by Warren Buffet in August 2011, it alone controlled $2.3 trillion in assets.

Making matters of re-regulation more difficult in balancing the contradictions between protecting investors and punishing securities fraudsters are the continued growth of these financial institutions. Furthermore, the past patterns in market relations continue to favor or privilege these financial firms' fast-track capital formation in borrowing and lending. For example, the central idea of too-big-to-fail organizations held by creditors and uninsured depositors was endorsed by credit-rating agencies when they gave "these organizations separate 'support' and 'standalone' ratings, which explicitly factor in the governmental support they likely will receive. The difference in these two ratings thus provides one measure of the funding advantages that too-big-to-fail organizations have over others."[7] For the twenty-eight largest banks in the world, Haldane estimated that this funding advantage amounted to about $250 billion in 2009.[8]

Similarly, the Federal Reserve Bank of Kansas City estimated that the ratings and funding advantage for the five largest U.S. banking organizations during the crisis were huge. For example, in June 2009, "these organizations had senior, long-term bank debt that was rated four notches higher on average than it would have been based on just the actual condition of the banks."[9] In a competitive marketplace, these rating returns yield a situation where the big banking organizations have significant advantages in not having to sell creditors on the strength of their condition and/or in competing for funds. Equally significant, these firms possess significant incentives to take on more risk, hold less capital, and book more assets.[10]

Prior to The Wall Street Financial Reform and Consumer Protection Act of 2010, there was Public Law 111-21 or the Fraud Enforcement and Recovery Act of 2009, signed by President Obama on May 20th to "improve enforcement of fraud, securities and commodities fraud, financial institution fraud, and other frauds related to Federal assistance and relief programs, for the recovery of funds lost to these frauds, and for other purposes."[11] As the previous chapters have shown, Public Law 111-21 has had at best a negligible impact on recovery for the vast majority of Americans victimized directly or indirectly by high-stakes securities fraud.

There had also been *A Joint Report of the SEC and the CFTC on the Harmonization of Regulation* issued October 16, 2009. This joint report was in response to an Obama administration white paper on financial regulatory reform released through the Treasury Department on June 17, 2009. The report requested that the U.S. Securities and Exchange Commission and the U.S. Commodity Futures Trading Commission identify "all existing conflicts in statutes and regulations with respect to similar types of financial instruments and either explain why those differences are essential to achieve underlying policy objectives with respect to investor protection, market integrity, and price transparency or make recommendations for changes to statutes and regulations that would eliminate the differences."[12] A brief overview and summary is presented in the next section on the findings from the special joint meetings held by the SEC and the CFTC on September 2nd and 3rd, 2009.[13]

"HARMONIZING REGULATION"

Present at the two-day conference were nine sitting commissioners and some thirty panelists, including members from the investor community, academics, industry experts, and market participants. In assisting the two agencies, those present helped to define the issues of greatest concern and to explore such topics as exchanges, markets, regulation, and enforcement. They also contributed to the production of the ninety-four-page joint report.[14] In spite of their comprehensive effort to discuss the similarities and dissimilarities between securities and futures, the joint report did not address all of the differences between the two regulatory regimes. Moreover, because these agencies traditionally have had no authority to regulate derivatives, the report did not address this key dimension of the financial crisis as did the Treasury white paper and the congressional deliberation before and after the passage of Dodd-Frank. Finally, for the purposes of enhancing customer protection and investor confidence, rendering compliance more efficient, and improving coordination and cooperation between agencies, the joint report concludes with a series of specific recommendations for strengthening the agencies' oversight and enforcement with respect to markets and financial intermediaries.

The joint report begins by emphasizing that since the 1930s "securities and futures have been subject to separate regulatory regimes. While both regimes seek to promote market integrity and transparency, securities markets are concerned with capital formation, which futures are not."[15] Furthermore, futures markets exist for the purpose of primarily facilitating the management and transfer of risk, and to manage positions in underlying assets of limited supply. Securities markets, with the exceptions of securities options and other securities derivative markets, are not concerned with facilitating the transfer of risk. Also, because of the role of some securities markets in capital formation, "securities regulation is concerned with disclosure—including accounting standards related to such disclosure, while commodities regulation is not."[16] What is noteworthy is that the "unique capital formation role of certain securities markets has informed the manner in which the two regulatory regimes have developed and, in part, explain differences between the regulatory structures of the CFTC and the SEC."[17]

The content of the joint report reviews and analyzes the statutory and regulatory structure of the CFTC and the SEC in the following areas:

- Oversight of New Products
- Review and Approval of Rules
- Financial Responsibility: Segregation, Insolvency, and Margin
- Markets and Clearing Systems
- **Manipulation, Insider Trading, and Fraud Enforcement**
- **Obligations to Customers**
- Registration and Recordkeeping Requirements
- **Regulation of Cross-Border Activity**
- Operational Coordination

Three of these are highlighted here: (1) "manipulation, insider trading and fraud enforcement," (2) "obligations to customers," and (3) "regulation of cross-border activity."

The manipulation of markets is unlawful under both securities and futures laws, although certain kinds of activity, such as "cornering the market," are unique to the futures markets. Enforcement in both of these areas of regulation requires both "legal action in response to violations and prescriptive action through proper market oversight."[18] However, when it comes to violating securities and futures laws, the two regulatory regimes approach matters very differently. Take the instances of insider trading.

The market integrity provisions of the securities laws prohibit insider trading. These provisions "do so in large part because securities laws are premised on a corporation's duties to disclose material information to protect shareholders from corporate insiders who have access to non-public information. Specifically, corporate officials and personnel of a firm who trade that firm's securities on the basis of inside information are viewed as breaching a fiduciary duty to the shareholders who hold those securities."[19] In contrast, the Commodity Exchange Act's insider trading prohibitions are focused on employees and agents of the CFTC and on self-regulating organizations (SRO) and markets that are regulated by the CFTC. This primary difference between the two regimes is also attributable to the historical functions of the futures markets: "These markets permit hedgers to use their non-public material information to protect themselves against risks to their commodity positions. Though counterparties to these kinds of transactions may not have access to the same non-public information, corporate officials and personnel generally do not have a similar fiduciary duty with respect to those counterparties; indeed, their duties are to ensure that the company properly manages its risks by trading on the best available information."[20]

As for fraud enforcement, there are also regulatory differences with respect to remedies as each are subject to different statutory rules. The "CFTC has specific statutory authority for aiding and abetting all violations of the CEA and CFTC regulations. The SEC has specific statutory authority for aiding and abetting under the Securities Exchange Act and the Investment Advisers Act but not under the Securities Act or the Investment Company Act."[21] One fundamental difference between the two regimes is that securities laws require "firewalls" between analysts and trading functions. No such parallel mechanism for avoiding conflicts of interest exists under trading laws or the CEA. One noteworthy similarity between the two regimes is that "neither agency has the ability to rely on whistleblowers to assist in detecting violations of their statutes."[22]

The obligations to customers are also subject to varying schemes under the two regulatory regimes, with risk built into commodity trading and the assumption that customers are in the best position to determine the propriety of a particular futures trade. These assumptions do not hold for securities, and the rules require much more customer protection or safety for investors in securities transactions. The CFTC requires

> financial advisors to determine an appropriate level of disclosure particularized to the client based on the "know your customer" information they have obtained. Because of the fundamental role of leverage and the inherent volatility of commodities markets, futures trading is considered "risky" by nature. Futures regulation, therefore, imposes an initial suitability determination before a customer even opens a futures trading account. However, once that threshold is crossed, the customer may engage in futures trade without a trade-by-trade suitability determination by the financial professional.[23]

By contrast, in the world of federal securities laws and SRO rules, "broker-dealers are required to deal fairly with their customers," which means "having a reasonable basis for recommendations given the customer's financial situation (suitability), engaging in fair and balanced communications with the public, providing timely and adequate confirmation of transactions, providing account statement disclosures, disclosing conflict of interest, and receiving fair compensation both in agency and principal transactions."[24] In addition, the SEC's suitability approach calls for broker-dealers to have adequately investigated the securities that they are recommending. These broker-dealers are "to determine whether a particular investment recommendation is suitable for a customer, based on customer-specific factors" and factors related to their customers' overall securities and investment strategies.[25]

In an age of globalizing financial markets, efforts of agency oversight of the regulation of cross-border activity is of increasing importance. In this area, both agencies have taken steps to "encourage cross-border flow of capital and trading while promoting adoption of robust regulatory standards throughout the world."[26] Once again, the agencies' approaches have differed, especially with regard to certain cross-border issues. The primary distinction is that federal securities laws require that those wishing to engage in such markets must register with the United States; there is no similar requirement for those who wish to engage in commodity markets or trading. "With regard to intermediaries, foreign broker-dealers' interaction with U.S. investors in securities transactions is facilitated primarily through the exemptions from U.S. broker-dealer registration offered under the Securities Exchange Act. The CFTC's regulatory regime allows for broader cross-border access by intermediaries."[27]

THE WALL STREET FINANCIAL REFORM AND CONSUMER PROTECTION ACT: A SYNOPSIS

The rationales for passing the Dodd-Frank Act of 2010 were to rein in Wall Street risk-taking and big bonuses, to end bailouts and too big to fail, to protect consumers, and to prevent another financial crisis. A familiar refrain is heard by those who favor regulation and re-regulation: The U.S. must "restore responsibility and accountability in our financial system to give Americans confidence that there is a system in place that works for and protects them."[28] In a 2010 overview of Dodd-Frank, the U.S. Senate Banking Subcommittee identified seven accomplishments of this gigantic piece of legislation as follows:[29]

1. **Consumer Protections with Authority and Independence**: Refers to the creation of a new independent "watchdog" agency, housed at the Federal Reserve, with "the authority to ensure American consumers get the clear, accurate information they need to shop for mortgages, credit cards, and other financial products, and protect them from hidden fees, abusive terms, and deceptive practices."

2. **Ends Too Big to Fail Bailouts**: Refers to ending the possibility that taxpayers will have to bail out financial firms that threaten the economy by "creating a safe way to liquidate failed financial firms; imposing tough new capital and leverage requirements that make it undesirable to get too big; *updating the Fed's authority to allow system-wide support but no longer prop up individual firms*; and establishing rigorous standards and supervision to protect the economy and American consumers, investors and businesses" (emphasis added).

3. **Advance Warning System**: Refers to the creation of a special interagency council to identify and address systemic risks imposed by "large, complex

companies, products, and activities before they threaten the stability of the economy."

4. **Transparency and Accountability for Exotic Instruments**: Refers to eliminating "loopholes that allow risky and abusive practices to go on unnoticed and unregulated—including loopholes for over-the-counter derivatives, asset-backed securities, hedge funds, mortgage brokers and payday lenders."

5. **Executive Compensation and Corporate Governance**: Refers to the provision of providing "shareholders with a say on pay and corporate affairs with a non-binding vote on executive compensation and golden parachutes."

6. **Protects Investors**: Refers to the provisions of "tough new rules for transparency and accountability for credit rating agencies to protect investors and businesses."

7. **Enforces Regulations on the Books**: Refers to the strengthening oversight and empowerment of "regulators to aggressively pursue financial fraud, conflicts of interest and manipulation of the system that benefits special interests at the expense of American families and businesses."

The Senate Banking Subcommittee's overview also discussed nineteen areas of related regulations:[30]

1. A Strong Consumer Financial Protection Watchdog

The establishment of a Consumer Financial Protection Bureau, led by an independent director appointed by the president and confirmed by the Senate, with a dedicated budget provided by the Federal Reserve and the authority to write rules for consumer protection governing all financial institutions, banks and non-banks alike (including mortgage-related businesses such as lenders and brokers), that offer consumer financial services or products, and have assets of over $10 billion. The creation of the bureau was to consolidate and strengthen the responsibilities heretofore handled by the Office of the Comptroller of the Currency, Office of Thrift Supervision, Federal Deposit Insurance Corporation, Federal Reserve, National Credit Union Administration, the Department of Housing and Urban Development, and the Federal Trade Commission.

2. Addressing Systemic Risk

The establishment of a Financial Stability Oversight Council, chaired by the Treasury secretary and made up of ten federal regulators from the Federal

Reserve Board, Office of the Comptroller of the Currency, National Credit Union Administration, Federal Housing Finance Agency, SEC, CFTC, FDIC, and the new Consumer Financial Protection Bureau, plus one independent member and five non-voting members. The overarching charge of the council is to identify and respond to emerging risks throughout the financial system. Toward this end, a new Office of Financial Research within the Treasury is called for to be staffed by economists, accountants, lawyers, former supervisors, and other specialists for the purposes of collecting and analyzing data to identify, monitor, and make more transparent emerging risks to the economy.

Within the basic charge are several related authorizations or tasks for specifically addressing companies that pose risks to the financial system as a whole. For example, the council is charged with making recommendations to the Federal Reserve for enhancing the rules for capital, leverage, liquidity, and risk management. The council is also authorized to require, with a two-thirds vote and vote of the chair, that a non-bank financial company be regulated if the council believes that there would be negative effects on the financial system if the company failed. Similarly, with the same number of votes, the council is able to require a large complex company to divest some of its holdings when viewed as posing a threat to the financial system should it fail.

3. Ending Too-Big-to-Fail Bailouts

Under the area of limiting large, complex financial companies and preventing future bailouts the overlapping objective with risk assessment/management is to discourage excessive growth and complexity and to facilitate the liquidation of failing companies, banking and non-banking, that systemically threaten the financial system. For example, the Volcker Rule requires that regulators implement regulations for banks, their affiliates, and holding companies, prohibiting proprietary trading and investment and sponsorship in hedge funds and private equity funds. Periodic "funeral plans" are now required of large, complex financial companies for their rapid and orderly shutdown should the company need to undergo bankruptcy. If firms fail to submit acceptable plans, they are to be hit with higher capital requirements and restrictions on growth and activity. Procedures are now in place for an orderly liquidation of companies once the Treasury, the FDIC, and the Federal Reserve agree that the time has come.

With respect to costing financial firms rather than taxpayers when these businesses are no longer too big to fail, the expectation now is supposed to be that failing companies are to be resolved through the bankruptcy process. For example, the new law significantly alters the Federal Reserve Emergency

Lending Rule 13(3) prohibiting the Fed from bailing out an individual company. Other restrictions are also now in place such as the FDIC can borrow only the amount of funds to liquidate a company that it expects to be repaid from the assets of the company being liquidated. Then again, the law permits with the approval of the secretary of Treasury lending programs that are broad based rather than aimed at aiding a particular financial company. A distinction, if you will, between "retail" and "wholesale" bailing out or between saving a single firm and saving a financial industry.

4. Reforming the Federal Reserve

As noted above, the new law limits emergency lending authority by prohibiting it to an individual entity or to insolvent firms. The law also calls for enough collateral to protect taxpayers from losses. From now on, the GAO will have ongoing authority not only to audit emergency lending under Rule13(3), but also for discount window lending and open market transactions. With respect to limits on debt guarantees, in order to prevent bank runs, the FDIC can guarantee debt of solvent insured banks, but only after (1) a two-thirds vote of the Federal Reserve Board and the FDIC board determine that there is a threat to financial stability, (2) the terms and conditions of the guaranteed amounts are approved by the Treasury secretary, and (3) the president initiates an expedited process for congressional approval. The other components of these reforms have to do with examining whether or not the current system effectively represents the pubic and/or conflicts of interests in relation to the daily operations of the Federal Reserve, such as supervisory accountability, bank governance, and the election of Federal Reserve bank presidents.

5. Creating Transparency and Accountability for Derivatives

Toward the goal of bringing transparency and accountability to the derivatives markets, the law establishes a not very impressive code of conduct for all registered swap dealers and major participants when advising their swap entities. When acting as counterparties, for example, to a pension fund, endowment fund, or state or local government, dealers are to have a "reasonable basis" to believe that the investors have independent representatives advising them. More substantively, the law does four other things:

1. **Closes Regulatory Gaps**: It gives the SEC and CFTC the authority to regulate over-the-counter derivatives.
2. **Central Clearing and Exchange Trading**: It requires central clearing and exchange trading for derivatives and the determination of which of those contracts should be cleared by both regulators and clearinghouses.

3. **Market Transparency**: To improve market transparency and to provide regulators with the tools for monitoring and responding to risks, the law requires data collection and publication through clearinghouses or swap repositories.
4. **Financial Safeguards**: Provides regulators with the authority to impose capital and margin requirements on swap dealers and major swap participants, and not on the end users, to ensure that these traders have adequate financial resources to meet their obligations.

6. Minority and Women Inclusion

For all banking and securities regulatory agencies, the law establishes an Office of Minority and Women Inclusion to address employment and contracting diversity matters. These offices will also coordinate technical assistance to minority-owned and women-owned businesses. Finally, these offices seek to diversify the workforce of regulators.

7. Mortgage Reform

In addition to establishing an Office of Housing Counseling within the Department of Housing and Urban Development, the law establishes penalties for irresponsible lending. The penalties hold lenders and mortgage brokers accountable to consumers by fining them as much as three years' of interest payments and damages plus attorney fees (if any). The law requires that lenders ensure a borrower's ability to repay the loans that he or she is sold. The law also requires lenders to disclose the maximum a consumer could pay on a variable rate mortgage. The law expands the consumer protections available under federal rules on high-cost loans—lowering the interest rate and the points and fee triggers that define the costs of these types of loans. Finally, the law goes after unfair lending practices. It specifically prohibits companies from instituting financial incentives that encourage lenders to steer borrowers into subprime and other costly loans. Similarly, the law prohibits those bonuses known as "yield spread premiums" that lenders pay to brokers to inflate the costs of loans. The law also prohibits pre-payment penalties that have trapped many borrowers into unaffordable loans.

8. Hedge Funds

The law raises some standards and fills some regulatory gaps in the "shadow" financial system by requiring hedge funds and private equity advisors to register with the SEC as investment advisors and to provide information about their trades and portfolios necessary to assess systemic risk. It also works to establish a division of labor among state and federal regulators by raising the assets threshold for SEC regulation of investment advisors from $30 million to $100 million, thereby significantly increasing the number of advisors under state supervision.

9. Credit Rating Agencies

In the area of credit rating agencies the law is especially proactive. It establishes new requirements and oversight of credit rating agencies. The law creates an Office of Credit Ratings at the SEC with expertise of its own and rating analysts who are to pass qualifying exams and have continuing education. The new office at the SEC will have its own compliance staff and the authority to fine agencies. The law further requires that the SEC examine all Nationally Recognized Statistical Ratings Organizations (NRSROs) at least once a year and make key findings public. It also requires that those rating organizations disclose their methodologies, their use of third parties for due diligence efforts, and their ratings track record. The law gives the SEC the authority to deregister a rating agency for providing bad ratings over time. The law incorporates the issues of liability by providing that investors can bring private rights of action against ratings agencies for a knowing or reckless failure to conduct a reasonable investigation of the facts or to obtain analysis from an independent source.

The law specifically addresses conflicts of interest by prohibiting compliance officers from working on ratings, methodologies, or sales. It also installs a new requirement for NRSROs to conduct one-year look-back reviews when an NRSRO employee goes to work for an obligor or underwriter of a security or money market instrument subject to a rating by that NRSRO. Similarly, the law mandates the reporting to the SEC of any NRSRO who goes to work for an entity that the NRSRO has rated in the previous twelve months. At the same time, the law reduces over-reliance on ratings and encourages investors to conduct their own analysis by eliminating many statutory and regulatory requirements to use NRSRO ratings.

Last but not least of all, the law seeks to end the game of shopping for ratings. After conducting a study and submitting a report to Congress, the SEC is required to create a new mechanism to prevent issuers of asset-backed securities from picking the agency they think will give the highest rating.

10. Executive Compensation and Corporate Governance

The law requires that federal financial regulators issue and enforce joint compensation rules specifically applicable to financial institutions. The law also directs the SEC to clarify disclosures relating to compensation, requiring that companies compare their executive compensation with stock performance over a five-year period. The law further requires that public companies establish policies to take back executive compensation if it was based on inaccurate (fraudulent) financial statements that do not comply with normal accounting standards. With respect to corporate governance there is the attempt to give shareholders a say on pay and greater accountability from executives. Although shareholders can certainly voice their disapproval of misguided incentive schemes and golden parachutes that threaten individual companies and in turn the broader economy, their rights consist of non-binding votes on these matters.

11. Improvements to Bank and Thrift Regulations

Implements a strengthened version of the Volcker rule to prohibit proprietary trading and investing a banking entity's own money in hedge funds, with the exception for funds where the investors are required by the investment advisor to have some "skin in the game" (up to 3 percent of tier 1 capital in the aggregate). The law establishes stronger lending limits by adding credit exposure from derivative transactions to banks' lending limits. It also repeals the prohibition on banks paying interest on demand deposits while removing a regulatory arbitrage opportunity by prohibiting a bank from converting its charter, unless both the "old" and "new" regulators do not object, in order to get out from under an enforcement action. Importantly, the act requires the Federal Reserve to examine non-bank subsidiaries that are engaged in the same activities that the subsidiary bank can perform, such as mortgage lending. Finally, the new law abolishes the Office of Thrift Supervision and transfers those authorities mainly to the Office of the Comptroller of the Currency while preserving the thrift charter.

12. Insurance

Historically, the law establishes the first Federal Insurance Office to be located within the Treasury Department. The charges of the new office are primarily two: First, to gather information about the insurance industry, especially concerning access to affordable insurance products for minorities, low- and moderate-income persons, and other underserved communities. Second, to monitor the insurance industry for systemic risk. The office will also work toward the streamlining of the regulation of surplus line insurance and reinsurance through state-based reforms. Lastly, the office will serve as a national voice on insurance matters for the United States on the international stage.

13. Interchange Fees

To protect small businesses from unreasonable fees, the law requires the Federal Reserve to issue rules to ensure that fees charged to merchants by credit card companies for business transactions are reasonable and proportional to the costs of processing those transactions.

14. Credit Score Protection

Helps to monitor personal financial ratings by giving consumers free access to their credit scores when their score has negatively affected them in a financial transaction or hiring decision.

15. SEC and Improving Investor Protections

Toward the goal of improving investor protections, the law does five things:

1. **Fiduciary Duty**: Gives the SEC the authority to impose a fiduciary duty on brokers who give investment advice, requiring that advice be in the best interest of their customers.
2. **Encouraging Whistleblowers**: Establishes a program within the SEC to encourage people to report securities violations, creating rewards of up to 30 percent of the funds recovered for the information provided.
3. **SEC Management Reform**: The law mandates three things in this area: a comprehensive outside consultant study of the SEC, an annual assessment of the SEC's internal supervisory controls, and a GAO review of SEC management.
4. **New Advocates for Investors**: Creates the Office of Investor Advocate to the SEC and the Investment Advisory Committee made up of investors. The charges of the former are to identify areas where investors have significant problems dealing with the SEC and to provide them with assistance. This office also has an ombudsman to handle investor complaints. The charges of the IAC are to advise the SEC on its regulatory priorities and practices.
5. **SEC Funding**: Provides "more" resources to the chronically underfunded agency to carry out its new duties.

16. Securitization

To reduce the risks posed by securities, such as selling products like mortgage-backed securities, the law requires "skin in the game" or retaining at least 5 percent of the credit risk, unless the underlying loans meet standards that reduce the riskiness. In other words, if these investments do not pan out, the company that packed and sold the investments will lose outright along with the people they sold them to. The law also calls for better disclosure by requiring the issuers to analyze the quality of the underlying assets involved in an investment and to disclose more information about those assets to their investors.

17. Municipal Securities

Improves oversight of the municipal securities industry by requiring the registration of municipal advisors, imposing a fiduciary duty on them, and subjecting them to rules written by the Municipal Securities Rulemaking Board. To better serve and protect the public interest the law also requires that the MSRB has a majority of independent members.

18. Tackling the Effects of the Mortgage Crisis

As already pointed out by the introduction of the Foreclosure Fraud and Homeowner Abuse Prevention Bill of 2011, Dodd-Frank was simply underwhelming in this area given the magnitude of the problem. For example, in the name of Emergency Mortgage Relief and a Neighborhood Stabilization Program, the law provides respectively $1 billion for bridge loans to qualified unemployed homeowners with reasonable prospects for re-employment to help tide them over between jobs and another $1 billion to the states and localities to combat the "ugly impact" on neighborhoods from the foreclosure crisis.

19. Transparency for Extraction Industry

Domestically, deposit insurance for banks, thrifts, and credit unions is increased to $250,000 per person. The law now requires SEC filing disclosure and public disclosure to the SEC about payments they or their subsidiaries have made to or received from U.S. and foreign governments related to the commercial development of oil, natural gas, and other minerals. Internationally, the law restricts U.S. funds for use by foreign governments, requiring the administration to evaluate proposed loans by the IMF to other nations based on their ratios of debt to GDP. The law also requires that the State Department submit a strategy to address the illicit minerals trade generally and specifically in relation to the links between conflict minerals and armed groups for the purpose of establishing a baseline against which to judge effectiveness.

CONCERNS AND CRITICISMS OF DODD-FRANK

"At the end of the day, the Dodd-Frank Wall Street Reform and Consumer Protection Act of 2010 is the keystone of the financial reform structure in the United States and will be influential worldwide."[31] The myriad of rules and initiatives that have been legislated and proposed by the act will undoubtedly have an impact on the operations of financial markets in the future, with anticipated as well as unanticipated consequences on the global economy. Nevertheless, by fall 2011, there were no shortage of concerns and criticisms addressing issues of substance, form, and implementation. The substantive issues had to do with arguments that the act could have been more constructive or effective.

For example, public interest critics of Dodd-Frank such as those faculty members from the Stern School of Business at NYU who contributed to the edited volume, *Regulating Wall Street: The Dodd-Frank Act and the New Architecture of Global Finance* (2010), have argued that the law needs amending. This is because the new law fails to regulate critical factors in the securities markets that lead both to moral hazard and to regulation by form rather than function. Three of these factors include: (1) large financial institutions can still finance their activities at below-market rates, (2) the shadow banking industry still persists, and (3) systemic risk remains virtually uninhibited. In addition, from the perspective of consumer protection not measuring up to the current foreclosure crisis, U.S. Senator Sherrod Brown, who chairs the Senate Banking Subcommittee on Financial Institutions and Consumer Protection, introduced the Foreclosure Fraud and Homeowner Abuse Prevention Bill of 2011. This legislation was designed to "prevent future servicer fraud and errors, improve foreclosure counseling and prevention, and reform oversight of mortgage-based investing" on behalf of both homeowners and investors.[32] If this bill passes into law some time in 2012, it should significantly augment Dodd-Frank in the area of consumer protection.

There were also procedural (e.g., form and implementation) concerns that much of the act had yet to be worked out or written and that these tasks had been essentially left to the regulators to accomplish. In effect, the new rules have been subject to the regulators at the Fed, the SEC, the CFTC, the FDIC, and the OCC to design and fine-tune. On the one hand, leaving the final regulatory touches to those enforcers who know the territories of securities makes sense. On the other hand, these are the same agencies and regulators who were not enforcing the existing rules prohibiting excessively risky behavior that helped to facilitate the financial meltdown of 2007–8. In addition, even if these regulators are successful in writing effective rules, implementation of these regulations will still face continuing "pressure from Wall Street lobbyists and mostly Republican legislators to soften restrictions and eliminate some of the critical ones. If the restrictions remain intact after the 2012 election, with at least a Democratic majority in the Senate, then the question remains whether the regulators will enforce them vigorously" given their record of the recent past.[33]

Many consumers are worried that vigorous lobbying by the financial industry may end up with Congress neutralizing the powers of the Consumer Financial Protection Bureau. For example, in July 2011 President Obama nominated former Ohio attorney general and head of enforcement for the bureau, Richard Cordray, to become the first director of the new agency. The move came after Wall Street interests and Republicans had strongly opposed the nomination of Elizabeth Warren, the bureau's creator and outspoken critic of megabanks. Since the Republicans were determined to block any nomination to direct the Consumer Protection Agency, President Obama was compelled to appoint Cordray to the new post during a congressional "recess" at the beginning of 2012.[34] However, as of the same time, regulators had issued 154 proposals, finalized 74 of them, and missed 200 deadlines as they moved through the complexity of some 30 federal agencies tasked with writing some 400 rules, to be implemented in 2012 and 2013.[35]

Another similarly related concern has to do with Dodd-Frank's answer to systemic risk, namely the creation of the Financial Stability Oversight Council and its charge to anticipate such problems and to reduce the risks taken by financial firms ahead of time. As a former economic columnist for the *New York Times*, Jeff Madrick has queried, "Will this prove to be more than a fantasy? When we consider how poorly the Fed and Treasury negotiated the AIG bailout, failing to stand up to Goldman Sachs and the other powers on Wall Street, there is little reason to have confidence that the new oversight institution will force the hands of the big banks and investment companies in the future."[36]

As for more general criticisms leveled at the Dodd-Frank Act, most of these center on coming up short or not doing enough to alter those financial relations responsible for the Wall Street collapse. For example, from the beginning, the act could have focused on setting higher capital requirements for the amount of money that banks and other financial institutions have to put aside for possible losses. Moreover, the law could have broken up today's megabanks that have only grown larger since the crisis. As noted elsewhere about the concentration of banking wealth since the crisis, the largest financial institutions in the U.S. now account for 55 percent of all banking assets, an increase of about 17 percent since before the crash. As Madrick stresses, the law could have

divided the banks by function in order to reduce the overlapping of investment activities, which increases the chances of damage to the financial system. For example, those banks that accept federally insured deposits from savers could have been restricted to making loans to consumers and businesses. Other institutions that

raise money independently of government guarantees could have been allowed to
sell more risky stocks or corporate bonds to investors or speculate in securities with
their shareholder capital.[37]

Or as suggested in *Regulating Wall Street*, taxes could have been levied to
discourage high-risk investing by Wall Street bankers. For example, a direct tax
on major financial institutions could have been imposed, based on how much
systemic risk they are creating, measured by the number of low-quality loans
and inadequate services provided. In another edited book, *Reforming U.S. Financial Markets*, based on a symposium held at Harvard University, economist
Robert Shiller has criticized Dodd-Frank for not establishing direct ways to
mitigate against future speculative bubbles. For example, he endorses raising
and lowering capital requirements as financial conditions change over time.[38]

POLITICAL REALITIES, RE-REGULATION,
AND STATE BANKING

Politically, the majority of the Republican party and the Wall Street financial
industry argues that Dodd-Frank goes too far in its proposed regulations.
These folks are working and lobbying respectively to block, change, or overturn the new rules and their implementation. From the point of view of the
politicians but not from the vantage point of Wall Street bankers, the irony
is that by nullifying these rules or by overturning the law altogether as many
Republicans would like, they would effectively preserve banking on the
state—with all of its negotiated bailouts, exemptions, and waivers between
the investment oligopoly in this nation and the Federal Reserve, the DOJ, and
the SEC. Such are the contradictions of advanced capitalism and bourgeois
legality, neither of which are addressed by Dodd-Frank.

On the other hand, there are not a few Democrats, a number of economists,
and others who argue that Dodd-Frank did not go far enough in its financial
reforms. These critics of financial regulation call for more as well as different types of reforms than Dodd-Frank, but certainly not for less regulations
or none at all as some extreme laissez-faire ideologues call for. In the book's
closing chapter, some of those proposed changes that go beyond Dodd-Frank
to take advantage of financial technologies that could help reduce the prospects for future financial collapses, bailouts, and reliance on state banking are
discussed. Nevertheless, none of these proposals contemplate the workings of
bourgeois legality as these affect the management of securities fraud and the
administration of financial justice.

Conclusion

The roots of the Wall Street collapse and economic crisis began in the 1980s and can be traced back to a rise in trade deficits, a deregulation of the financial sector, and an intensification of capital inequality. Research has documented that among developed nations, the more financially unequal ones experience slower economic growth on average than the more equal ones. Likewise, in periods when incomes are more equal individual countries develop more rapidly. Conversely, during periods when incomes are more unequal economic growth slows.[1] This has certainly been true of the United States since World War II. From the 1940s through the 1970s the United States enjoyed considerable equality and growth in the GDP was strong. Over the past three decades as inequality in income and wealth has surged, economic growth in the United States has slowed down.

Wealth inequality is also linked to policies of lowered and regressive taxation. Over time, the escalating economic inequality has been linked to financial bankruptcies, to financial distress, to financial panics, and to financial crises. In human terms, financial inequality leads to stress, early deaths, more divorces, and increased violence. The outcomes of these heightened disparities anger both Occupy Wall Street and the Tea Party. These widening inequities and the growing numbers of poor and near poor in this nation are increasingly victimizing the American people and the economy as a whole. In this regard, Andrew Berg and Jonathan Ostry of the International Monetary Fund have been quoted as saying, "The recent global economic crisis, with its roots in U.S. financial markets, may have resulted, at least in part, from the increase in inequality."[2]

What is known for certainty about U.S. financial markets is that with the ascendance of Reaganomics and neo-liberalism, usury laws were knocked down and end runs around Glass-Steagall began. Therein lies the seeds of liquidity preference, the spread of speculative markets, and the aversion to keeping money locked up in long-term investments, like infrastructure or manufacturing. Those legal changes accounted initially in the 1980s for the fraudulent Savings and Loans epidemic and their record-setting bailouts at the time.

Both the recent Great Recession and the TARP bailouts were the result of a wider epidemic of Wall Street banking fraud and abuse, high-risk and fraudulent mortgage lending, inflated and fraudulent credit ratings, and fraudulent regulation/deregulation. This widespread untrustworthy behavior was set into motion in 1999 when Glass-Steagall was overturned completely. Even before the formal elimination of the separation between commercial and investment banking, most of the "large commercial banks, facing the need to raise their own capital in speculative securities markets, were increasingly relying on trading profits to enhance their returns."[3] In effect, these banks had turned themselves into giant hedge funds. Meanwhile, most of the large investment banks already had substantial trading operations, and they were increasingly funding themselves with what amounted to short-term deposits as part of the "the shadow banking system."[4]

The increased competition between the biggest banks and other financial firms, in turn, pressured these institutions not only to boost their returns to shareowners, but also to swell their leverage—the amount of assets they hold compared to the base of invested capital that supports them—to record levels. Leverage of "twelve- or fifteen-to-one was not uncommon among the large U.S. commercial banks, and many investment banks had ratios of twenty-five- or even thirty-to-one. As a result, once these firms began to incur losses on their trading operations, they had little cushion with which to absorb them."[5]

On top of these old leverage risks there were the new risks attached to the developing markets for financial derivatives. Those financial instruments, based once again on the value of other financial instruments, allowed select financial institutions and some investors to hedge those risks that they already bore with new, unrelated risks. As a consequence, "many of the risks to which investors of all kinds became exposed bore little or no connection to fluctuations in any component of the economy's actual wealth, such as housing prices or the value of companies issued shares. The risks borne were, increasingly, merely one side of the other of zero-sum bets."[6] In a relatively short time, the interconnected risks and vulnerabilities let loose by deregulation were accumulating everywhere. These developments in financial markets along with the rising rate of mortgage delinquencies and defaults that they yielded, beginning in 2005, would shortly thereafter spark a financial collapse of mammoth proportions.

Ultimately, as the value of securities backed by packages of subprime mortgages declined in value, leveraged derivative claims against these securities declined even more. Those investors who held these toxic instruments, whether they be very rich individuals or the pooled retirement funds of firefighters, experienced huge losses. As for those highly leveraged financial institutions that saw their investments/capital erode to the point of insolvency and probable failure, they were bailed out in 2008 to the tune of $680 billion (a figure large enough to cover the U.S. trade deficit of $680.9 billion in July 2011).[7]

After the bailouts, however, without any significant changes in investing incentives or structures, banks were still not lending and the markets in which many firms regularly issued commercial paper were also effectively shut down. By the fall of 2011, despite an impending global financial crisis, Wall Street profits and bonuses for the few were as good or better than they had ever been. As for Main Street, unable to borrow, small businesses were flat at best and average families were cutting their spending because of real declines in income of 10 percent on average since 2007.

ON THE CONTRADICTIONS OF
DODD-FRANK AND BOURGEOIS LEGAL-JUSTICE

The Dodd-Frank Act in its conceptually comprehensive approach to financial regulatory reform has many worthwhile reforms—short of any fundamental or structural reform of financial markets. At the same time, there are other reforms that are hollow or have no teeth as in the areas of executive compensation and corporate governance. More significantly, Dodd-Frank provides several loopholes or escape clauses to bail out the financial industry as a whole and to reproduce the recent history of banking on the state. Contradictorily, forcing insolvency and bankruptcy, breaking up the too-big-to-fail institutions, ending taxpayer bailouts, and eliminating certain types of derivative practices are all conditional. None of these changes are a done deal. Consequently, the new law is not likely to do very much to hedge against or to reduce moral hazards, high-risk betting, or the next financially driven bubble in the economy. Finally, Dodd-Frank and most regulatory legislation is silent on the workings of the contradictions of bourgeois legal-justice, high-stakes securities fraud, and the super-financialization of capital at the turn of the twenty-first century.

In October 2011, President Obama gave a press conference on the importance of passing his subsequently defeated American Jobs Act of that year. During the Q & A, journalist Jake Tapper queried the president:

One of the reasons why so many of the people in the Occupy Wall Street protests are so angry is because, as you say, so many people on Wall Street did not follow the rules, but your administration hasn't really been very aggressive in prosecuting. In fact, I don't think any Wall Street executives have gone to jail despite the rampant corruption and malfeasance that did take place. So I was wondering if you would comment on that.[8]

President Obama:

> On the issue of prosecutions on Wall Street, one of the biggest problems about the collapse of Lehman's and the subsequent financial crisis and the subprime lending fiasco is that a lot of that stuff wasn't necessarily illegal, it was immoral or inappropriate or reckless. That's exactly why we needed to pass Dodd-Frank to prohibit some of these practices.
>
> The financial sector is very creative and they are always looking for ways to make money. And if there are loopholes and rules that can be bent and arbitrage to be had, they will take advantage of it. So without commenting on particular prosecutions—obviously that's not my job; that's the Attorney General's job—I think part of people's frustrations, part of my frustration, was a lot of practices that should not have been allowed weren't necessarily against the law, but they had a huge destructive impact. And that's why it was important for us to put in place financial rules that protect the American people from reckless decision-making and irresponsible behavior.[9]

Let's "deconstruct" the president's whitewashing rhetoric on the lack of criminal charges in the absence of what he failed to acknowledge about the factual realities of zero federal criminal prosecutions against the Wall Street banking elite:

- "a lot of that stuff wasn't necessarily illegal, it was immoral or inappropriate or reckless" and "that's exactly why we needed to pass Dodd-Frank"

As for needing new regulations, for example, to prohibit certain kinds of derivative practices, as Dodd-Frank will try to accomplish, the president was essentially correct. As for a lot of other "stuff" that the president preferred not to identify by name, such as full disclosure securities violations, fraudulent sales of real estate mortgage-backed securities, robo-signing loans, or filing false affidavits in foreclosure proceedings, these actions were unequivocally illegal both civilly and criminally. While these illegalities were not prosecuted by the U.S. Department of Justice, it is also true that these criminal behaviors were immoral, inappropriate, and reckless behavior.

- "if there are loopholes and rules that can be bent and arbitrage to be had, they will take advantage of it"

This is probably true of many, but certainly not all, or even most individual bankers. More importantly, the president's rhetoric of defending or justifying these activities as shrewd financial deal-making was a political deflection away from the institutionalized levels of securities fraud that were at work systemically leading up to the Wall Street collapse. Most Americans are aware of these crimes of capitalist control but not by my socially constructed phrase that also refers to criminal banking on the state. After all, as this inquiry and others on Wall Street looting all agree, there have been throughout the financial services industry no shortages of documented evidence of securities fraud. From the Financial Crisis Inquiry Commission to Senators Carl Levin (MI) and Tom Coburn (OK), to *ProPublica*, and to every other independent investigation of Wall Street, not to mention the numerous "prima facie" civil lawsuits that have triumphed over the nation's biggest banks.

These fraudulent offenses, however, were not about loopholes nor were they about bending the rules. As chapters 4–6 demonstrated, many of the legal settlements and litigated lawsuits were open-and-shut cases of securities fraud. Since the law already prohibited these behaviors, the passage of Dodd-Frank was not relevant to those legal cases and did nothing to shore up or amend those laws. The new law did not repeal or even overturn parts of the Gramm-Leach Bliley/Financial Services Modernization Act of 1999, nor reinstate portions of the 1933 Glass-Steagall Act that made "it a felony for anyone—banker, broker, dealer in securities, or savings institution—to engage in the deposit-taking and securities businesses at the same time."[10] In effect, the enactment in 1999 of the FSMA decriminalized the mixing of investment and commercial banking activities. In turn, this allowed for financial instruments, such as toxic residential mortgage-backed securities that facilitated the housing bubble, which shortly thereafter demanded the massive bailouts of a collapsed Wall Street. These catastrophic events occurred essentially because of the deregulation of the separation of commercial and investment banking.

- "without commenting on particular prosecutions—obviously that's not my job"

First, since the DOJ has not criminally prosecuted any of the biggest Wall Street investment banking firms, the president could not have commented on a particular criminal prosecution nor for that matter could his attorney general. Second, because the job had belonged to AG Holder for close to three years at the time, perhaps the president had not noticed that the Justice Department had not bothered to conduct any FBI investigations or criminal inquiries. Nor had the DOJ issued Wall Street any grand jury subpoenas, apparently ignoring all the "hot spots" where plenty of securities fraud evidence had accumulated.

- "it was important for us to put in place financial rules that protect the American people from reckless decision-making and irresponsible behavior"

While it was certainly the case that new rules were needed to protect both investors and non-investors from future victimization, once again all kinds of financial laws against securities fraud were already in place. Nevertheless, very creative financial traders understand what average Americans understand as well. Without application of those laws or any criminal prosecutions, those penal sanctions have little if any deterrent or enforcement value. Hence, the repeated failures by law enforcers and regulators alike to use these adversarial weapons against these habitual securities fraudsters have neutralized these potential punishments.

FREE MARKETS AND RE-REGULATION

In "Democratizing and Humanizing Finance" in the edited volume *Reforming U.S. Financial Markets*, economist Robert Shiller has argued that markets and regulation are inseparable. He has also emphasized that the "free market is one of the most important inventions in human history. It is indeed an invention, and the invention takes the form of regulation and standards enforced by some form of government."[11] For free markets to exist they have always needed to disconnect transactions from relationships and to formalize those into rules and regulations. This has also meant that "there has to be trust in rules, trust that others one hardly knows will uphold the rules."[12]

Financial regulation of banks and stocks can be traced back to the collapse of the tulip market in 1637 when the Dutch government shut down the speculative flower market. In 1720, the stock market crashes in both France and the United Kingdom were responsible for the establishment of "a new set of regulations to try to prevent a repetition of such an event."[13] These financial crashes also introduced the term "bubble" referring to the lack of substance or to trade irrationally based on nothing more than air. In the United States, as described in chapter 3, the stock market crash of 1929 led to the recognition of behavioral and systemic risks to the financial system. The Great Depression that followed also prompted massive increases in financial regulation. It is "not surprising that such regulation took place, for the Depression was a time when financial institutions were seen as failing on an international level, much as they are seen today."[14]

Historically, periods of regulatory innovation have occurred in waves that are followed by long periods of relative inattention. After World War II, a period of financial and economic stability over subsequent decades in the United States helped support an intellectual drift toward the belief in the natural well functioning of markets and to the eventual dismantling of many regulatory controls. For example, in *Capitalism and Freedom*, Friedman depicted most regulation as a ruse for special interests to secure their own benefits. Similarly, in their 1963 book, *A Monetary History of the United States*, Friedman and Anna Schwartz argued that the Federal Reserve's mismanagement of the money supply caused the Great Depression. By 1966, Friedman, who not too long before had been thought of as eccentric in his economic views, was elected president of the American Economic Association. Ten years later he was the recipient of the Nobel Memorial Prize in Economics.

Armed with his anti-Keynesian macroeconomic theory known as "monetarism," Friedman became the economic advisor to President Reagan. In the 1970s and 1980s deregulation was further aided and abetted by the popularity of "efficient markets theory" or the idea that financial markets work perfectly, in pooling information and in price discovery, without any need for human intervention.[15] Together, these still unproven theories serve as part of the foundational mantra for a conservative revolution in economics. Ultimately, they helped to spur on both privatization and an age of deregulation, which peaked with the passage of Gramm-Leach-Bliley in 1999. In turn, this deregulatory law enabled the housing bubble and bust (2000–2006) that still plagues the housing recovery and ongoing financial crisis in the United States.

Governmental regulation operates on a myriad of levels, both publicly and privately, and not only at the federal, but also at the state and local levels. During flattened or heightened periods of regulation, doing good government regulation means applying both "a theory of mind and a theory of finance as only skilled regulators" are capable of.[16] In the regulation of finance as well as in other areas of human activity, there are also "industry groups (sometimes designated SROs) which represent private interests of an industry group and set rules for their proper behavior. The government delegates authority to SROs because there is a sense that rules that serve a certain purpose are better made by people who understand that purpose."[17]

As an advocate of SROs and other trade organizations that he believes are essential to a functioning democracy, Shiller emphasizes an inclusive approach to regulation: "Any discussion of regulation should not really be centered on federal government interventions, but about finding new rules for an economy, rules that may be implemented at various governmental levels and that may also be adopted by the private sector without government intervention."[18] Shiller also contends, "Some of the most serious shortcomings of regulation lie in the rigidity and arbitrariness of laws and rules within which regulators must operate."[19] Thus, viable re-regulation of finance capital or other industries for that matter should take such issues as these into consideration.

As depicted in the previous chapter and elsewhere there are serious coordination and fragmentation problems across and between all the different regulators that make "it difficult for them to stop bad practices," especially as "the regulation of one sector" only puts "the others at a competitive advantage."[20] Mortgage-lending regulation leading up to the financial collapse certainly exemplified this problem. Once again, regulation of mortgage lenders has been traditionally divided up among the Federal Reserve, the Office of the Comptroller of the Currency, the Federal Deposit Insurance Corporation, the Office of Thrift Supervision, the National Credit Union Administration, and numerous state regulatory authorities. Unfortunately, Dodd-Frank did little in the way of dealing with this separation-of-powers problem as the law only consolidated one of these five regulators.

The lack of coordination between these agencies or the dispersion of mortgage regulation made it very difficult, for example, to address the bad lending practices that infected mortgage loans.[21] In short, there were no government regulators or SROs that could stop the proliferation of unsuitable mortgage loans. Similarly, there were no SROs in place to reduce real estate appraisal fraud that helped support the housing bubble. Perhaps more significantly, there were no effective regulators or SROs in place to stop the proliferation of collateralized mortgage obligations. Synergistically, this lack of regulation on multiple trading fronts accommodated the largest theft in U.S. history.

Other inadequacies of the existing regulatory framework include:

- The division of risk management regulation between the SEC and the CFTC.
- The division of insurance regulation across fifty state regulators.
- The division of insurance regulation from securities regulation.
- The division of systemically important failing firms between the FDIC and bankruptcy courts.

In response to the financial collapse and to the failures of the regulatory regime to adequately regulate Wall Street, former Treasury Secretary Henry Paulson and his colleagues called for objective-based regulation in their treatise on re-regulation, *Blueprint for a Modernized Financial Regulatory Structure*.[22] Among their recommended types of regulators were a systemic risk regulator, a prudential financial regulator, and a business conduct regulator. Similarly, in *Financial Regulatory Reform: A New Foundation*, President Obama and the Treasury Department proposed the creation of an agency whose charges would be to identify emerging systemic risks and improving interagency cooperation.[23]

As pointed out in chapter 7, Dodd-Frank did, indeed, charge the Federal Reserve with the authority to supervise non-bank firms that could pose a threat to financial stability. The 2010 law also established the Financial Services Oversight Council, chaired by the Treasury Secretary and composed of the heads of the different inter-regulatory agencies. Critics of Dodd-Frank such as Robert Pozen have argued that the law did not go far enough with the consolidation of regulatory agencies and with the appointment of one director whose only task would be to pursue unification between these agencies.[24]

Naturally, the efficacy of regulatory rules and re-regulation can only be as effective as its regulators are. Like other law enforcers, regulators require adequate resources to do their jobs. When it comes to the SEC and other regulatory agencies, they have been conveniently underfunded and understaffed by Congress for their many tasks. Regulators also require a certain degree of respect. Unfortunately, regulators not unlike the police of the past have been portrayed all too negatively. The reasons for these negative stereotypes are admittedly different. In the case of the regulators, they are often dismissed as mindless government bureaucrats who are not up to the job of taking on the brilliant quants of Wall Street. However, these popularly derogatory characterizations of regulators as well as those who foolishly advocate for doing away with most, if not all, regulations miss the whole point of regulation. Not having regulations or regulators would be

> like saying we shouldn't have a referee in a sporting event because the referees are inherently less capable at playing the game than the players are. In fact, referees are of fundamental importance to sporting events, for only when there are referees can the best players show their real talents. Referees, and a good set of rules, prevent the rough play and cheap moves that would actually compromise the abilities of the best players.[25]

Moreover, part of "good" regulation is

> seeing through the artifices and deliberate manipulations that some in the financial sector will promote. Professional regulators develop special expertise (just as sports regulators do) to detect shenanigans and assess ethical behavior, or to distinguish behavior that is in good faith from behavior which shows artifice. Just as a referee at a soccer match will recognize that certain players are deliberately hurting others, or deliberately feigning injuries, and attempt to temper his judgments to sensibly enforce a rule of law, so too must financial regulators use their judgment as to motives and artifices.[26]

On the other hand, Shiller's democratizing and humanizing model of finance reform like Dodd-Frank ignores the contradictions of bourgeois legality that places high-stakes securities fraud beyond incrimination.

POST-CRISIS FINANCIAL REFORM AND
VICTIM REDUCTION

The financial crisis that began with the housing-mortgage crisis in mid-year 2006 and still persists today has set in motion a regimen of regulatory reforms not seen since the Great Depression. Had the regulatory regime of the past engaged in better risk management, the current financial crisis may not have occurred in the first place. Had the financial collapse not occurred, then the uncomfortable sequence of bailouts and exceptional favors for the privileged U.S. banking oligopoly in order "to right the system" would not have occurred. Now consider the fact that Dodd-Frank all but ignores the speculative bubbles that caused the financial debacle. While authorizing studies on the subject, the act is silent about how the newly reformed agencies are to recognize these problems in the future. Moreover, while the new law has also introduced numerous legal reforms, these still represent only a starting place for a dialogue on how to move our financial system safely into the twenty-first century.

Not surprisingly, the Occupy Wall Street protestors were in agreement with the testimony of Treasury Secretary Timothy Geithner before the House Financial Services Committee when he claimed that the recent financial crises "have caused a great loss of confidence in the basic fabric of our financial system." OWS was also in agreement with Geithner when he called for comprehensive reform—not "modest repairs at the margin, but new rules of the game."[27] What seems to be missing so far from both the popular outrage and discussions, as well as from the massive regulatory reforms of Dodd-Frank, are an articulation of any overarching principles to guide the new rules of finance capital.

Regarding re-regulation, economist Shiller has offered two guiding principles. According to these principles, new regulations should serve to

1. Democratize finance by making the technology of finance work better for the *people*.
2. Humanize finance by making our financial institutions better able to respond to the way people actually *think and act* regarding financial institutions, so that they are really and effectively incentivized and to make it more natural for them to take proper actions to deal with risks.[28]

The materialization of these two ideas could indeed alter some of the contemporary relations of finance capitalism. At the same time, even if there were a political consensus around the governing principles of democratizing and humanizing financial capital, their implementation and enforcement would still be subject to the diversity of competing capitalist-regulatory interests and to the contradictions of bourgeois legal-justice.

More specifically, democratizing finance "means creating an environment where technology is applied effectively to kinds of risks that are not managed well today, risks that impinge on the welfare of individuals and their businesses."[29] Of course, while it is people that matter to our economy, to date, regulation has not "really focused as much as it should on making changes to enable the full power of financial theory to work for everyone."[30] In other words, there needs to be the creative extension of the capitalist principles of risk management for average people. Similarly, humanizing finance "means taking account of the actual incentives that are created by financial institutions, something that economists are already wont to do, but also taking account of them in a deeper way that is cognizant of human psychology and of those behavior patterns that lead some people to get themselves into trouble, and that at other times lie behind speculative bubbles."[31] More fundamentally, regulating financial institutions have to come to terms with "the reality of human nature, taking account of how people are motivated and steering around human foibles."[32] Finally, this means applying "the various branches of cognitive science into a plan for improved human-factors financial engineering."[33]

Had these two guiding principles been in place, Schiller contends that the current financial crisis would have been less likely to have occurred. Surely, there would have been a lot less than 28 percent of the mortgages in this country that are underwater, not to mention fewer than some fifteen million mortgage delinquencies and foreclosures.[34] For example, had democratized practices of finance capital been operating, hundreds of thousands of relatively low income, African American, Hispanic, and less sophisticated homebuyers would not have been "taken to the cleaners" by unscrupulous mortgage lenders who were only doing what their fellow incentivized mortgage writers were doing. Even "middle" income persons might have availed themselves of strategies that would have helped them hedge their own real estate risks. Instead, they were "advised to take out high, and increasingly, leveraged positions in local real estate, even if the amount invested was their entire life savings."[35] Many of these homebuyers, some two million, were totally wiped out financially.

At the same time, those businesses that dealt with these individual clients regarding their real estate risks were not "incentivized properly to help them do better" nor did they "offer tools to enable them."[36] In addition, had the relations of finance capital been humanized or had they taken human nature into account, monetary authorities would have taken action against the unrestrained bubbles that were "operating through various feedbacks including psychological contagion" and that "took place in stock markets and housing markets around the world."[37] Likewise, regulators would have also been "organized to resist the complacency encouraged by the bubbles regarding counterparty risk and systemic risks."[38]

Though modern financial theory provides technology for the advancement of human welfare that can reduce risks and incentivize constructive work that will not be diminished by moral hazard, research in behavioral finance has shown how difficult it is "to develop a system that does a semblance of adoption of these basic finance principles."[39] As challenging as the transition to these guiding principles has and will be, there has been an evolving, but not a linear, history of doing precisely this. In fact, there are elements within Dodd-Frank that actually advance the cause of democratizing and humanizing finance.

In the not so distant past, the role of government intervention into financial innovation on the behalf of average people had been relatively active. For example, before 1980 the defined contribution pension fund (or the 401K plans of the IRS Code) did not exist. Similarly, in 1960 Congress invented the Real Estate Investment Trust (REIT) that allowed small investors to participate in commercial real estate. The mutual fund industry was created when Congress by way of the Investment Company Act of 1940 and by way of new regulatory interpretations of the law combined to establish the original 401K. These were all steps in the democratization of finance capital as they helped more people to own diversified portfolios of riskier assets with higher returns, thereby helping average people hedge their investments. By 2011, the government-sponsored mutual funds, for example, were owned by nearly half of American households, either directly or as part of their defined contribution pension plan, to the tune of $7.89 trillion at its peak in the third quarter of 2007 before the market crash.[40]

In terms of Dodd-Frank, the enactment of the Bureau of Consumer Financial Protection is a step in the right direction. It has the authority to collect information about financial practices. It also has the power to enact new rules to protect individuals against bad practices in credit cards, home mortgages, account overdrafts, payday loans, and other financial products. These rule changes should help focus the attention of financial regulators to include the problems of common consumers/investors. These changes would also facilitate the implementation of objectives-based financial regulation. At least this is the way Elizabeth Warren envisioned her proposed Financial Products Safety Commission, upon which the BCFP has been modeled. Another agency to protect consumers from financial abuse not unlike the successful Consumer Products Safety Commission to protect consumers from product abuse.[41]

On the other hand, there are other rules in place that need to be changed in the spirit of democratizing and humanizing finance capital. The government already mandates extensive disclosure, and one could argue that government policies have endorsed disclosure as central to regulatory processes. However, much of those unread disclosures by investors who rely on word of mouth, news media, and investment advisors for information effectively make it harder for investors to sue issuers of credit. As Warren has emphasized, these lengthy contracts are full of legalese designed to skirt consumer protection laws and class-action lawsuits. The same has been true for some of the tort lawsuits involving securities fraud as chapter 6 disclosed. Hopefully, re-regulation will deal with these needed reforms. There are also other innovations to help democratize finance and to reduce the human costs of financial victimization. These include proposals to extend unemployment insurance, to provide livelihood insurance against the vicissitudes of earning a living, and to develop infrastructure to "facilitate these activities, such as the creation of a new system of economic units of measurement."[42]

Beyond these financial steps, the government should have a broader role in promoting the better management of individual-specific risks and the reduction of victimization and suffering in society overall. For example, Obama's Patient Protection and Affordable Care Act of 2010 was a positive exercise in basic risk management reducing costs as it expands the number of Americans covered by health care by an additional forty-five million people. The law "creates new National Health Exchanges, creating new avenues for competition in providing low-cost health care, and limits insurance companies' latitude to charge higher premia for preexisting conditions, thereby making for more fundamental risk management."[43]

However, Republican and Democratic proposals to shrink Medicare represent a negative exercise in the world of health management and cost containment. Aside from leaving more people uncovered, shrinking coverage means shrinking the government's power to dictate the price. It also leaves employers and the rest of us exposed to higher health care costs subject to the dictates of the insurance industry standing between our doctors and us. To paraphrase labor lawyer and writer Thomas Geoghegan: "If the president [and the Congress] wanted to increase the trade deficit, the best thing [they] could do would be to cut Medicare coverage and give the government even less power to hold down the healthcare costs that make us even less competitive abroad than we are now."[44]

The positive course in health risk management would be to copy what other developed nations have done to keep health care affordable for all their citizens—provide a universal system of coverage, whether private or public. As Geoghegan contends, "If our government could deliver just one Keynesian 'shock' to make us more competitive, it would be single payer national health-care. At least right now, we should expand Medicare (lower the eligibility age) and adopt a public option, so that government can have more bargaining leverage to beat down by degree the stupefying prices we pay to get well in an ever more concentrated healthcare sector."[45]

A FANTASY BAILOUT FOR THE AMERICAN PEOPLE

In terms of the larger structural contradictions of finance capital, regulatory questions remain about the possibility or inevitability of either breaking up or nationalizing the banking oligopoly in America as an alternative to high-stakes, high-risk finance capitalism. In the spirit of democratizing finance and achieving a fairer America, I end this inquiry into Wall Street looting by trying to imagine what a redistribution of the bailouts on behalf of the citizens of Main Street might look like. I do so through the imaginary creation of a National Tribunal for Reparations for the Crimes of Securities Fraud Com-mitted against the American People.

These tribunal-like reparative actions are oriented primarily toward alleviat-ing the pain of those Americans who came up financially short, lost their home or job, or were otherwise victimized by the Wall Street–invoked housing and fi-nancial crises. The objective is not to criminally punish the perpetrators of these illegalities. Rather, by providing reparations for the victims of Wall Street, bankers attempt to remedy or compensate for the imposed damages/harms/in-juries. In the spirit and mode of a restorative justice that strives to make victims and investors whole again, this tribunal is not unlike those conciliatory efforts to reconstruct better future scenarios, and to encourage the participation by as many collective stakeholders, victims, and perpetrators as possible.

During this "people's tribunal," those large financial firms that were the benefactors of the bailouts have pleaded guilty to the "crimes of capitalist control." Or, more specifically in the case of the Wall Street collapse of 2008, to an epidemic of securities, mortgage, and other fraudulent practices. None of these fraudsters throughout the financial services industries will be imprisoned for their past crimes leading up to the financial collapse nor will their corporate charters expire unless they revert back to their "old" ways of high-finance fraud. Accordingly, these culpable fraudsters have all signed anti-securities-fraud agreements that in the event of the next illegal transac-tion or fraudulent case successfully brought against them or their corporation that the firm will be broken up and its charter permanently dissolved.

For openers, Wall Street has agreed to a financial transactions tax, to the abolishment of the carried-interest tax loophole, and to an end to the Bush tax cuts for those making over $250,000 a year. In addition, those working in the securities industries on Wall Street have agreed to cap their salaries to 3 times rather than the present 5.5 times the average private-sector salaries in New York. The savings in these salaries will go into a special bank to assist victims of the financial crisis. The CEOs of the large Wall Street firms have also agreed that their salary and bonuses can never exceed more than 20 percent of the total sum paid in their firm's federal corporate taxes. Furthermore, the billions of dollars in bonuses that were originally distributed to those institutions that had looted themselves into insolvency will be turned over to the special bank. At the same time, Wall Street has agreed to a "debt forgiveness" program for millions of Americans who are facing foreclosures and a "housing refinancing" program for millions more whose homes are worth less than they owe. For these homeowners, lenders have agreed to write down the principal people owe on their mortgages to match the current market value of their homes so that they are no longer underwater.

Recall the rationale for bailing out those too big to fail or jail; namely, rescuing bankers first was necessary because the economy could not recover until after the financial system was healed. The same rationale or logic applies to failing homeowners. To put it simply, a heavy blanket of bad debt is suffocating economic activity. Until this debt "is lifted from the housing market and the financial sheets, the economy is unlikely to regain its normal energies. So debt forgiveness is not just a moral imperative; it's also an economic necessity."[46]

The benefits from these debt forgiveness reparations are straightforward. By lending institutions refinancing loans with reduced interest rates that struggling homeowners can afford, families will be able to stay in their homes. These otherwise defaulting homeowners are now able to make their monthly payments and to build equity in their real estate. In the process, the public commons benefit from owner-occupied properties rather than boarded-up homes inviting vandalism and crime that lower neighborhood property values. As the surplus of foreclosed homes are reduced and eventually disappear, property values everywhere will start to rise in value as demand once again grows.

Lastly, in the spirit of restoring America's middle class, a couple of significant pieces of legislation have been agreed to by the U.S. Congress. First, the Comprehensive Infrastructure–Human Development Fund and American Jobs Act of 2012, which will appropriate $1 trillion over the next ten years. Second, the Forgive Student Loan Debt Act of 2012, which would have an immediate stimulus effect as millions of Americans would suddenly have hundreds of extra dollars in their pockets each and every month with which to invest or spend.[47] With a refurbished infrastructure, millions of re-employed workers, and with debt-free students, the ailing sectors of the economy would be revived, creating a new era of innovation and prosperity for all.

Postscript

Given the historical record of not punishing high-stakes financial fraud for its periodic devastating consequences to our and other economies, and given the nature of the most recent financial meltdown—a product of both the de-regulation of the securities industry and the merging of investment and commercial banks—many sensible persons call for criminal punishment as some kind of deterrent to Wall Street looting and/or they call for a new regulatory regime capable of reining in the wayward wizards of Wall Street. Even if both of these realities would materialize—an impossibility without changing the present political and economic arrangements in the United States—it is still highly unlikely that the megabanks or any large corporations, for that matter, will ever abandon their capitalist mantra of "grow or die."

Just as antitrust laws have failed miserably to stop corporate monopolies from controlling markets, better regulatory laws will not effectively manage the vagaries of the enforcement of high-stakes securities markets and/or securities fraud. Without fundamental changes in the relations between finance capital and government intervention, the very same rationales—too big to fail or jail—would be used to excuse these financial institutions the next time. This is not only the case because the concentration of financial power of the megabanks has grown since the Wall Street meltdown of 2007–8, but also because even with Dodd-Frank, the mega investment banks are being allowed by the Federal Reserve, the FDIC, and the Treasury Department's Office of the Comptroller of the Currency to transfer their high-risk derivatives to FDIC-insured status, which when established during the New Deal was designed to protect the savings of small depositors from panicky bank runs. Presently, however, thanks to federal regulatory collusion this status has been corrupted for the purposes of helping to protect/insure the balance sheets of Wall Street financial institutions.

The reasonable alternatives to this financial dilemma call for structural changes in the securities markets, including the breakup of the too big to fail institutions—as supported by Alan Greenspan and Lawrence Summers—and/or the public ownership of these institutions—as supported by Gar Alerpovitz and Lawrence E. Mitchell.

In the case of publicly owned banks, since 2010 seventeen states have explored and/or introduced legislation to establish state-owned banks like the one in North Dakota, including: Arizona, California, Connecticut, Hawaii, Idaho, Illinois, Louisiana, Maine, Maryland, Massachusetts, Montana, New Hampshire, New Mexico, New York, Oregon, Virginia, and Washington. If these efforts to create social ownership of banking are successful, then the United States would not only find itself in the company of the world's biggest public bank (Japan Post Bank) and more than two hundred public and semi-public banks (plus another eighty-one funding agencies), which account for one-fifth of all banking assets in the European Union, but also, more important, the United States would be on the path to confronting, if not overcoming, a banking oligopoly that has been all too consumed with enriching itself while depressing the American economy as a whole.

Notes

ACKNOWLEDGMENTS

1. Hyman Gross, *A Theory of Criminal Justice* (Oxford, UK: Oxford University Press, 1979), 382.

2. Wayne Morrison, "What Is Crime? Contrasting Definitions and Perspectives," in *Criminology*, edited by C. Hale, K. Hayward, A. Wahidin, and E. Wincup (Oxford, UK: Oxford University Press, 2005), 12.

3. Louk Hulsman, "Critical Criminology and the Concept of Crime," *Contemporary Crisis* 10 (1986): 64.

4. Simon Hallsworth, "Street Crime: Interpretation and Legacy in Policing the Crisis," *Crime, Media, and Culture* 4 (2008): 1.

INTRODUCTION

1. Gary Fields and John Emshwiller, "As Criminal Laws Proliferate, More Ensnared," *Wall Street Journal*, July 23–24, 2011, A10.

2. Fields and Emshwiller, "As Criminal Laws Proliferate."

3. As chapter 5 will discuss, law varies inversely with stratification, meaning that it is always easy to prosecute and criminally convict a powerless person and always difficult to prosecute and secure a penal punishment beyond compensation for a powerful person. See Donald Black, *The Behavior of Law*, Special Edition (Bingley, UK: Emerald, 2010 [1976]).

4. Henry Pontell, *A Capacity to Punish: The Ecology of Crime and Punishment* (Bloomington: Indiana University Press, 1984).

5. Securities are negotiable financial instruments that represent financial value, such as bonds, stocks, options, or swaps. Securities fraud is a "serious white-collar crime in which a person or company, such as a stockbroker, brokerage firm, corporation

or investment bank, misrepresents information that investors use to make decisions." Specifically, the "types of misrepresentation involved in this crime include providing false information, withholding key information, offering bad advice, and offering or acting on inside information." Usually investigated by the Securities and Exchange Commission (SEC) and the National Association of Securities Dealers (NASD), these crimes "can carry both criminal and civil penalties, resulting in imprisonment and fines." "Securities Fraud," Investopedia, accessed August 13, 2010, http://www.investopedia.com/terms/s/securities-fraud.asp. These cases may also be criminally prosecuted by U.S. attorneys representing the DOJ or by local and state criminal prosecutors representing the people of individual states.

6. For example, *Morrison v. National Australia Bank Ltd* [561 U.S.____ (2010), 130 S. Ct. 2869 (2010)] denied foreign defendants the right to sue executives for fraudulent activities and violation of Rule 10(b)(5) of the Security and Exchange Act of 1934.

7. Mark Kennedy, "Beyond Incrimination: Some Neglected Aspects of the Theory of Punishment, *Catalyst* 5 (Summer 1970): 1–30.

8. "Federal Prosecutions of Financial Frauds Falls to 20-Year Low, New Report Shows," *Huffington Post*, November 15, 2011. Shanny Basar, "SEC Enforcement Cases Hit Record Levels," *Financial News*, November 10, 2011.

9. For example, during a CBS *60 Minutes* interview in 2009, President Obama criticized "fat cat bankers" who had received bailout money and then lobbied against Wall Street. In November of the same year, Obama signed an executive order establishing a specialized financial crime unit—the Financial Fraud Enforcement Network (FFEN)—within the DOJ whose raison d'être was to hold accountable those who helped bring about the devastating financial crisis of 2008–9 and to prevent future financial crises. However, the end of 2010 could hear Obama publicly defending the bonuses handed out to the same Wall Street bankers. By the beginning of 2012, the specialized financial crime unit had not prosecuted a single case against anyone working for one of the six largest banks in America. Obama played the same déjà vu rhetorical card of getting tough on Wall Street during his 2012 State of the Union address: "It was wrong. It was irresponsible. And it plunged our economy into a crisis that put millions out of work, saddled us with more debt, and left innocent, hard-working Americans holding the bag." Without bringing up the irrelevance of his previously created FFEN in the war against financial crime, Obama informed the American people that he was establishing a Financial Crimes Unit within the DOJ "to crack down on large-scale fraud," "to protect people's investments," and "to expand our investigations into the abusive lending and packaging of risky mortgages that led to the housing crisis." The president went on to say that this "new unit will hold accountable those who broke the law, speed assistance to homeowners, and help turn the page on an era of recklessness that hurt so many Americans." All quotes are from Zach Carter and Loren Berlin, "State of the Union: President Obama's Financial Fraud Team Tied to Banks," *Huffington Post*, January 25, 2012, http://www.huffingtonpost.com/2012/01/24/state-of-the-union-obama-financial-bank-fraud_n_1229798.html.

10. Bertell Ollman, *Alienation: Marx's Conception of Man in Capitalist Society*, 2nd ed. (New York: Cambridge University Press, 1976).

11. Max Weber, *The Protestant Ethic and the Spirit of Capitalism* (London: Allen and Unwin, 1976 [1904]).

12. Adam Davidson, "It's Not Technically an Oligopoly," *New York Times Magazine*, December 11, 2011, 16–18.

13. William Cohan, "How Wall Street Turned a Crisis into a Cartel," *Bloomberg*, January 8, 2012, http://www.bloomberg.com/news/2012-01-09/cohan-how-wall -street-turned-a-crisis-into-a-cartel.html.

14. Cohan, "How Wall Street Turned a Crisis into a Cartel."

15. Quoted in Cohan, "How Wall Street Turned a Crisis into a Cartel."

16. Cohan, "How Wall Street Turned a Crisis into a Cartel."

17. Barry Ritholtz, "The Big Picture," December 25, 2011, http://www.ritholtz .com/blog/2011/12/the-banking-oligopoly.

18. Critique of Law Editorial Collective, *Critique of Law: A Marxist Analysis* (Kensington, Australia: UNSW Critique of Law Society, 1978), 18.

19. William Chambliss, "On Lawmaking," *British Journal of Law and Society* 6, no. 2 (1979): 149–71. See also, William Chambliss and Marjorie Zatz, eds., *The State, The Law, and Structural Contradictions* (Bloomington: Indiana University Press, 1993).

20. Raymond J. Michalowski, *Order, Law, and Crime: An Introduction to Criminology* (New York: Random House, 1985), 318.

CHAPTER 1:
LAW, POWER, AND WEALTH

1. Attorney General John Ashcroft, "Enforcing the Law, Restoring Trust, Defending Freedom," *United States Attorney's Bulletin*, May 2003, 4.

2. Francis Cullen, Gray Cavender, William Maakestad, and Michael Benson, *Corporate Crime Under Attack: The Fight to Criminalize Business Violence*, 2nd ed. (Cincinnati, OH: Anderson Publishing, 2006), 323.

3. William Jackson, *Glass-Steagall Act: Commercial vs. Investment Banking* (Economics Division, Congressional Research Service, 1987), 3.

4. A derivative instrument is a financial contract between parties that specifies the conditions and terms under which payments, or payoffs, are to be made between parties. "Under US law and the laws of most other developed countries, derivatives have special legal exemptions that make them a particularly attractive legal form through which to extend credit. However, the strong creditor protections afforded to derivatives counterparties, in combination with their complexity and lack of transparency, can cause capital markets to underprice credit risk. This can contribute to credit booms, and increase systemic risks." For example, the use of derivatives to mask credit risk from third parties while protecting counterparties has contributed to several financial crises, including one in 2008 in the United States (quoted from "Derivative [finance]," Wikipedia, http://en.wikipedia.org/wiki/Derivative_%28finance%29).

5. Lynn Turner, "The Systematic Dismantling of the System," *CPA Journal* May (2009): 16–17.

6. Daphne Eviatar, "What's Behind the Drop in Corporate Fraud Indictments?" *Corporate Counsel*. November 1, 2007, http://www.law.com/jsp/cc/PubArticleCC .jsp?id=1193821429242.

7. Quoted in Eviatar, "What's Behind the Drop in Corporate Fraud Indictments?"

8. Quoted in Eviatar, "What's Behind the Drop in Corporate Fraud Indictments?"

9. Eviatar, "What's Behind the Drop in Corporate Fraud Indictments?"

10. Eviatar, "What's Behind the Drop in Corporate Fraud Indictments?"

11. John Hueston quoted in Eviatar, "What's Behind the Drop in Corporate Fraud Indictments?"

12. Quoted in Eviatar, "What's Behind the Drop in Corporate Fraud Indictments?"

13. Pub. L. No. 111-121, 123 Stat. 1617 (2009).

14. Deputy Attorney General, *Memorandum for the Attorney General*, November 13, 2009.

15. Deputy Attorney General, *Memorandum for the Attorney General*.

16. Quoted in Joe Palazzolo, "DOJ Unveils Financial Crime Task Force," November 17, 2009, http://www.mainjustice.com/2009/11/17doj-to-unveil-financial-on.

17. Palazzolo, "DOJ Unveils Financial Crime Task Force."

18. OSD was the brainchild of the Financial Fraud Enforcement Task Force's Mortgage Fraud Working Group to target fraudsters across the nation.

19. California RealEstateRama, "U.S. Attorney Announces Results of Mortgage Fraud Prosecutions in 12 Months Since Operation Stolen Dreams," 2011, http://california.realestaterama.com.

20. California RealEstateRama, "U.S. Attorney Announces Results of Mortgage Fraud Prosecutions."

21. Quoted in California RealEstateRama, "U.S. Attorney Announces Results of Mortgage Fraud Prosecutions."

22. Quoted in California RealEstateRama, "U.S. Attorney Announces Results of Mortgage Fraud Prosecutions."

23. William Black, "Why Greenspan's & Bush's Regulatory Failure Allowed a 'Criminogenic Environment.'" Paper presented at the Levy Institute's Minsky Conference, Annandale-on-the Hudson, NY, June 28, 2008.

24. Matt Stoller, "Lanny Breuer, Task Force Leader, Doesn't Bother Showing Up for Mortgage Fraud Press Conference," Guest Blog at *Naked Capitalism*. January 27, 2012, http://www.nakedcapitalism.com/2012/01/lanny-breuer-task-force-leader -doesnt-bother-showing-up-for-mortgage-fraud-press-conference.html.

25. Stoller, "Lanny Breuer, Task Force Leader."

26. Peter Goldmann, *Fraud in the Markets: Why It Happens and How to Fight It* (Hoboken, NJ: John Wiley & Sons, 2010).

27. Edward Kaplan, *The Bank of the United States and the American Economy* (Santa Barbara, CA: Greenwood Publishing Group, 1999), 3.

28. Kaplan, *The Bank of the United States*, xx.

29. Kaplan, *The Bank of the United States*, xx–xi.

30. "Say Money Trust Is Now Exposed," *New York Times*, January 12, 1913, http://query.nytimes.com/mem/archive-free/pdf?_r=2&res=9F00E2DB163FE633A2 5751C1A9679C946296D6CF.

31. Goldmann, *Fraud in the Markets*, xv.

32. Goldmann, *Fraud in the Markets*, xxvi.

33. Association of Certified Fraud Examiners (ACFE), *2008 Report to the Nation on Occupational Fraud and Abuse*, 8, http://www.acfe.com/uploadedFiles/ACFE_Website/Content/documents/2008-rttn.pdf.

34. Cited in Goldmann, *Fraud in the Markets*, 6.

35. Henry Pontell, "White-collar Crime or Just Risky Business? The Role of Fraud in Major Financial Debacles," *Crime, Law, and Social Change* 42 (2004): 310. In this and a companion article by Pontell, "Control Fraud, Gaming for Resurrection, and Moral Hazard: Accounting for White-Collar Crime in the Savings and Loan Crisis," *Journal of Socio-Economics* 34 (2005): 756–70, the author uses actual data to demystify the rhetorically based "minimal fraud model" exemplified by legal economists Frank Easterbrook and Daniel Fischel in their 1991 classic text, *The Economic Structure of Corporate Law* (Cambridge, MA: Harvard University Press, 1991).

36. "Moral hazard" refers to the behavior of parties who would act differently if they were fully exposed to or not insulated from the risks involved. In terms of rational economic theory, "gambling for resurrection" refers to those parties who when faced with extreme moral hazard are seen as desperately gambling in futile attempts to save their institutions.

37. "Wall Street and the Financial Crisis: Anatomy of a Financial Collapse," *U.S. Senate Permanent Subcommittee Investigative Report* (Washington, DC, 2011), 4–14.

38. National Commission of Financial Institutional Reform, Recovery and Enforcement (NCFIRRE), *Origins and Causes of the S&L Debacle: A Blueprint for Reform. A Report to the President and Congress of the United States* (Washington, DC: Government Printing Office, 1993).

39. In chapters 2 and 3 where appropriate these reports and their relevant findings and interpretations will be discussed.

40. A CMO is a type of mortgage-backed security that is supported by a wide pool of mortgage loans that allegedly lower the risks against default.

CHAPTER 2:
BERNIE MADOFF'S PONZI SCHEME AND
WALL STREET'S FINANCIAL MELTDOWN

1. *New York Times*, "Bernard L. Madoff," updated May 25, 2010, http://topics.nytimes.com/top/reference/timestopics/people/m/bernard_l_madoff/index.html.

2. Probably the closest thing to an autobiographical account comes from senior financial writer for the *New York Times*, Diana Henriques. Her book, *The Wizard of Lies: Bernie Madoff and the Death of Trust* (New York: Times Books/Henry Hold & Company, 2011) provides the simplest explanation: Sometime in the early 1990s or late 1980s after losing a lot of money on his investments, rather than coming clean to his clients, he fudged the numbers, hoping to recoup the losses later and get back on track. Instead, he ended up digging himself deeper and deeper into debt. After a while,

he stopped investing in the market altogether, relying on new investors' monies to pay out fictitious returns or profits to old investors.

3. Quoted in Diana Henriques, "From Prison, Madoff Say Banks 'Had to Know' of Fraud," *New York Times*, February 15, 2011, http://www.nytimes.com/2011/02/16/business/madoff-prison-interview.html?pagewanted=all.

4. In June 2011, a second-generation employee of Madoff's, thirty-seven-year-old Eric S. Lipkin, became the third person in addition to Madoff to plea guilty. He pleaded guilty to bank fraud, conspiracy, and falsifying financial records as part of an agreement in which he agreed to cooperate with prosecutors. "Lipkin also agreed to surrender any property related to the fraud, including his Ridgewood, N.J., home and accounts held in the names of his wife and children. He also will pay a $1.4 million judgment. U.S. District Judge Laura Taylor Swain permitted him to remain free on $2.5 million bail, secured by $800,000 in cash or property," until December 15, 2011, when sentencing was scheduled. "The charges carry a potential penalty of 70 years in prison and $7 million in fines, though cooperation was likely to earn Lipkin a substantial reduction." Associated Press, "Member of Madoff's 'Inner Circle' Pleads Guilty to Fraud, Conspiracy," OregonLive.com, June 6, 2011, http://www.oregonlive.com/business/index.ssf/2011/06/member_of_madoffs_inner_circle.html.

5. Henk van de Bunt, "Walls of Secrecy and Silence: The Madoff Case and Cartels in the Construction Industry," *Criminology & Public Policy* 9, no. 3 (2010): 591–612.

6. Harry Markopolos, *No One Would Listen: A True Financial Thriller* (Hoboken, NJ: Wiley, 2010).

7. Nancy Reichman, "Getting Our Attention," *Criminology & Public Policy* 9, no. 3 (2010): 483–96. Quote from page 485.

8. Those relevant legal issues at the heart of the matter will be examined in some detail in chapters 5 and 6.

9. A derivative "product" is not the easiest idea to grasp. Here are a couple of different but overlapping ways to think about derivatives: "a financial instrument whose value is derived from the price of another financial asset. Derivatives are contracts that can refer to a vast array of financial products, from standard equity options such as puts or calls to much more complex instruments such as credit default swaps, which are linked to the value of an underlying debt instrument. Derivatives are typically used for hedging or speculative purposes. Derivatives are contracts, not securities, and are not regulated as such by the SEC." Charles Gasparino, *The Sellout: How Three Decades of Wall Street Greed and Government Mismanagement Destroyed the Global Financial System* (New York: Harper Business, 2009), 502. "A type of financial instrument whose value is derived from something else," usually a stock, bond, or other asset, for example, "a stock index is a derivative based on a group of underlying stocks. When you buy an index, you are not buying the stocks that make up that index. Yet your index security goes up and down based on the value of the stocks it tracks." This contrasts, for example, with a mutual fund where you actually own a piece of a pool of real stocks and bonds. "Think of fantasy baseball. It's a derivative game of betting based on statistics based on the behavior of real major league players. You don't own the real players, or even a piece of them as in a mutual fund. When you own a fantasy baseball team, you don't really own anything except your derivative

statistics compiled for you by a service. Yet your bet has value because other players and their derivative teams are willing to bet with you. There can be tens of thousands of fantasy baseball leagues based on only the two major leagues. Similarly, there are tens of thousands of derivative securities based on combinations of the same underlying real securities." Les Leopold, *The Looting of America: How Wall Street's Game of Fantasy Finance Destroyed Our Jobs, Pensions, and Prosperity (and What We Can Do About It)* (White River Junction, VT: Chelsea Green Publishing, 2009), 193–94.

10. John K. Galbraith, *The Great Crash, 1929* (New York: Pelican, 1961). Leverage is the use of financial instruments or borrowed capital to increase the size and potential of returns on an investment, most commonly used in real estate transactions.

11. Mark Seal and Eleanor Squillari, "'Hello, Madoff!'—What the Secretary Saw," *Vanity Fair*, June 2009, http://www.vanityfair.com/politics/features/2009/06/madoff200906.

12. At the court proceeding where Madoff pleaded guilty. Quoted in Robert Frank and Amir Efrati, "Madoff Plays Fate Like His Fraud," *Wall Street Journal*, June 27–28, 2009, B1, B3.

13. Quoted in Robert Frank and Amir Efrati, "'Evil' Madoff Gets 150 Years in Epic Fraud," *Wall Street Journal*, June 30, 2009, Front Page, A12.

14. Quoted in Peter Lattman and Annelena Lobb, "Victims' Speeches in Court Influenced Judge's Ruling," *Wall Street Journal*, June 30, 2009, A12.

15. Lattman and Lobb, "Victims' Speeches in Court Influenced Judge's Ruling."

16. Hon. Donald E. Shelton has been a felony trial judge in Michigan since 1990. Personal e-mail to author, August 21, 2010.

17. Quoted in Lattman and Lobb, "Victims' Speeches in Court Influenced Judge's Ruling," A12.

18. Frank and Efrati, "'Evil' Madoff Gets 150 Years."

19. David Kauzlarich, "Victimisation and Supranational Criminology," in *Supranational Criminology: Towards a Criminology of International Crimes*, eds. A. Smeulers and R. Haveman (Antwerp: Intersentia, 2008).

20. Andrew Karmen, *Crime Victims: An Introduction to Victimology* (Belmont, CA: Wadsworth Cengage Learning, 2010), 4.

21. There is an old saying, "If it sounds too good to be true, it probably is." As far back as the 1970s in an interview that appeared in the *Wall Street News*, Madoff had discussed how he had invested funds in convertible arbitrage positions in large-cap stocks, with promised investment returns of 18 percent to 20 percent. Typical Ponzi schemes usually offer returns of 20 percent on an investment and usually collapse within several months. Madoff never paid near that; however, he always paid to his exclusive customers far more than the competition. For example, one of his funds that focused on shares in the Standard & Poor's 100-stock index reported 10.5 percent for seventeen straight years (which should have sent up a red flag to anybody who knows anything about high-stakes investments). Moreover, in November 2008, the same fund reported it was up 5.6 percent while at the time the total return to the S&P 500 was down 38 percent. The "bottom line" being that wealthy investors and savvy wealth management folks like de la Villehuchet should have known that neither Madoff's explanations for high returns nor his investments were kosher.

22. Karmen, *Crime Victims*, 4–5.

23. Jane Kim, "Hunt Goes on for Missing Madoff Money," *Wall Street Journal*, June 29, 2009, CI.

24. Kim, "Hunt Goes on for Missing Madoff Money."

25. Amir Efrati, "Madoff Trustee Seeks $7.2 Billion from Florida Investor," *Wall Street Journal*, October 1, 2009, WSJ.com.

26. Raphael Minder and Diana B. Henriques, "Overseas Madoff Investors Settle with Banks," May 24, 2010, http://www.nytimes.com/2010/05/25/business /global/25madoff.html?_r=1&dbk.

27. Jim Ottewill, "Bernie Madoff Trustee to File Suits against Victims, Newspaper Report States," May 24, 2010, BobsGuide.com, http://www.bobsguide.com/guide/ news/2010/Jul/27/bernie-madoff-trustee-to-file-suits-against-victims-newspaper -report-states.html.

28. Michael Rothfeld and Tom Herman, "Trustee Aims to Begin Payouts," *Wall Street Journal*, May 5, 2011, C3.

29. Rothfeld and Herman, "Trustee Aims to Begin Payouts."

30. Michael Rothfeld, "Madoff Claims Lure Banks," *Wall Street Journal*, June 17, 2011, A1.

31. Tomson H. Nguyen and Henry N. Pontell, "Mortgage Origination Fraud and the Global Economic Crisis: A Criminological Analysis," *Criminology & Public Policy* 9 no. 3 (2010): 591–612.

32. Greg Hunter, "The Perfect No-Prosecution Crime," *USAWatchdog*, October 25, 2010, http://usawatchdog.com/the-perfect-no-prosecution-crime.

33. Greg Hunter, "The Six Trillion Dollar Problem," *USAWatchdog*, October 27, 2010, http://usawatchdog.com/mortgage-crisis-the-six-trillion-dollar-problem.

34. A collateralized mortgage obligation is a mortgage-backed security that "creates separate pools of pass-through rates for different classes of bondholders with varying maturities, called tranches. The repayment from the pool of pass-through securities are used to retire the bonds in the order specified by the bonds' prospectus." "Collateralized Mortgage Obligation," Investopedia, retrieved from http://www .investopedia.com/terms/c/cmo.asp#axzz1kwpZjF5W.

35. U.S. Senate, *Wall Street and the Financial Crisis: Anatomy of a Financial Collapse*, April 13, 2011. The ratings by Moody's and S&P's will be discussed in detail in Chapter 3.

36. Stephen Pizzo, Mary Fricker, and Paul Muolo, *Inside Job: The Looting of America's Savings & Loans* (New York: Harper Perennial, 1991).

37. Matt Taibbi, "The Great American Bubble Machine," *Rolling Stone*. Originally published July 2009, the article was reposted April 5, 2010, and retrieved on August 12, 2010, from http://www.rollingstone.com/plitics/news/12697/64796.

38. A credit default swap is a type of swap (e.g., the exchange of one security for another security to change the nature of the investment) that is designed to transfer the exposure of fixed income products between parties to a contract. The buyer of the credit swap receives credit protection; the seller of the swap guarantees the credit worthiness of the product. "Credit Default Swap," Investopedia, http://www.investo pedia.com/terms/c/creditdefaultswap.asp#axzz1kwpZjF5W.

39. This type of insurance betting dates back to Lloyd's of London in the late seventeenth century when they insured slave ships and bet that they would not sink and the owners of the ships bet that they would. J. P. Van Niekerk in his classic treatment on the subject has argued that there is no conceptual distinction between insurance and wagering and that the only reason the law created such a distinction was "because of the increasingly different moral values attached to them: the economically justifiable compensatory aim of insurance as opposed to the possibility of profit and enrichment in the case of wagering" (145). *The Development of the Principles of Insurance Law in the Netherlands: From 1500 to 1800* (UK: Hart Publishing Company, 1999). Nevertheless, the law invented a distinction between an "insurable interest" or to protect against a loss as opposed to creating an opportunity for speculative gain.

40. Taibbi, "The Great American Bubble Machine."

41. Goldman Sachs was not alone. The other major investment banks during the run-up to the crisis were also engaging in a long list of abuses, "including mortgage bonds having more dodgy loans in them than they were supposed to, banks selling synthetic or largely synthetic collateralized debt obligations as being just the same as ones made of real bonds when the synthetics were created for the purpose of making bets against the subprime market and selling BBB risk at largely AAA prices, and of course, phony accounting at the banks themselves." Yves Smith, "Why Are the Big Banks Getting off Scot-Free?" *Salon.com*, August 8, 2011, http://www.salon.com/news/opinion/glenn_greenwald/2011/08/08/sec_fraud.

42. Charles Gasparino, *The Sellout: How Three Decades of Wall Street Greed and Government Mismanagement Destroyed the Global Financial System* (New York: Harper Business, 2009). See the Prologue or the Epilogue.

43. John Cassidy, *How Markets Fail: The Logic of Economic Calamities* (New York: Farrar, Straus, and Giroux, 2009).

44. Quoted in Graham Bowley, "People Power: Taking Spin out for a Spin," *New York Times*, November 22, 2009, Week in Review, 1.

45. Taibbi, "The Great American Bubble Machine."

46. Liz Rappaport, Aaron Lucchetti, and Stephen Grocer, "Wall Street Pay: A Record $144 Billion," *Wall Street Journal*, October 11, 2010, http://online.wsj.com/article/SB10001424052748704518104575546542463746562.html.

47. Steven Brill, "Government for Sale: How Lobbyists Shaped the Financial Reform Bill," *Time*, July 24, 2010, http://www.time.com/time/politics/article/0,8599,2000880,00.html#ixzz0wh4805Pf.

48. William Greider, "The Money Man's Best Friend: Blue Dog Democrats Are Undermining Prospects for Financial-Industry Regulation and Reform," *The Nation*, November 30, 2009, 22.

49. Paul Barrett, "Rational Irrationality: The Story of 2008's Crash, and an Effort to Size up the Problem," *New York Times Book Review*, November 15, 2009, 19.

50. Andrew R. Sorkin, *Too Big to Fail: The Inside Story of How Wall Street and Washington Fought to Save the Financial System—and Themselves* (New York: Viking, 2009).

51. These totals in loans include major programs of the U.S. Treasury Department, the Federal Reserve, and other government agencies to assist the financial sector and

institutions that had a role in the crisis. These numbers come from The Wall Street Bailout Cost Table, produced and updated monthly by the Real Economy Project of the Center for Media and Democracy, which publishes the website *SourceWatch*. Retrieved on June 18, 2010, from http://www.sourcewatch.org/index.php?title=Total_Wall_Street_Bailout_Cost.

52. Michael Levi, "Giving Creditors the Business: The Criminal Law in Inaction," *International Journal of the Sociology of Law* 12 (1984): 321–33. Quote from page 322.

53. Robert Merton, *Social Theory and Social Structure* (New York: Free Press, 1968), 190.

54. Mark Lanier and Stuart Henry, *Essential Criminology*, 2nd ed. (Boulder, CO: Westview, 2004), 8–9.

55. Steven Messner and Richard Rosenfeld, *Crime and the American Dream*, 3rd ed. (Belmont, CA: Wadsworth Group, 2001), 64.

56. Adam Trahan, James Marquart, and Janet Mullings, "Fraud and the American Dream: Toward an Understanding of Fraud Victimization," *Deviant Behavior* 26 (2005): 601–20.

57. Trahan, Marquart, and Mullings, "Fraud and the American Dream," 618.

58. Carol Lloyd, "Mortgage Fraud—The Worst Crime No One's Heard Of," *San Francisco Chronicle*, 2006.

59. Trahan, Marquart, and Mullings, "Fraud and the American Dream," 603.

60. Quoted in Trahan, Marquart, and Mullings, "Fraud and the American Dream," 603.

61. Peter Grabosky and Neal Shover, "Forestalling the Next Epidemic of White-Collar Crime: Linking Policy to Theory," *Criminology & Public Policy* 9, no. 3 (2010): 641–54. Quote from page 642.

62. Grabosky and Shover, "Forestalling the Next Epidemic of White-Collar Crime."

CHAPTER 3:
UNENLIGHTENED SELF-INTEREST, UNREGULATED FINANCIAL MARKETS, AND UNFETTERED VICTIMIZATION

1. Investment brokers are individuals who bring together buyers and sellers of investments. Arbitrage dealers are individuals who are engaged in taking advantage of price differences between two or more markets, creating the possibility of a risk-free profit at zero cost. Derivative traders are individuals who specialize in financial instruments that are usually designed to hedge against risks, and/or for speculative purposes.

2. Simon Johnson and James Kwak, *13 Bankers: The Wall Street Takeover and the Next Financial Meltdown* (New York: Pantheon Books, 2010), 109.

3. An asset-backed security (ABS) is a security whose value and income payments are derived from a collateralized (or "backed") pool of underlying assets. A

mortgage-backed security (MBS), for example, refers to an asset-backed security that represents a claim on the cash flows from mortgage loans. Collateral debt obligations (CDOs) are structured asset-backed securities with multiple layers or "tranches" representing different risks and payoffs to investors.

4. For example, the third quarter for 2009 showed 937,840 foreclosure filings, a 5 percent increase from the previous quarter and an increase of nearly 23 percent from Q3 in 2008. "Foreclosure Activity Hits Record High in Third Quarter," RealtyTrac, October 15, 2009, accessed July 12, 2010, http://www.realtytrac.com/foreclosure/foreclosure-rates.html.

5. Quoted in Christopher Hayes, "Subprime Contagion," *The Nation*, August 29/September 5 (2011): 6.

6. Johnson and Kwak, *13 Bankers*, 17.

7. Quoted in Johnson and Kwak, *13 Bankers*, 13.

8. "Glass-Steagall Act," Investopedia, accessed July 21, 2010, http://www.investopedia.com/terms/g/glass_steagall_act.asp.

9. Quoted in Johnson and Kwak, *13 Bankers*, 141.

10. Elizabeth Bumiller, "Bush Signs Bill Aimed at Fraud in Corporations," *New York Times*, July 31, 2002, A1.

11. Yves Smith, *Econned: How Unenlightened Self Interest Undermined Democracy and Corrupted Capitalism* (New York: Palgrave McMillan, 2010). See chapter 2.

12. Stephen Pizzo, Mary Fricker, and Paul Muolo, *Inside Job: The Looting of America's Savings and Loans* (New York: Harper Perennial, 1991). See 104–5 and 14–15 as well as Chapter 3: Shades of Gray.

13. Milton Friedman, *Capitalism and Freedom* (Chicago: University of Chicago Press, 1982).

14. Ragoucy Yulia, "Jeffrey Sachs, The Evolution of an American Economist," Memoire de Maitrise en Civilisation americaine, Universite Stendhal Grenoble3, UFR d'Etudes Anglophones, September 2008.

15. Despite these and other documented cases and well-known examples of free-enterprise failure found in Johnson and Kwak, *13 Bankers*, and in Smith, *Econned*, and the works of many historians, economists, and commentators, such as Jeff Faux's *The Global Class War: How America's Bipartisan Elite Lost Our Future and What It Will Take to Win It Back* (Hoboken, NJ: Wiley, 2006) or Naomi Klein's *The Shock Doctrine: The Rise of Disaster Capitalism* (New York: Picador, 2007), the ideology and belief in the philosophy of free markets lives on in the minds of most Americans.

16. Leverage refers to the amount of debt used to finance a firm's assets. A firm is considered highly leveraged when it has significantly more debt than equity. "Leverage," Investopedia, http://www.investopedia.com/terms/l/leverage.asp#axzz1l39YYy5J.

17. Smith, *Econned*, 4.

18. Smith, *Econned*, 4.

19. Smith, *Econned*, 4–5.

20. Smith, *Econned*.

21. Quoted in Johnson and Kwak, *13 Bankers*, 48.

22. Smith, *Econned*, 145.

23. Smith, *Econned*, 146.

24. Money market funds are open-ended mutual funds that are invested in short-term debt securities and that provide liquidity to financial intermediaries.

25. Pizzo, Fricker, and Muolo, *The Looting of America's Savings and Loans*, 24.

26. Pizzo, Fricker, and Muolo, *The Looting of America's Savings and Loans*, 24. At the time, as these investigative journalists parenthetically noted, "Thrift lobbyists were said to have more influence over their regulators than any other regulated industry, and the U.S. League of Saving Institutions had traditionally participated in regulatory and legislative decisions, even going so far as to write some of the regulations. Bankers complained that they did not get treated as generously by Congress as did savings and loans because their lobbyists were not as powerful" (24–25). Twenty-five years later, thrifts were all but history and megabank lobbying power would be second to none.

27. Pizzo, Fricker, and Muolo, *The Looting of America's Savings and Loans*, 25.

28. Quoted in Pizzo, Fricker, and Muolo, *The Looting of America's Savings and Loans*, 25.

29. Pizzo, Fricker, and Muolo, *The Looting of America's Savings and Loans*, 15. See also Kitty Calavita, Henry N. Pontell, and Robert Tillman, *Big Money Crime: Fraud and Politics in the Savings and Loan Crisis* (Berkeley, CA: UC Press, 1999) for the distinction between traditional and collective embezzlement and its application to the vagaries of Wall Street in chapter 3 of this book.

30. Johnson and Kwak, *13 Bankers*, 152.

31. David Wessel, *In Fed We Trust: Ben Bernanke's War on the Great Panic* (New York: Crown Business, 2009).

32. Smith, *13 Bankers*, 151.

33. Smith, *13 Bankers*, 151.

34. Gillian Tett, *Fool's Gold: How the Bold Dream of a Small Tribe at J. P. Morgan Was Corrupted by Wall Street Greed and Unleashed a Catastrophe* (New York: Free Press, 2009), 34–35.

35. Johnson and Kwak, *13 Bankers*, 142.

36. "Brooksley Born Interview," *Frontline*, PBS, August 28, 2009. Transcript available at http://www.pbs.org/wgbh/pages/frontline/wanring/interview/born.html.

37. The report is available at http://search.treas.gov/search/press/releases.

38. See Johnson and Kwak, *13 Bankers*, "Chapter 5: The Best Deal Ever," and Smith, *Econned*, "Chapter 9: The Heart of Darkness."

39. Quoted in *Washington Post*, April 27, 2010, and shared on *Morning Joe*, MSNBC, April 28, 2010.

40. Editorial Board, "Maurice Allais: An Economic Visionary," Focus on Issues, *Momagri.org*, February 2, 2009, http://www.momagri.org/UK/focus-on-issues/Maurice-Allais-An-Economic-Visionary_429.html on 7/26/10.

41. Ellen Brown, "How Financial Brokers Became Bookies: The Insidious Transformation of Markets into Casinos," *Global Research*, July 13, 2010, accessed August 3, 2010, http://globalresearch.ca/PrintArticle.php?articledd=20121.

42. Brown, "How Financial Brokers Became Bookies."

43. "The Feinberg Report and the 'Wisdom of TARP," *The Daily Bail*, accessed July 26, 2010, http://dailybail.com/home/the-feinberg-report-and-the-wisdom-of-tarp.html?utm_source=feedburner&utm_medium=email&ut.

44. Shahien Nasiripour, "Pay Czar Criticizes 17 Bailed-Out Banks for Huge Pay Packages—But Won't Go After Money Already Paid," *Huffington Post*, July 23, 2010, accessed July 26, 2010, http://www.huffingtonpost.com/2010/07/23/pay-czar-names-17-banks-t_n_656988.html.

45. All quotes in this paragraph are from Nasiripour, "Pay Czar Criticizes 17 Bailed-Out Banks."

46. Quoted in Nasiripour, "Pay Czar Criticizes 17 Bailed-Out Banks."

47. Nasiripour, "Pay Czar Criticizes 17 Bailed-Out Banks."

48. Quoted in Nasiripour, "Pay Czar Criticizes 17 Bailed-Out Banks."

49. Julianna Goldman and Ian Katz, "Obama Doesn't 'Begrudge' Bonuses for Blankfein, Dimon," *Bloomberg News*, July 10, 2010, accessed July 26, 2010, http://www.bloomberg.com/apps/news?pid=newsarchive&sid=aTwD6RCGR6PA.

50. Goldman and Katz, "Obama Doesn't 'Begrudge' Bonuses for Blankfein, Dimon."

51. Quoted in Goldman and Katz, "Obama Doesn't 'Begrudge' Bonuses for Blankfein, Dimon."

52. Smith, *Econned*, 27.

53. Smith, *Econned*, 3.

54. The eleven CEOs and their banks included: Ken Chenault, American Express; Ken Lewis, Bank of America; Robert Kelly, Bank of New York Mellon; Vikram Pandit, Citigroup; John Koskinen, Freddie Mac; Lloyd Blankfein, Goldman Sachs; Jamie Dimon, JP Morgan Chase; John Mack, Morgan Stanley; Rick Waddell, Northern Trust; James Rohr, PNC; Ronald Logue, State Street; Richard Davis, US Bank; and John Stumpf, Wells Fargo. Smith, *Econned*, 4.

55. Smith, *Econned*, 4.

56. Smith, *Econned*, 5.

57. Smith, *Econned*, 3–4.

58. Smith, *Econned*, 4.

59. Dan Fitzpatrick and Robin Sidel, "A City Feels the Squeeze in the Age of Mega-Banks," *Wall Street Journal*, July 20, 2010, A1, A14. Quote from A14.

60. Fitzpatrick and Sidel, "A City Feels the Squeeze."

61. Fitzpatrick and Sidel, "A City Feels the Squeeze."

62. Fitzpatrick and Sidel, "A City Feels the Squeeze."

63. Smith, *Econned*, 6.

64. Smith, *Econned*, 6.

CHAPTER 4:
THEORIES OF WHITE-COLLAR ILLEGALITIES AND THE CRIMES OF THE POWERFUL

1. For three representative white-collar crime typologies, see James Coleman, *The Criminal Elite: Understanding White Collar Crime*, 5th ed. (New York: St. Martin's, 2002); David Friedrichs, *Trusted Criminals: White Collar Crime in Contemporary Society*, 3rd ed. (Belmont, CA: Wadsworth, 2007); and S. M. Rosoff, H. N. Pontell, and R. H. Tillman, *Profit without Honor: White-Collar Crime and the Looting of America*, 3rd ed. (Upper Saddle River, NJ: Pearson-Prentice Hall, 2004).

2. Gilbert Geis, "White-Collar Crime: What Is It?" in *White-Collar Crime Reconsidered*, eds., K. Schlegel and D. Weisburd (Boston: Northeastern University Press, 1992), 31–52.

3. Joseph Sheley, "Critical Elements of Criminal Behavior Explanation," *The Sociological Quarterly* 24 (1983): 161–86.

4. John Braithwaite and Toni Makkai, "Testing an Expected Utility Model of Corporate Deterrence," *Law & Society Review* 25 (1991): 7–41; Toni Makkai and John Braithwaite, "The Dialectics of Corporate Deterrence," *Journal of Research in Crime and Delinquency*, 31 (1994): 347–73.

5. Ray Paternoster and Sally Simpson, "Sanction Threats and Appeals to Morality: Testing a Rational Choice Model of Corporate Crime," *Law and Society Review*, 30 (1996): 549–83; Ray Paternoster and Sally Simpson, eds. *A Rational Choice Theory of Corporate Crime* (Oxford: Oxford University Press, 2000).

6. In *U.S. v. Bank of New England* (1987) the doctrine of collective knowledge was adopted and applied to cases of corporate criminality because as an institution the bank's knowledge consisted of the sum of all the knowledge of its employees, not any particular employee.

7. Diane Vaughn, "The Macro-Micro Connection in White Collar Crime Theory," in *White-Collar Crime Reconsidered*, eds. K. Schlegel and D. Weisburd (Boston: Northeastern University Press, 1992), 124–48.

8. David Friedrichs, *Trusted Criminals: White Collar Crime in Contemporary Society*, 3rd ed. (Belmont, CA: Wadsworth, 2007), 207.

9. Edwin Sutherland, "White-Collar Criminality," *American Sociological Review* 5 (1940):1–12.

10. Gresham Sykes and David Matza, "Techniques of Neutralization: A Theory of Delinquency," *American Sociological Review* 22 (1957): 664–70.

11. Michael Gottfredson and Travis Hirschi, *A General Theory of Crime* (Stanford: Stanford University Press, 1990).

12. Robert Merton, "Social Structure and Anomie," *American Sociological Review* 3 (1938): 672–82.

13. Albert Cohen, *Delinquent Boys: The Culture of the Gang* (New York: Free Press, 1955).

14. Richard Cloward and Lloyd Ohlin, *Delinquency and Opportunity* (Glencoe, IL: Free Press of Glencoe, 1960).

15. Terance Miethe and Robert Meier, "Opportunity, Choice, and Criminal Victimization: A Test of a Theoretical Model," *Journal of Crime and Delinquency* 27, no. 3 (1990): 243–66.

16. Braithwaite and Makkai, "Testing an Expected Utility Model of Corporate Deterrence."

17. Ronald Clarke and Derek Cornish, eds., *The Reasoning Criminal* (New York: Springer Verlag, 1986).

18. Marcus Felson, "Routine Activities, Social Controls, Rational Decisions, and Criminal Outcomes," *Criminology* 25, no. 4 (1987): 911–31.

19. Marcus Felson and Ronald Clarke, *Opportunity Makes the Thief: Practical Theory for Crime Prevention*. Police Research Series, Paper 98. Policing and Reducing Crime Unit. (London, UK: Home Office, 1998).

20. Gregg Barak, *Integrating Criminologies* (Boston: Allyn & Bacon, 1998). See also, Gregg Barak, *Criminology: An Integrated Approach* (Lanham, MD: Rowman & Littlefield, 2009).

21. Richard Quinney, *Class, State, and Crime: On the Theory and Practice of Criminal Justice* (New York: David McKay, 1977).

22. Stephen Box, *Power, Crime, and Mystification* (London: Tavistock, 1983).

23. John Braithwaite, *Crime, Shame, and Reintegration* (Cambridge: Cambridge University Press, 1989); John Braithwaite, "Criminological Theory and Organizational Crime," *Justice Quarterly* 6 (1989): 333–58.

24. David Friedrichs, *Trusted Criminals*, 221.

25. David Friedrichs, *Trusted Criminals*, 221.

26. John Braithwaite, *Inequality, Crime, and Public Policy* (London: Routledge and Kegan Paul, 1979).

27. Kitty Calavita and Henry Pontell, "Heads I Win, Tails You Lose: Deregulation, Crime, and Crisis in the Savings and Loan Industry," *Crime and Delinquency* 36 (1990): 309–41; Henry Pontell and Kitty Calavita, "White-collar Crime in the Savings and Loan Scandal," *The Annals* 525 (1993): 31–45.

28. Ke Wang, *Securities Fraud, 1996–2001: Incentive Pay, Governance, and Class Action Lawsuits* (El Paso, TX: LFB Scholarly Publishing, 2010).

29. Wang, *Securities Fraud, 1996–2001*, 33.

30. Wang, *Securities Fraud, 1996–2001*, 32.

31. Wang, *Securities Fraud, 1996–2001*, 32–33.

32. Wang, *Securities Fraud, 1996–2001*, 33.

33. Wang, *Securities Fraud, 1996–2001*, 34.

34. Maureen Cain and Alan Hunt, *Marx and Engels on Law* (London: Academic Press, 1979). See also Raymond Michalowski, *Order, Law and Crime* (New York: Random House, 1985).

35. Ronald Kramer, Raymond Michalowski, and David Kauzlarich, *Toward an Integrated Theory of State-Corporate Crime*. Presented at the American Society of Criminology, Baltimore, MD, 1990; David Kauzlarich and Ronald Kramer, "State-Corporate Crime in the U.S. Nuclear Weapons Complex," *Journal of Human Justice* 5, no. 1 (1993): 1–26; and Ronald Kramer, Raymond Michalowski, and David Kauzlarich, "The Origins and Development of the Concept and Theory of State-Corporate Crime," *Crime and Delinquency* 48, no. 2 (2000): 263–82.

36. Dawn Rothe and Christopher Mullins, "Toward a Criminology for International Criminal Law: An Integrated Theory of International Criminal Law Violations," *International Journal of Comparative and Applied Criminal Justice* 33, no. 1 (2009): 97–118.

37. Raymond Michalowski and Ronald Kramer, eds. *State-Corporate Crime: Wrongdoing at the Intersection of Business and Government* (New Brunswick, NJ: Rutgers University Press, 2006).

38. James Galbraith, "How Fraud and Bad Economic Thinking Got Us in This Mess," Keynote Speech, 5th Annual "Dijon" Conference on Post Keynesian Economics, Denmark, May 12–13, 2011, accessed August 7, 2011, http://www.nakedcapital ism.com/2011/08/james-galbraith-on-fraud-and-how-bad-economic-thinking-got-us -in-this-mess.html.

39. Stanton Wheeler and Mitchell Rothman, "The Organization as Weapon in White Collar Crime," *Michigan Law Review* 80, no. 7 (1982): 1403–26.

40. William Black, *The Best Way to Rob a Bank is to Own One: How Corporate Executives and Politicians Looted the S&L Industry* (Austin: University of Texas Press, 2005), xiii.

41. Black, *The Best Way to Rob a Bank is to Own One.*

42. Black, *The Best Way to Rob a Bank is to Own One*, xiv.

43. Black, *The Best Way to Rob a Bank is to Own One*, xiv.

44. Alan Block and Constance Weaver, *All Is Clouded by Desire: Global Banking, Money Laundering, and International Organized Crime* (Westport, CN: Praeger, 2004).

45. Michael Johnston, *Syndromes of Corruption: Wealth, Power, and Democracy* (Cambridge, UK: Cambridge University Press, 2005), 42.

46. Johnston, *Syndromes of Corruption.*

47. Johnston, *Syndromes of Corruption*, 11.

48. Johnston, *Syndromes of Corruption.*

49. Dennis Thompson, "Mediated Corruption: The Case of the Keating Five," *American Political Science Review* 87 (1993): 369–81.

50. Johnston, *Syndromes of Corruption*, 12.

51. For examples: Henry Pontell, "Deterrence: Theory and Practice," *Criminology* 16 (1978): 3–22; Henry Pontell, *A Capacity to Punish: The Ecology of Crime and Punishment* (Bloomington: Indiana University, 1982).

52. For examples: Pontell and Calavita, "Heads I Win, Tails You Lose," 309–41; Henry Pontell, Kitty Calavita, and Robert Tillman, "Corporate Crime and Criminal Justice System Capacity: Government Response to Financial Institution Fraud," *Justice Quarterly* 11, no. 3 (1994): 384–409; Henry Pontell, "White-collar Crime or Just Risky Business? The Role of Fraud in Major Financial Debacles," *Crime, Law, and Social Change* 44 (2004): 309–24; Henry Pontell, "Control Fraud, Gambling for Resurrection, and Moral Hazard: Accounting for White-collar Crime in the Savings and Loan Crisis," *Journal of Socio-Economics* 34 (2005): 756–70.

53. Pontell, *A Capacity to Punish*, 36.

54. Pontell, *A Capacity to Punish*, 33.

55. Pontell, Calavita, and Tillman, "Corporate Crime and Criminal Justice System Capacity," 384–85.

56. Pontell, Calavita, and Tillman, "Corporate Crime and Criminal Justice System Capacity," 384.

57. Galbraith, "How Fraud and Bad Economic Thinking Got Us in This Mess," 2011.

58. These were the four causes of the financial meltdown according to the U.S. Senate's official report, *Wall Street and the Financial Crisis: Anatomy of a Financial Collapse*, April 13, 2011. I think two of the causes could have been labeled a bit differently. Specifically, "investment bank abuse" could have been "investment bank fraud" and "high-risk mortgage lending" could have been "fraudulent mortgage lending."

59. U.S. Senate, *Wall Street and the Financial Crisis*, 13.

60. U.S. Senate, *Wall Street and the Financial Crisis*, 6.

61. U.S. Senate, *Wall Street and the Financial Crisis*, 9.

62. U.S. Senate, *Wall Street and the Financial Crisis*, 7.

63. U.S. Senate, *Wall Street and the Financial Crisis*, 10.

64. U.S. Senate, *Wall Street and the Financial Crisis*, 10.

65. U.S. Senate, *Wall Street and the Financial Crisis*, 10.

66. In finance, it refers to the practice of selling assets, usually securities, that have been borrowed from a third party, to be sold back at a later date to the lender with the intent of profiting from a decline in the price of the assets between the sale and repurchase.

67. U.S. Senate, *Wall Street and the Financial Crisis*, 10.

68. U.S. Senate, *Wall Street and the Financial Crisis*, 11.

69. U.S. Senate, *Wall Street and the Financial Crisis*, 11.

70. A synthetic collateralized debt obligation is a complex financial security used to speculate or manage the risk that an obligation will not be paid in full and whose derived value may or may not be owned by the involved parties.

71. U.S. Senate, *Wall Street and the Financial Crisis*, 13.

72. "Securities Fraud," Investopedia, accessed August 13, 2010, http://www.investopedia.com/terms/s/securities-fraud.asp.

73. U.S. Senate, *Wall Street and the Financial Crisis*, 6.

74. U.S. Senate, *Wall Street and the Financial Crisis*, 5.

75. U.S. Senate, *Wall Street and the Financial Crisis*, 5.

76. U.S. Senate, *Wall Street and the Financial Crisis*, 4.

77. Quoted in U.S. Senate, *Wall Street and the Financial Crisis*, 5.

78. Jean Eaglesham, "Criminal Mortgage Probes Fizzle Out," *Wall Street Journal*, August 6–7, 2011: B1–2.

79. Quoted in Eaglesham, "Criminal Mortgage Probes Fizzle Out," B1.

80. Eaglesham, "Criminal Mortgage Probes Fizzle Out," B2.

81. Eaglesham, "Criminal Mortgage Probes Fizzle Out," B2.

82. "SEC Enforcement Chief Defends Record Under Fire From Rakoff, Critics," *Huffington Post*, January 18, 2012, accessed February 3, 2012, http://www.huffingtonpost.com/2012/01/18/sec-mounts-defense-of-enforcement_n_1205318.html.

83. U.S. Senate, *Wall Street and the Financial Crisis*, 8.

84. U.S. Senate, *Wall Street and the Financial Crisis*, 9.

85. *Reuters*, "Lawsuit against Moody's, S&P Dismissed," April 1, 2010, accessed August 7, 2011, http://www.reuters.com/article/2010/04/01/ratings-lawsuit-idUSN0112717020100401.

86. *Huffington Post*, "SEC Enforcement Chief Defends Record Under Fire."

87. *Huffington Post*, "SEC Enforcement Chief Defends Record Under Fire."

88. U.S. Senate, *Wall Street and the Financial Crisis*, 6.

89. U.S. Senate, *Wall Street and the Financial Crisis*, 7.

CHAPTER 5:
FINANCIAL LOOTING, VICTIMIZATION, AND LEGAL INTERVENTION

1. David Simon, *Elite Deviance*, 8th ed. (Boston: Pearson/Allyn & Bacon, 2006), 211.

2. Simon, *Elite Deviance*.

3. Simon, *Elite Deviance*, 212.

4. Simon, *Elite Deviance*, 212.

5. David Matza, *Becoming Deviant* (Englewood Cliff, NJ: Prentice-Hall, 1969), 144.

6. Matza, *Becoming Deviant*, 143.

7. Donald Black, "How Law Behaves: An Interview with Donald Black," reprinted in *The Behavior of Law*, Special Education (Bingley, UK: Emerald Group Publishing, 2010 [1976]), 180.

8. Black, "How Law Behaves."

9. Dietrich Rueschemeyer, Review of *The Behavior of Law* (New York: Academic Press, 1976), in *American Journal of Sociology* January (1978): 1042.

10. Mark Cooney, Foreword to *The Behavior of Law*, Special Education (Bingley, UK: Emerald Group Publishing, 2010), xii. See also the thirteen positive testimonials, 193–201. One testimonial of particular relevance for this study of regulating Wall Street crime was made by Peter Grabosky: "When John Braithwaite and I were seeking to make sense of variation in the enforcement strategies of regulatory agencies, we turned immediately to *The Behavior of Law*. Our data fit like a glove" (201). See also Peter Grabosky and John Braithwaite, *Of Manners Gentle: Enforcement Strategies of Australian Business Regulatory Agencies* (Oxford, UK: Oxford University Press, 1986).

11. Rueschemeyer, Review of *The Behavior of Law*, p. 1040.

12. Personally, I want it both ways. That is to say, I believe it is necessary to study the behavior of law both with *and* without an examination of the thoughts, values, and motives of the individuals involved. I also believe that the understanding of the law in action divorced from normative aspirations may be used in the development of policy formulations to bring about changes in the social geometry of law.

13. Black, "How Law Behaves," 3.

14. Black, "How Law Behaves," 180.

15. Black, "How Law Behaves," 180.

16. Black, "How Law Behaves," 180.

17. Rueschemeyer, Review of *The Behavior of Law*, 1042.

18. Ralph Taylor, "Student Guide to Accompany Donald Black's *The Behavior of Law*," (unpublished manuscript, Temple University, Department of Criminal Justice, 2008), 11.

19. Black, "How Law Behaves," 4.

20. Black, "How Law Behaves," 4.

21. Black, "How Law Behaves," 5.

22. Black, "How Law Behaves," 5.

23. The Sarbanes-Oxley Act of 2002, Section 804—Statute of Limitations for Securities Fraud, July 30, 2002, 107 P.L. 204, Title VIII, § 804, 116 Stat. 745.

24. After more than eighteen months a deal was finally struck on February 8, 2012. More about this settlement later in the chapter. See also endnote 50 below.

25. *New York Times*, "Tracking Financial Crisis Cases," June 2011, accessed June 24, 2011, http://www.nytimes.com/interactive/business/financial-crisis-cases.html.

26. Susanne Craig and Peter Lattman, "Goldman's Shares Tumble as Blankfein Hires Top Lawyer," *New York Times DealBook*, August 22, 2011, accessed Au-

gust 23, 2011, http://dealbook.nytimes.com/2011/08/22/goldmans-shares-tumble-as
-blankfein-hires-lawyer.

27. U.S. Securities and Exchange Commission, "Goldman Sachs to Pay Record $550 Million to Settle SEC Charges Related to Subprime Mortgage CDO,"
Press Release July 15, 2010, accessed August 25, 2011, http://www.sec.gov/news
/press/2010/2010-123.htm.

28. U.S. Securities and Exchange Commission, "Goldman Sachs to Pay Record
$550 Million."

29. Lea Winerman, "Goldman Sachs, SEC Reach $550 Million Settlement," *The
Rundown* (blog), *PBS NewsHour*, July 15, 2010, accessed February 7, 2012, http://
www.pbs.org/newshour/rundown/2010/07/goldman-sachs-sec-reach-550-million-
settlement.html.

30. U.S. Securities and Exchange Commission, "Goldman Sachs to Pay Record
$550 Million."

31. U.S. Securities and Exchange Commission, "Goldman Sachs to Pay Record
$550 Million."

32. U.S. Securities and Exchange Commission, "Goldman Sachs to Pay Record
$550 Million."

33. U.S. Securities and Exchange Commission, "Goldman Sachs to Pay Record
$550 Million."

34. U.S. Securities and Exchange Commission, "Goldman Sachs to Pay Record
$550 Million."

35. U.S. Securities and Exchange Commission, "Goldman Sachs to Pay Record
$550 Million."

36. Craig and Lattman, "Goldman's Shares Tumble as Blankfein Hires Top Lawyer."

37. Craig and Lattman, "Goldman's Shares Tumble as Blankfein Hires Top Lawyer."

38. Gretchen Morgenson and Louise Story, "As Wall St. Polices Itself, Prosecutors Use Softer Approach," *New York Times*, July 7, 2011, accessed August 23,
2011, http://www.nytimes.com/2011/07/08/business/in-shift-federal-prosecutors-are-
lenient-as-companies-break-the-law.html?pagewanted=all.

39. Morgenson and Story, "As Wall St. Polices Itself, Prosecutors Use Softer Approach."

40. Morgenson and Story, "As Wall St. Polices Itself, Prosecutors Use Softer Approach."

41. Morgenson and Story, "As Wall St. Polices Itself, Prosecutors Use Softer Approach."

42. Morgenson and Story, "As Wall St. Polices Itself, Prosecutors Use Softer Approach."

43. Gretchen Morgenson and Louise Story, "In Financial Crisis, No Prosecutions
of Top Figures," *New York Times*, April 14, 2011, accessed August 23, 2011, http://
www.nytimes.com/2011/04/14/business/14prosecute.html?pagewanted=all.

44. Quoted in Morgenson and Story, "In Financial Crisis, No Prosecutions of Top
Figures."

45. Morgenson and Story, "In Financial Crisis, No Prosecutions of Top Figures."

46. Morgenson and Story, "In Financial Crisis, No Prosecutions of Top Figures."

47. Morgenson and Story, "In Financial Crisis, No Prosecutions of Top Figures."

48. Morgenson and Story, "In Financial Crisis, No Prosecutions of Top Figures."

49. Ruth Simon and Rick Timiraos, "New York Spars in Foreclosure Talks," *Wall Street Journal*, August 25, 2011, C3.

50. Nelson Schwartz and Shaila Dewan, "States Negotiate $26 Billion Deal for Homeowners," *New York Times*, February 8, 2012. "After months of painstaking talks, government authorities and five of the nation's biggest banks have agreed to a $26 billion settlement" that "will help a relatively small portion of the millions of borrowers who are delinquent and facing foreclosure." About "one million home owners are expected to have their mortgage debt reduced by lenders or [be] able to refinance their homes at lower rates. Another 750,000 people who lost their homes to foreclosure from September 2008 to the end of 2011 will receive checks for about $2000" distributed over three years. $3.5 billion will go to governments that lost investments. All and all the settlement represents only a small fraction of the monies lost to the mortgage crisis. However, in many instances investors can still sue to re-coup their losses. Accessed February 9, 2012, http://www.nytimes.com/2012/02/09/business/states-negotiate-25-billion-deal-for-homeowners.html?_r=1. The five firms included were Ally Financial, Bank of America, Citigroup, JP Morgan, and Wells Fargo, who combined handle the payments on 55 percent of all outstanding loans, or about twenty-seven million mortgages, according to *Inside Mortgage Finance*. *Wall Street Journal*, "WSJ News Alert: U.S. Banks Seal $26 Billion Settlement on Foreclosures," February 9, 2012. Fannie Mae and Freddie Mac, who hold nearly all of the rest of the outstanding mortgage loans, were not part of the deal, so no relief for those homeowners.

51. Matt Taibbi, "Obama Goes All Out for Dirty Banker Deal," *Rolling Stone*, July 24, 2011, accessed August 25, 2011, http://www.rollingstone.com/politics/blogs/taib blog/obama-goes-all-out-for-dirty-banker-deal-20110824.

52. David Friedrichs, *Trusted Criminals: White Collar Criminals in Contemporary Society*, 3rd ed. (Belmont, CA: Thomas/Wadsworth, 2007), 173.

53. Shahien Nasiripour, "New York Attorney General Kicked off Government Group Leading Foreclosure Probe," *Huffington Post*, 2011, accessed August 23, 2011, http://www.huffingtonpost.com/2011/08/23/new-york-attorney-general-eric-schneiderman_n_934517.html.

54. Quoted in Taibbi, "Obama Goes All Out For Dirty Banker Deal."

55. Morgenson and Story, "As Wall St. Polices Itself, Prosecutors Use Softer Approach."

56. Peter Lattman, "Fugitive Moody's Analyst Ordered to Pay $35 Million to S.E.C." *New York Times*, *DealBook*, August 24, 2011, accessed August 25, 2011, http://dealbook.nytimes.com/2011/08/24/fugitive-moodys-analyst-ordered-to-pay-35-million-to-s-e-c.

57. Louise Story and Gretchen Morgenson, "S.E.C. Case Stands Out Because It Stands Alone," *New York Times*, May 31, 2011, accessed August 23, 2011, http://www.nytimes.com/2011/06/01/business/01prosecute.html?pagewanted=all.

58. Quoted in Story and Morgenson, "S.E.C. Case Stands Out Because It Stands Alone."

59. According to an analysis by the *New York Times*, "Nearly all of the biggest financial companies—Goldman Sachs, Morgan Stanley, JP Morgan Chase and Bank of America among them—have settled fraud cases by promising that they would never again violate an antifraud law, only to have the S.E.C. conclude that they did it again a few years later." Between 1996 and 2011 the *Times* analysis of SEC enforcement actions found at least fifty-one cases where Wall Street firms had broken antifraud laws that they had already agreed not to breach again. In response to these repeated breaches, the SEC does not target repeat violators. Nor does the SEC typically bring civil contempt charges against these companies for violating previous orders or even refer publicly to those past violations when filing new charges. See Edward Wyatt, "Promises Made, and Remade, by Firms in S.E.C. Fraud Cases," *New York Times*, November 7, 2011, accessed November 8, 2011, http://www.nytimes .com/2011/11/08/business/in-sec-fraud-cases-banks-make-and-break-promises.html.

60. Edward Wyatt, "S.E.C. Is Avoiding Tough Sanctions for Large Banks," *New York Times*, February 3, 2012, accessed February 9, 2012 http://www.nytimes .com/2012/02/03/business/sec-is-avoiding-tough-sanctions-for-large-banks.html.

61. Wyatt, "S.E.C. Is Avoiding Tough Sanctions for Large Banks."

62. Wyatt, "S.E.C. Is Avoiding Tough Sanctions for Large Banks."

63. Wyatt, "S.E.C. Is Avoiding Tough Sanctions for Large Banks."

64. Ryan Chittum, "*NYT* With More on the SEC's Soft Touch with Big Banks," *Columbia Journalism Review*, February 3, 2012, accessed February 9, 2012, http:// www.cjr.org/the_audit/nyt_with_more_on_the_secs_soft.php.

65. Wyatt, "S.E.C. Is Avoiding Tough Sanctions for Large Banks."

66. Quoted in Wyatt, "S.E.C. Is Avoiding Tough Sanctions for Large Banks."

67. See Johannes Andenaes, "The General Preventive Effects of Punishment," *University of Pennsylvania Law Review* 114 (May 1966): 949–83, or William Chambliss, "Types of Deviance and the Effectiveness of Legal Sanctions," *Wisconsin Law Review* (Summer 1967): 703–19.

68. Black, "How Law Behaves," 105.

69. Black, "How Law Behaves," 111.

70. Matt Taibbi, "Is the SEC Covering Up Wall Street Crimes?" *Rolling Stone*, August 17, 2011, accessed August 27, 2011, http://www.rollingstone.com/politics /news/is-the-sec-covering-up-wall-street-crimes-20110817?print=true.

71. Taibbi, "Is the SEC Covering Up Wall Street Crimes?"

72. Taibbi, "Is the SEC Covering Up Wall Street Crimes?"

CHAPTER 6:
CONSUMING VICTIMS AND
VICTIMLESS IDENTITIES

1. Arline Geronimus, Margaret Hicken, Danay Keene, and John Bound, "Weathering and Age-Patterns of Allostatic Load Scores among Blacks and Whites in the United States," *American Journal of Public Health* 96 (2006): 826. See also, Arline

Geronimus, Cynthia Colen, Tara Schochet, Lori Barer Ingber, and Sherman James, "Urban-Rural Differences in Excess Mortality among High-Poverty Populations: Evidence from Harlem Household Survey and the Pitt County, North Carolina Study of African American Health," *Journal of Health Care for the Poor and Underserved* 17, no. 3 (2006): 532–58.

2. Ryan Blitstein, "Racism's Hidden Toll," *Miller-McCune*, July–August, 2009, 53.

3. Gregg Barak, Paul Leighton, and Jeanne Flavin, *Class, Race, Gender, and Crime: The Social Realities of Justice in America*, 3rd ed. (Lanham, MD: Rowman and Littlefield, 2010).

4. Leslie Kennedy and Vincent Sacco, *Crime Victims in Context* (Los Angeles, CA: Roxbury Publishing, 1998), 209.

5. Marilyn McShane and Traqina Emeka, *American Victimology* (El Paso, TX: LFB Scholarly Publishing, 2011), 61.

6. McShane and Emeka, *American Victimology*.

7. As Erik Eckholm and Timothy Williams wrote in their article, "Anti-Wall Street Protests Spreading to Cities Large and Small," in *New York Times*, October 3, 2011: "A loose-knit populist campaign that started on Wall Street three weeks ago has spread to dozens of cities across the country, with protesters camped out in Los Angeles near City Hall, assembled before the Federal Reserve Bank in Chicago and marching through downtown Boston to rally against corporate greed, unemployment and the role of financial institutions in the economic crisis." Accessed October 4, 2011, http://www.nytimes.com/2011/10/04/us/anti-wall-street-protests-spread-to-other-cities.html?_r=1&ref=business.

8. Jo-Anne Wemmers, "Where Do They Belong? Giving Victims a Place in the Criminal Justice Process," *Criminal Law Forum* 20, no. 4 (2009): 395.

9. Robert Davis and Carrie Mulford, "Victim Rights and New Remedies: Finally Getting Victims Their Due," *Journal of Contemporary Criminal Justice* 24, no. 2 (2008): 198.

10. Wemmers, "Where Do They Belong?"

11. Davis and Mulford, "Victims Rights and New Remedies."

12. Kathleen Daly and Russ Immarigeon, "The Past, Present, and Future of Restorative Justice: Some Critical Reflections," *Contemporary Justice Review* 1, no. 1 (1998): 21–45. See also Barak, Leighton, and Flavin, *Class, Race, Gender, and Crime*, 296–99.

13. Robert Elias, *The Politics of Victimization: Victims, Victimology and Human Rights* (New York: Oxford University Press, 1986), 18.

14. McShane and Emeka, *American Victimology*.

15. McShane and Emeka, *American Victimology*, 177.

16. Thorsten Sellin and Marvin Wolfgang, *The Measurement of Delinquency* (New York: Wiley, 1964).

17. McShane and Emeka, *American Victimology*, 9.

18. Elizabeth Moore and Michael Mills, "The Neglected Victims and Unexamined Costs of White-Collar Crime," *Crime and Delinquency* 36, no. 3 (1990): 408–18.

19. Jason Davis, "Seeking Justice: An Analysis of Victim Impact Statements in the Bernie Madoff Ponzi Scheme." Paper presented at the annual meetings of the American Society of Criminology, Washington, DC, November 2011.

20. Basia Spalek, "White-Collar Crime Victims and the Issue of Trust." Paper presented at the British Society of Criminology Conference, Leicester, July 2000, in *British Society of Criminology Conference: Selected Proceedings*, vol. 4 (October 2001): 10.

21. Spalek, "White-Collar Crime Victims and the Issue of Trust."

22. *The Politics of Victimization*, 33.

23. *The Politics of Victimization*, 3–4.

24. *The Politics of Victimization*, 4.

25. Quoted in Matthew Hall, *Victims and Policy Making: A Comparative Perspective* (New York: Willan Publishing, 2010), 54.

26. Hall, *Victims and Policy Making*, 52.

27. Kennedy and Sacco, *Crime Victim in Context*, 204.

28. Kennedy and Sacco, *Crime Victim in Context*, 204.

29. Kennedy and Sacco, *Crime Victim in Context*, 203.

30. H.R. 5107, Chapter 237—Crime Victims' Rights.

31. David Friedrichs, *Trusted Criminals: White Collar Crime in Contemporary Society*, 3rd ed. (Belmont, CA: Thomson/Wadsworth, 2007), 326–27.

32. Friedrichs, *Trusted Criminals*, 326.

33. Susan Shapiro, *Wayward Capitalists: Targets of the Securities and Exchange Commission* (New Haven, CT: Yale University Press, 1984).

34. Kennedy and Sacco, *Crime Victim in Context*, 149.

35. Kennedy and Sacco, *Crime Victim in Context*, 149.

36. For important clarification purposes, my indictment about a lack of criminal prosecution refers to the U.S. Attorney General and the DOJ. It does not pertain to regulatory actions, for example, the SEC and its agreement announced on June 21, 2011, with JP Morgan to pay $153.6 million to settle charges related to a $1.1 billion heavily synthetic CDO called Squared or with the comparably higher SEC settlement of $550 million with Goldman Sachs to resolve its notorious Abacus transactions. There are also those rogue state attorney generals like New York's Eric Schneiderman and Nevada's Catherine Cortez Masto, who both in late 2011 went after BAC/Countrywide units for their practices of predatory lending, refinancing, robo-signing, and more in 2008 and thereafter in violation of loan modification agreements struck with the states and/or between the banks during the collapse of the mortgage bubble at the time. Similarly, the Federal Reserve announced in September 2011 an enforcement action against Goldman for unspecified damages for the same type of violations, involving mortgage-servicing irregularities after the financial collapse. See also chapter 4 of this book.

37. William Doerner and Steven Lab, *Victimology*, 5th ed. (Newark, NJ: LexisNexis Group, 2008), 92.

38. Office for the Victims of Crime, *Civil Legal Remedies for Crime Victims*, 2nd ed. (Washington, DC: U.S. Department of Justice, 1997).

39. Bottom line: Between 2006 and 2010, the SEC ordered $11.3 billion in penalties for wrongdoing, but had only received two-thirds of the sum by July 2011. Jean Eaglesham, "Chasing Fraud, then Chasing Cash," *Wall Street Journal*, July 8, 2011, C1.

40. Tom Weidlich, "Banks May Fight Banks as Mortgage Securities Investors Try for Class Suits," *Bloomberg News*, 2011, accessed September 9, 2011, http://www.bloomberg.com/news/2011-09-09/banks-may-fight-banks-as-mortgage-securities-investors-try-for-class-suits.html.

41. Quoted in Weidlich, "Banks May Fight Banks."

42. Weidlich, "Banks May Fight Banks."

43. Weidlich, "Banks May Fight Banks."

44. Doerner and Lab, *Victimology*, 92.

45. Nelson Schwartz and Eric Dash, "Bank of America Settles Claims Stemming from Mortgage Crisis," *New York Times*, June 29, 2011, accessed August 23, 2011, http://www.nytimes.com/2011/06/30/business/30mortgage.html?pagewanted=all.

46. Schwartz and Dash, "Bank of America Settles Claims Stemming From Mortgage Crisis."

47. Schwartz and Dash, "Bank of America Settles Claims Stemming From Mortgage Crisis."

48. In fact, back in January 2011, BAC had settled civil suits from Fannie Mae and Freddie Mac for $2.5 billion.

49. Eric Morath, "Ex-Lehman Officers Seek $90 Million to End Lawsuit," *Wall Street Journal*, August 26, 2011, C2.

50. Joseph Checkler, "Lehman Retirees' Push to Sue CEO Is Denied," *Wall Street Journal*, Money & Investing, October 7, 2011, C5.

51. Reuters, "Washington Mutual Settles Fraud Suits for $208 Million," *New York Times*, July 1, 2011, accessed July 2, 2011, http://www.nytimes.com/2011/07/02 /business/02wamu.html.

52. Reuters, "Washington Mutual Settles Fraud Suits for $208 Million."

53. Reuters, "F.D.I.C. Must Face WaMu Suit, Judge Rules," *New York Times*, August 23, 2011, accessed August 24, 2011, http://www.nytimes.com/2011/08/24 /business/fdic-must-face-wamu-suit-judge-rules.html.

54. Louise Story and Gretchen Morgenson, "A.I.G. Sues Bank of America over Mortgage Bonds," *New York Times*, August 8, 2011, accessed August 23, 2011, http://www.nytimes.com/2011/08/08/business/aig-to-sue-bank-of-america-over -mortgage-bonds.html?pagewanted=all.

55. Story and Morgenson, "A.I.G. Sues Bank of America over Mortgage Bonds."

56. Story and Morgenson, "A.I.G. Sues Bank of America over Mortgage Bonds."

57. Story and Morgenson, "A.I.G. Sues Bank of America over Mortgage Bonds."

58. Mark Jewell, "Allstate Sues Goldman Sachs over Toxic Investments," *Huffington Post*, August 16, 2011, accessed October 7, 2011, http://www.huffingtonpost .com/2011/08/16/allstate-sues-goldman-sachs-over-toxic-investments_n_928550 .html.

59. Quoted in Jewell, "Allstate Sues Goldman Sachs over Toxic Investments."

60. Jewell, "Allstate Sues Goldman Sachs over Toxic Investments."

61. Bret Philbin, "Morgan Stanley Ends Suit," *Wall Street Journal*, May 10, 2011, C3.

62. Quoted in Philbin, "Morgan Stanley Ends Suit."

63. Philbin, "Morgan Stanley Ends Suit."

64. Randall Smith and Suzanne Barlyn, "Citigroup Loses Muni Case," *Wall Street Journal*, April 13, 2011, C2.

65. Smith and Barlyn, "Citigroup Loses Muni Case," C1.

66. Quoted in Smith and Barlyn, "Citigroup Loses Muni Case," C1.

67. Smith and Barlyn, "Citigroup Loses Muni Case," C2.

68. Yves Smith, "Bank of America Deathwatch: $50 Billion Fraud Suit over Merrill Acquisition," *Naked Capitalism*, September 28, 2011, accessed September 30, 2011, http://www.nakedcapitalism.com/2011/09/bank-of-america-deathwatch -50-billion-securities-fraud-suit-over-merrill-acquisition.html.

69. Quoted in Smith, "Bank of America Deathwatch."

70. Smith, "Bank of America Deathwatch."

CHAPTER 7:
THE WALL STREET FINANCIAL REFORM AND
CONSUMER PROTECTION ACT OF 2010

1. Thomas Hoenig, "Financial Reform: Post Crisis?" Paper delivered by the president of the Federal Reserve Bank of Kansas City, February 23, before Women in Housing and Finance, Washington, DC, 2011, 6.

2. Andrew Haldane, "Banking on the State." Paper presented at the Federal Reserve Bank of Chicago, Conference on "The International Financial Crisis: Have the Rules of Finance Changed?" September 25, 2009, 11, accessed August 29, 2011, http://www.bis.org/review/r091111e.pdf.

3. Hoenig, "Financial Reform," 3.

4. Hoenig, "Financial Reform," 3–4.

5. Hoenig, "Financial Reform," 4.

6. Quoted in Jeff Madrick, "The Wall Street Leviathan," *New York Review of Books*, April 28, 2011, accessed August 29, 2011, http://www.nybooks.com/articles /archives/2011/apr/28/wall-street-leviathan.

7. Hoenig, "Financial Reform," 5.

8. Haldane, "Banking on the State."

9. Hoenig, "Financial Reform," 5.

10. Hoenig, "Financial Reform," 5.

11. Fraud Enforcement and Recovery Act of 2009, 111th Congress, Pub. L. No. 111-21, 123 Stat. 1617 (May 20, 2009).

12. *Financial Regulatory Reform—A New Foundation: Rebuilding Financial Supervision and Regulation*, U.S. Department of the Treasury White Paper, June 17, 2009, 50–51, accessed August 30, 2011, http://www.financialstability.gov/docs/regs /FinalReport_web.pdf.

13. The next section is presented as a means of highlighting the differences in emphases between securities and commodities trading. It does not really address the harmonizing aspects between the SEC and the CFTC, but its recommendations for doing so are incorporated along with other recommendations for addressing financial reform from a variety of sources in the conclusion of this book.

14. Transcripts of the September meeting are available on the agencies' websites: at the SEC, http://www.sec.gov/spotlight/harmonization.htm, and at the CFTC, http:// www.cftc.gov ("Transcripts").

15. SEC and CFTC, *A Joint Report of the SEC and CFTC on Harmonization of Regulation*, October 16, 2009, 1.

16. SEC and CFTC, *A Joint Report of the SEC and CFTC on Harmonization of Regulation*.

17. SEC and CFTC, *A Joint Report of the SEC and CFTC on Harmonization of Regulation*.

18. SEC and CFTC, *A Joint Report of the SEC and CFTC on Harmonization of Regulation*, 7.

19. SEC and CFTC, *A Joint Report of the SEC and CFTC on Harmonization of Regulation*, 7.

20. SEC and CFTC, *A Joint Report of the SEC and CFTC on Harmonization of Regulation*, 7.

21. SEC and CFTC, *A Joint Report of the SEC and CFTC on Harmonization of Regulation*, 7–8.

22. SEC and CFTC, *A Joint Report of the SEC and CFTC on Harmonization of Regulation*, 8.

23. SEC and CFTC, *A Joint Report of the SEC and CFTC on Harmonization of Regulation*, 8.

24. SEC and CFTC, *A Joint Report of the SEC and CFTC on Harmonization of Regulation*, 8.

25. SEC and CFTC, *A Joint Report of the SEC and CFTC on Harmonization of Regulation*, 8.

26. SEC and CFTC, *A Joint Report of the SEC and CFTC on Harmonization of Regulation*, 10.

27. SEC and CFTC, *A Joint Report of the SEC and CFTC on Harmonization of Regulation*, 10.

28. U.S. Senate Banking Subcommittee, *Brief Summary of the Dodd-Frank Wall Street Reform and Consumer Protection Act*, 2010, 1, accessed August 31, 2011, http://banking.senate.gov.

29. U.S. Senate Banking Subcommittee, *Brief Summary of the Dodd-Frank Wall Street Reform and Consumer Protection Act*, 1–2.

30. U.S. Senate Banking Subcommittee, *Brief Summary of the Dodd-Frank Wall Street Reform and Consumer Protection Act*, 2–14.

31. Viral Acharya, Thomas Cooley, Matthew Richardson, and Ingo Walter, eds. *Regulating Wall Street: The Dodd-Frank Act and the New Architecture of Global Finance* (Hoboken, NJ: Wiley, 2011), xviii.

32. Sherrod Brown, "In the Wake of Enforcement Actions against Mortgage Servicers, Brown Introduced Bill to Keep Ohioans in Their Homes; Stem Foreclosure Crisis," Press Release, April 14, 2011, accessed August 29, 2011, http://brown.senate.gov/newsroom/press_releases/release/?id=e0bc8b2a-4947-4b32-bc9d-fefda5bc132e.

33. Madrick, 2011.

34. Jim Puzzanghera and Lisa Mascaro, "Obama Bypassing Senate to Appoint Richard Cordray Consumer Chief," *Los Angeles Times*, January 4, 2012, accessed February 10, 2012, http://articles.latimes.com/2012/jan/04/business/la-fi-obama-cordray-20120104.

35. Danielle Douglas, "Banks Still Waiting on Most Dodd-Frank Rules," *Washington Post*, December 25, 2011, accessed December 26, 2011 http://www.washingtonpost.com/business/capitalbusiness/banks-still-waiting-on-most-dodd-frank-rules/2011/1.

36. Madrick, "The Wall Street Leviathan."

37. Madrick, "The Wall Street Leviathan."

38. Randall Kroszner and Robert Shiller, eds. *Reforming U.S. Financial Markets: Reflections Before and Beyond Dodd-Frank* (Cambridge, MA: MIT Press, 2011).

CONCLUSION

1. Robert Frank, *The Darwin Economy: Liberty, Competition, and the Common Good* (Princeton, NJ: Princeton University Press, 2011).

2. Quoted in Nicholas Kristof, "America's Primal Scream," *New York Times*, October 16, 2011, SR11.

3. Benjamin Friedman, Introduction to *Reforming U.S. Financial Markets: Reflections Before and Beyond Dodd-Frank* by Randall Kroszner and Robert Shiller (Cambridge, MA: MIT Press, 2011), xi.

4. "Shadow banks are highly leveraged financial institutions that perform functions historically relegated to the commercial banking system." Traditionally, these financial concerns did "not have access to the conventional means of Fed support. Nor were they ever really regulated or supervised by the Fed. They engaged in risky behavior that in large part led to the global financial crisis." And, when the crisis hit the Fed quietly spent/lent as little as a couple trillion dollars according to the Fed, some $7.1 trillion according to *Bloomberg News*, and as high as $29 trillion as calculated by some number crunchers. Quotes are from J. Andrew Felkerson, "Bail-out Bombshell: Fed 'Emergency" Bank Rescue Totaled $29 Trillion Over Three Years," *AlterNet*, December 16, 2011.

5. J. Andrew Felkerson, "Bail-out Bombshell."

6. J. Andrew Felkerson, "Bail-out Bombshell," xii.

7. Thomas Geoghegan, "What Would Keynes Do?" *The Nation*, October 17, 2011, 11–17.

8. MarketWatch, "Transcript of Obama's Press Conference," provided by the White House, October 6, 2011, accessed October 11, 2011, http://www.marketwatch.com/story/transcript-of-obamas-press-conference-2011-10-06.

9. MarketWatch, "Transcript of Obama's Press Conference."

10. William Jackson, *Glass-Steagall Act: Commercial vs. Investment Banking* (Economics Division, Congressional Research Service, 1987), 3.

11. Robert Shiller, "Democratizing and Humanizing Finance," in *Reforming U.S. Financial Markets: Reflections Before and Beyond Dodd-Frank* by Randall Kroszner and Robert Shiller (Cambridge, MA: MIT Press, 2011), 14.

12. Shiller, "Democratizing and Humanizing Finance," 15.

13. Shiller, "Democratizing and Humanizing Finance," 16.

14. Shiller, "Democratizing and Humanizing Finance," 16.

15. Richard Brealey and Stewart Myers, *Principles of Corporate Finance*, 2nd ed. (New York: McGraw-Hill, 1984).

16. Shiller, "Democratizing and Humanizing Finance," 25.

17. Shiller, "Democratizing and Humanizing Finance," 8.

18. Shiller, "Democratizing and Humanizing Finance," 9.

19. Shiller, "Democratizing and Humanizing Finance," 9.

20. Shiller, "Democratizing and Humanizing Finance," 9.

21. Edward Gramlich, *Subprime Mortgages: America's Latest Boom and Bust* (Washington, DC: Urban Institute Press, 2007).

22. Henry M. Paulson, Robert K. Steel, and David G. Nason, *Blueprint for a Modernized Financial Regulatory Structure*, U.S. Department of the Treasury, March 2008.

23. U.S. Treasury, *Financial Regulatory Reform: A New Foundation; Rebuilding Financial Supervision and Regulation* (Washington, DC, 2009).

24. Robert Pozen, *Too Big to Save? How to Fix the Financial System* (New York: John Wiley, 2010).

25. Shiller, "Democratizing and Humanizing Finance," 24.

26. Shiller, "Democratizing and Humanizing Finance," 24.

27. From Tim Geithner's written testimony presented to the House Financial Services Committee Hearing, March 26, 2009, and quoted in Shiller, "Democratizing and Humanizing Finance," 3.

28. Shiller, "Democratizing and Humanizing Finance," 4.

29. Shiller, "Democratizing and Humanizing Finance," 4.

30. Shiller, "Democratizing and Humanizing Finance," 4.

31. Shiller, "Democratizing and Humanizing Finance," 4.

32. Shiller, "Democratizing and Humanizing Finance," 4.

33. Shiller, "Democratizing and Humanizing Finance," 43.

34. John Prior, "Foreclosures in 2011 to Break Last Year's Record: RealtyTrac," *Housingwire*, January 12, 2011, accessed October 16, 2011, http://www.housingwire.com/2011/01/12/foreclosures-reach-record-high-in-2010-realtytrac.

35. Shiller, "Democratizing and Humanizing Finance," 5.

36. Shiller, "Democratizing and Humanizing Finance," 5.

37. Shiller, "Democratizing and Humanizing Finance," 5.

38. Shiller, "Democratizing and Humanizing Finance," 6.

39. Shiller, "Democratizing and Humanizing Finance," 7.

40. Shiller, "Democratizing and Humanizing Finance," 33.

41. Elizabeth Warren, "Unsafe at Any Rate," *Democracy Journal.org*, 5 (Summer 2007): 8–19.

42. Shiller, "Democratizing and Humanizing Finance," 36.

43. Shiller, "Democratizing and Humanizing Finance," 36.

44. Geoghegan, "What Would Keynes Do?" 17.

45. Geoghegan, "What Would Keynes Do?" 17.

46. William Greider, "Debt Jubilee, America Style," *The Nation*, November 14, 2011, 12.

47. Robert Applebaum, "Want a Real Economic Stimulus and Jobs Plan? Forgive Student Loan Debt!" *SignOn.org*, 2011, accessed October 17, 2011, http://signon.org/sign/want-a-real-economic?source=mo&id=32074-1706635-UivpPNx.

Glossary of Financial Terms

Arbitrage Dealers Financiers who take advantage of price differences between two or more markets, creating the possibility of a risk-free profit at zero cost.

Asset-Backed Security (ABS) A security whose value and income are "backed" or derived from a collateralized pool of underlying assets.

Collateral Debt Obligation (CDO) A structured asset-backed security with multiple layers or "tranches" representing different risks and payoffs to investors.

Collateralized Mortgage Obligation (CMO) A type of mortgage-backed security that is supported by a wide pool of mortgage loans that allegedly lower the risks against defaults, usually divided up into tranches.

Credit Default Swap (CDS) A type of derivative that acts as a form of insurance against the default on anything from a corporate loan to a mortgaged-backed security. Should a bond or the structured loan default, the seller of the CDS pays the buyer for his/her losses.

Derivative Traders Are financiers who specialize in derivative instruments designed either to hedge against risks and/or for speculative ("gambling") purposes.

Derivatives Financial contracts that are designed to allow investors to insure themselves against future changes in prices, first used in trading as a means of speculating on exchange or interest rates and later expanding to virtually all markets, real and synthetic (think "fantasy" baseball).

Hedge Funds Are typically illiquid partnerships limited to a small number of wealthy investors employing sophisticated investment strategies, such as taking leveraged, long, short, and derivative positions in both domestic and international markets.

Investment Brokers   Financiers who bring together buyers and sellers of investments.

Leverage   Refers to the number of borrowed dollars for every dollar a firm owns or the amount of debt used to finance a firm's assets. When the ratios of debt to equity exceed sevenfold, these are considered highly leveraged entities.

Money Market Funds   Open-ended mutual funds that are invested in short-term debt securities, which provide liquidity to the financial intermediaries between buyers and sellers.

Moral Hazard   Refers to those behaviors that would be otherwise if the parties were fully exposed to or not insulated from the market risks involved.

Mortgage-Backed Security (MBS)   An asset-backed security that represents a claim on the cash flow from mortgaged pooled loans.

Mutual Funds   Refer to the professionally organized investments of pooled monies from many investors for the purposes of buying stocks, bonds, open-ended money markets, and/or other securities.

Securities   Marketable or negotiable instruments that represent financial value such as bonds, stocks, options, or swaps.

Securities Fraud   A financial crime in which a person or company, such as a stockbroker, a trader, brokerage firm, corporation, or investment bank, misrepresents information that investors use to make decisions.

Securitization   Refers to the process of structuring and redirecting the cash flow of an asset to create multiple securities that may be bought or sold by investors, as when banks seek to capture the cash flow of any type of receivable, such as mortgages or credit card loans.

Shadow Banking   Refers to highly leveraged financial institutions that perform functions that were historically restricted to commercial banks. Traditionally, these firms operated outside and did not have access to the Federal Reserve. These institutions often participated like Goldman Sachs in "hidden" structured investment vehicles.

Short Sales   Refers to those investment strategies that allow investors to profit from the decline in the value of a security. Typically, these deals involve the practice of selling assets, usually securities, that have been borrowed by a third party, to be sold back at a later date to the lender, with the intent to profit from the decline in the prices of the assets between the sale and repurchase.

Structured Investment Vehicles (SIV)   Refers to those large pools of investment assets that are kept off the balance sheets of firms whose intent is to benefit from the difference between the short- and long-term rates of return.

Synthetic Collateralized Debt Obligation (SCDO) Refers to a complex financial security used to speculate on or manage the risk that the obligation will not be paid in full and whose derived value may or may not be owned by the parties involved.

Tranche A "slice" or *tranche* in French refers to a section of mortgage-related securities that create separate pools of pass-through rates for different classes of bondholders with varying maturities, risks, and payoffs.

Subject Index

Name Index

About the Author

Gregg Barak is professor of criminology and criminal justice at Eastern Michigan University and the former visiting distinguished professor in the College of Justice & Safety at Eastern Kentucky University. He received his PhD in criminology from the University of California at Berkeley. In 2003 he became the twenty-seventh Fellow of the Academy of Criminal Justice Sciences, and in 2007 he received the Lifetime Achievement Award from the Critical Division of the American Society of Criminology. Barak is the author and/or editor of numerous books on crime, justice, media, violence, criminal law, homelessness, human rights, and related topics, including his award-winning *Gimme Shelter: A Social History of Homelessness in Contemporary America* (1991).

CPSIA information can be obtained at www.ICGtesting.com
Printed in the USA
BVOW010617300712

296499BV00001B/4/P

9 781442 207783